Law and Society
Recent Scholarship

Edited by Eric Rise

A Series from LFB Scholarly

Women's Rights in Native North America
Legal Mobilization in the US and Canada

Judith H. Aks

LFB Scholarly Publishing LLC
New York 2004

Library of Congress Cataloging-in-Publication Data

Aks, Judith H.
  Women's rights in Native North America : legal mobilization in the
US and Canada / Judith H. Aks.
      p. cm. -- (Law and society)
Includes bibliographical references and index.
  ISBN 1-59332-012-4 (alk. paper)
  1. Indian women--Legal status, laws, etc.--United States. 2. Women's
rights--United States. 3. Indian women--Legal status, laws,
etc.--Canada. 4. Women's rights--Canada. I. Title. II. Series: Law and
society (New York, N.Y.)
  KDZ483.D64A83 2004
  342.708'78'08997--dc22

2003026275

ISBN 1-59332-012-4

Printed on acid-free 250-year-life paper.

Manufactured in the United States of America.

For Diana

CONTENTS

ACKNOWLEDGEMENTS

There are many people whose assistance was crucial to the creation of this book. Michael McCann, Nancy Hartsock, and Stuart Scheingold guided me through writing my Ph.D. dissertation, which is the foundation for this book. My colleagues at the University of Washington provided an exciting and engaging intellectual community. Lennie Feldman, Beth Harris, Margaret Hobart, Danielle Lavaque-Manty, Kimberley Manning, Lisa Miller, Niall O'Murchu, Sarah Pralle, Karin Roberts, Norma Rodriguez, and Steve Sandweiss were a great support system. Jan Bultmann is an ace editor, who really cleaned up my prose.

I am deeply grateful to brave women like Julia Martinez, Jeannette Lavell, Yvonne Bedard, and Sandra Lovelace, whose quests for justice inspired this project. Richard Collins and Alan Taradash cleared time from their very busy schedules to talk to me about their involvement in the *Santa Clara Pueblo v. Martinez* case. Their hard work gave Julia Martinez's claims a legal voice, and the arguments that they presented before the Supreme Court form the foundations for the framework that I present in this study.

I would also like to thank my family for all of their love and support. Debbie Aks, Frank Aks, Gloria Aks, Jake Aks, Steve Aks, Julie Bokser, Ray Cangemie, Bob Goodman, and the Rosenberg gang were all very encouraging throughout the years. Sebastian David Pallais-Aks provided encouraging prods from in utero and made his grand entrance just as I was putting the final touches on the manuscript. And finally, I dedicate this book to Diana Pallais, my partner in all of life's adventures.

LIST OF TABLES

xi

LIST OF ACRONYMS

ICRA	Indian Civil Rights Act
UN HRC	United Nations Human Rights Committee
IRA	Indian Reorganization Act
DIAND	Department of Indian Affairs and Northern Development
IAA	Indian Association of Alberta
IRIW	National Committee on Indian Rights for Indian Women
NIB	National Indian Brotherhood
QNWA	Quebec Native Women's Association
WNWA	Winnipeg Native Women's Association
NWAC	Native Women's Association of Canada

Indigenous Women's Legal Mobilization

Introduction

In 1939, the Santa Clara Pueblo amended its constitution to stipulate that children "born of marriages between female members of the Santa Clara Pueblo and non-members shall not be members of the Santa Clara Pueblo."[1] Meanwhile, children of male members and female non-members were still granted membership in the Santa Clara Pueblo. In 1941, Julia Martinez married a Navajo man and subsequently had children with him. While those children lived on the Santa Clara Pueblo reservation and were culturally, linguistically, and religiously tied to the community, they were denied official membership in the Pueblo and were probably going to be evicted from the reservation upon their mother's death. Julia Martinez and her daughter Audrey filed suit under Title I of the Indian Civil Rights Act (ICRA), claiming that the Santa Clara Pueblo's membership rules denied her equal protection of the law. Ultimately, her case reached the US Supreme Court. To acknowledge that Indian tribes were sovereign entities and to defer to Congressional plenary authority, the Court ruled against Martinez, stating that the suit was out of its jurisdiction, because Indian tribes were immune to lawsuits. This bow to Indian sovereignty prevented Martinez from making a claim against her tribe's sexist membership rule. There was no subsequent mobilization to change this rule, and it continues to guide Santa Clara Pueblo membership policy today.

The lack of mobilization after the *Santa Clara Pueblo v. Martinez* case starkly contrasts with indigenous women's continuing struggles in Canada. Section 12(1)(b) of Canada's 1951 Indian Act[2] states, "The following persons are not entitled to be registered [as an Indian:] . . . a woman who married a person who is not an Indian, unless that woman is subsequently the wife or widow of [an Indian]."[3] This section of the Indian Act spurred a great deal of legal and political mobilization because, while it denied aboriginal status to indigenous women who married out of their bands, it also allowed indigenous men to pass their aboriginal status onto the non-aboriginal women that they married. In

1

1973, the Canadian Supreme Court upheld the sexist section 12(1)(b) in a consolidated case *Attorney General of Canada v. Lavell-Bedard.* This negative ruling acted as a catalyst for further mobilization and, eventually, a woman named Sandra Lovelace, with the help of the New Brunswick Human Rights Commission, questioned the sexism of the Indian Act before the United Nations Human Rights Committee (UN HRC). In 1982, in *Lovelace v. Canada,* the UN HRC found that 12(1)(b) violated the *International Covenant on Civil and Political Rights* because it denied Lovelace and similarly situated indigenous women contact with their natal culture. This UN declaration sparked the reformation of Canada's Indian Act, which eventually would allowed many indigenous women who had married out of their band to regain their aboriginal status and move back to their reserves. The process of reforming the Indian Act was long and complicated, with many important consequences for indigenous women. There was great resistance from indigenous bands, who feared that enforcing sex equality norms would tax their limited resources with an influx of new reinstated members. Thus, the compromises of the reform process included some expanded aboriginal rights, which complicated indigenous women's gender-based claims.

These "marrying out" cases in the US and in Canada illustrate how difficult it is for political and legal institutions to simultaneously recognize indigenous and gender identity. This study explores how competing strands of power, or the intersection of racism and sexism,[4] affect indigenous women's legal mobilization. An analysis of the legal logics used in these cases will explicate some of the conflicting forces that indigenous women must balance when they act politically. I argue that indigenous women, like most women of color, experience their intersectional identity as a kind of double bind: Often their race and gender interact in complex ways, sometimes causing remedies for one structure of power to reinforce the dominating effects of the other. In light of this double bind of intersectionality, the cases I discuss exemplify how legal mobilization might simultaneously reinforce domination and plant the seeds for indigenous women's future resistance.

Annette Jaimes Guerrero observes the complicated relationship that indigenous women have with tribal and federal governments: "Sexism and racism in the American State and sexism within tribal contexts operate more often than not to nullify any demands Native women can make as citizens."[5] This leads her to a very pessimistic view of indigenous women's political clout. In contrast, Michael McCann describes the "catalyst" or symbolic effect of legal mobilization in his book, *Rights at Work*. He writes that, in some cases, "taking legal rights seriously has opened up more than closed debates, exposed more than masked systemic injustices, stirred more than pacified discontents, and nurtured more than retarded the development of solidarity."[6] Jaimes Guerrero's account of indigenous women's intersectional identities forces theorists of legal mobilization to consider the multiplicity of power. This study brings two sets of literature together to assess when and how legal tactics alleviate and reinforce the burden of the double bind of intersectional power. The comparison between the US and Canadian cases sheds empirical light on these theoretical questions.

The Intersections of Power

Kimberlé Crenshaw labels the combined effect of racism and sexism "intersectionality."

> Intersectionality captures the way in which the particular location of black women in dominant American social relations is unique and in some senses unassimilable into the discursive paradigms of gender and race domination . . . The marginalization of black women in antidiscrimination law is replicated in the realm of oppositional politics; black women are marginalized in feminist politics as a consequence of race, and they are marginalized in antiracist politics as a consequence of their gender. The consequences of this multiple marginality are fairly predictable—there is simply silence of and about black women.[7]

Crenshaw[8] shows that the "intersections" of oppression and the nuance of identity exclude many groups or individuals from both legal remedies and transformative social movements. She notes that African-American women often must choose between their race and their gender to fight political battles, because existing political and legal discourses focus on singular strands of power.

Crenshaw hopes to push the boundaries of how we conceive of political identity to try to include the complicated identities of women of color.

In mapping the intersections of race and gender, the concept does engage dominant assumptions that race and gender are essentially separate categories. By tracing the categories to their intersections, I hope to suggest a methodology that will ultimately disrupt the tendencies to see race and gender as exclusive or separable. [9]

Indigenous women comprise another group that falls through (legal) categorical cracks; existing legal tools either speak to their gender or their racial identity, but not to both simultaneously. Indigenous women contest feminist theories because they feel that "western feminism" proposes solutions that oppress indigenous women on racial grounds. Such feminists ignore tribal sovereignty claims and often even dismiss them as archaic.[10] These critiques of feminism show how groups that are struggling only against one strand of power (gender) sometimes frame their analysis using discourses which dominate others. Patricia Hill Collins, among others, points out that white feminists often do not realize the power that they wield when they describe women's experience in a way that ignores racial inequity.[11] By universalizing white women's experiences in their battle against sex discrimination, some feminists augment the power that dominates women of color.

When referring to indigenous women's intersectional identity, it is not clear whether "race" or "ethnicity" is a better signifier because both represent structures of power that affect them. Since race and ethnicity are both social constructions, the two terms themselves exert power over people. I could write a whole study on the meaning of the terms "race" and "ethnicity" and which better describes the domination of indigenous peoples, but that is not the aim of this project. That said, for the purpose of this study, both racial and ethnic domination affect indigenous women's lives.[12] There is a racial element to discrimination against indigenous women because colonial forces focused upon skin color and biology in the process of defining certain groups as Indian. Yet, there is more to discrimination against indigenous people than race. Because there has been historical control over their cultural practices, contemporary battles are often about ethnic autonomy or freedom. These issues often fall under the broad umbrella of sovereignty, which involves both racial and ethnic domination. Yet, indigenous peoples are unlike other ethnic minorities because indigenous peoples are historically 'original' peoples and nations, their rights have a kind of historical precedence and, for that reason, the collective rights they struggle for are not conceived by them as rights to be granted to them, but rather as rights they had always enjoyed before they were taken away from them by conquerors, settlers, missionaries or merchants coming from afar . . . [Also] among all the collective rights of indigenous peoples, the right to land, to their ancestral territory and its resources is paramount.[13]

Thus, when describing the multiplicity of domination against indigenous peoples, I refer to the combined forces of ethnic and racial subordination, all the while acknowledging their unique history. All of these forms of power combine with gender to create indigenous women's intersectional identity.

In her discussion of the *Lavell* case in Canada, Kathleen Jamieson describes the double bind of intersectionality quite well.

The stand taken by Jeannette Lavell was itself first of all a manifestation of the resurgence of pride in Indian identity. It was an affirmation by an Indian woman of belief that the concept of 'citizen plus' and the desirability of retaining Indian status. To pose this case as it has been, as one of Indians' rights v. women's rights, is to assume that all Indians are male.[14]

A zero-sum conception of power requires issues to be labeled as either indigenous rights or women's rights, which ignores the multiplicity of power that affects indigenous women's lives. To characterize Lavell's action against the Canadian government's sexist Indian Act as a "resurgence of pride in Indian identity" shows that, in Lavell's mind, fighting sex discrimination was a way to actualize her ethnic identity. This disturbed many status Indians because it threatened the benefits that they reaped from their existing relationship with the Canadian government, and thus the dichotomy between indigenous and women's rights became even more pronounced. The prevailing legal protections prevented the consideration of simultaneous race and sex discrimination. Jaimeson's characterization of this case attempts to offer a more nuanced account of intersectional identity. Her point is echoed by many indigenous women.

Lorelei Means articulates some indigenous women's feelings about feminism:

> White women . . . tell us we have to move 'beyond our culture to be 'liberated' like them . . . What we need to be is *more*, not less Indian. But every time we try to explain this to our self-proclaimed 'white sisters,' we either get told we're missing the point—we're just dumb Indians, after all—or we're accused of 'self-hatred' as women. A few experiences with this sort of arrogance and you start to get the idea maybe all this feminism business is just another extension of the same old racist, colonialist mentality.[15]

And Pam Colorado, an Oneida scholar adds, "[F]eminism is essentially a Euro-supremacist ideology and is therefore quite imperialist in its implications."[16] To fully understand indigenous women's political identity, it is necessary to consider it as a whole that is greater than the sum of its constituent parts: race, ethnicity, and gender.[17]

Gender and race-based domination and their corresponding remedies are both part of the "power" that figures prominently in the everyday lives of indigenous women. I argue that domination can derive from certain conceptions of justice and "right" as much as it comes from outright discrimination or subjugation. Dominant legal remedies to gender inequality (through individual rights as found in the Indian Civil Rights Act or the Canadian Bill of Rights) are sometimes a form of colonial domination, and sometimes colonized indigenous practices (via constructions of sovereignty rights) exacerbate gender inequality (i.e. sexist membership rules). Likewise, resistance can work to challenge existing dominant norms, but it can also further entrench the very forces that it aims to change.

To better explain the double bind of intersectionality, I must describe the conception of power that informs this study. Michel Foucault complicates our understanding of power, challenging the idea that it is neatly explained in a top-down or dichotomous manner. Several aspects of Foucault's relational model of power are useful for understanding indigenous women's legal mobilization. First, for Foucault, power is exercised rather than possessed. This allows individuals and groups to temporarily deploy power, sometimes in subversive ways. There is a temporal contingency to exercising, rather than possessing power, which opens up space for power dynamics to be more fluid and ever-changing.

Second, Foucault's notion of power is diffuse—not centralized—so it must be studied both at the grassroots capillaries, as well as the more disciplinary institutional levels. By discipline, Foucault means coalescing power relations that guide behavior and constrain actors. Finally, Foucauldian power is productive rather than repressive. Discipline and repression are found in patterned behaviors that are deemed "normal." Thus, enforcement happens at many sites, virtually in every social interaction. While disciplinary power normalizes particular behaviors and meanings, it also creates—rather than curbs—new activities and discursive practices.[18] Since Foucault sees power as being exercised at many sites, rather than being possessed by any monolithic, easily identifiable entity, it becomes multiple and generative. He writes:

> [P]ower must be understood . . . as the multiplicity of force relations immanent in the sphere in which they operate and which constitute their own organization; as the process which, through ceaseless struggles and confrontations, transforms, strengthens, or reverses them; as the support which these force relations find in one another, thus forming a chain or a system, or on the contrary, the disjunctions and contradictions which isolate them from one another; and lastly, as the strategies in which they take effect, whose general design of institutional crystallization is embodied in the state apparatus, in the formulation of the law, in the various social hegemonies . . . Power is everywhere; not because it embraces everything, but because it comes from everywhere . . . [P]ower is not an institution, and not a structure; neither is it a certain strength we are endowed with; it is the name that one attributes to a complex strategical situation in a particular society. [19]

With a diffuse conception of power, it is possible to articulate both the overwhelming constraints experienced by women of color, and also to uncover modes of resistance in unpredictable sites.

If one reads the Foucauldian power matrix literally, actors (both the more "powerful" and the "powerless") seem to have no agency to change or even to define their reality. Nancy Hartsock believes that Foucault's vision of power means that "[p]ower is everywhere, and so ultimately nowhere."[20] Thinkers such as Hartsock believe that actors are unable to move in Foucault's power web. To the contrary, he states, "As soon as there's a relation of power there's a possibility of resistance. We're never trapped by power; it's always possible to modify its role, in determined conditions and following a precise strategy."[21] He wants to reformulate power in order to see how it constitutes subjects and how that affects the ability to resist. If power is truly everywhere, those traditionally painted as powerless can realize the power that they can exercise. At the same time, due to the complexity of power, those who attempt to resist sometimes reassert power in an oppressive way.

Joan Cocks echoes this point:

> The inappropriate if still magnetic image of power and resistance is then, that of a unitary resisting self pitted against a unitary power, or that of an oppressed group pitted against an oppressor in a monolithic/reverse-monolithic way . . . Several major systems of power can be operating simultaneously in one society, with any individual implicated in power and resistance in a multiplicity of different ways at once.[22]

While Cocks's conception of power is less "capillary" or diffuse than Foucault's, she also captures the multiplicity of forces that affect people's lives. While Foucault's reading of power is central to this study, I argue that scholars must try to name particular stands of power that operate in different contexts to try to observe domination and resistance more systematically. Cocks's language, which points to "systems of power," allows for more structured analysis than Foucault's capillaries. To paint a more concrete picture of the intersectional power matrix, I'll next describe some of the forces that mediate indigenous women's lives.

Indigenous women's experience of intersectionality is distinct because of their unique legal status and because of the many cultural strands that define their identity. To disaggregate the complicated web that affects indigenous women's lives, it is important to distinguish pre-colonial indigenous culture from colonized indigenous culture and the dominant colonial culture. None of these forces are unitary or monolithic, because they are all the products of multiple and often contradictory historical inputs. This study attempts to systematically assess how these multiple cultural forces interact with gender to illustrate the web of power described above. All of these cultural strands can serve both as coercive forces and terrains for resistance. The interaction between indigenous and colonial cultures shows how productive power can be, and the affect that this interaction has upon indigenous women is often unpredictable.

Pre-colonial indigenous culture—I'll call this "tradition"—is what indigenous tribes were like prior to colonial conquest. It is often invoked to justify the use of particular legal logics in contemporary conflicts. According to some, cultural survival depends on preserving a particular account of tradition. It is very difficult to know the status of "true tradition" because much cultural history has been altered, destroyed, or selectively restructured by the colonial experience. Boaventura de Sousa Santos echoes this point:

> What are seen (and [indigenous peoples] themselves see) today as their traditions, customs and economies are indeed the sedimentation of resistances, survival strategies and adaptive responses in the face of mass destruction of their ancestral communal life by modern conquerors and settlers of all denominations.[23]

This historically reconstructed tradition is important nonetheless, because it forms the foundation for many contemporary demands for tribal self-determination. For instance, traditional gender roles often are invoked by various political actors either to contest or to enforce current tribal practices that appear to be sexist.

Second, colonized indigenous culture is the product of historical relations with the dominant culture; the amalgam of indigenous culture which has been salvaged and reconstructed after conquest. Many treaties were signed between indigenous tribes and colonial forces. While these might have been part of an agenda of forced assimilation, they also sometimes serve as the foundation for contemporary legal claims to sovereignty rights. Many legal arguments and political acts draw upon this very oppressive historical legacy, and play upon the contradictions found in the dominant culture. For instance, current versions of indigenous sovereignty are constructed by US and Canadian edicts. Rather than being separate nations, indigenous nations are "domestic dependents" or protectorates of an overarching federal force. Given this shaky legal foundation, self-determination is subject to the whims of legislatures, and indigenous self-government depends on federal approval. The resulting political culture is, by necessity, a patchwork of provisional acts that attempt to make the best of a very oppressive situation. One aim of this project is to identify how dominant norms and institutions have affected the construction of indigenous tradition over time. The net result is what I label "colonized indigenous culture."

Third, the "dominant (colonial) culture" in the US and Canada is a patchwork of norms that have developed over time. This dominant culture has been influenced by the colonial experience, and the need to account for indigenous peoples' existence has produced a variety of often contradictory policies.   The dominant culture is an amalgam of many ideological inputs, including egalitarian ideals, notions of representative democracy, individual civil rights, Christianity, individual property rights, and free market capitalism. Often these ideals contradict one another and compete for primacy in the political agenda. This ideological competition is apparent in the different stances taken toward indigenous groups over time.[24] Competing ideologies often legitimate various kinds of domination while providing tools for political resistance. Since the dominant legal logics are multiple, political actors can draw upon different aspects of them to make their claims. Current constructions of individual and sovereignty rights[25] are a result of the historical competition between these forces.[26] Thus, when one places these rights discourses into the power matrix that I have described above, it is possible to see where they might be combined and rearticulated in a way that might begin to capture the double bind of intersectionality.

These three forces—traditional, colonized indigenous, and dominant culture—mediate the kinds of claims that indigenous women can make. Or, as Inderpal Grewal and Caren Kaplan argue, "[T]he multidirectional flow of culture . . . provides both hegemonic and counter-hegemonic possibilities."[27] Contemporary battles combine these forces in creative and sometimes contradictory ways. Some women make gender-based claims using several different discourses. They might invoke tradition by pointing to historical matrilineal practices. They sometimes stress indigenous sovereignty by saying that colonialism created patriarchy and gender equality can fall into place once sovereignty has been attained. Or, indigenous women might draw upon individual rights discourses, arguing that female indigenous people deserve the same government protections as male indigenous people. There are also creative combinations of these discourses. Some argue that since gender discrimination did not exist under the "authentic" historical practice of matrilineal tribes, then gender equality will fall into place once "true" sovereignty has been achieved. For these indigenous women, this turn to (a constructed version of) pre-colonial tradition offers a convenient way to assert present day racial and gendered identity simultaneously. Thus, the litigants in the cases that I examine draw upon the rhetoric of individual rights to uphold their version of "tradition" (which is not sexist). But because these individual rights claims echo western liberal democratic norms, many indigenous sovereignty advocates claim that they fly in the face of "traditional communal values."

Male sovereignty advocates also feel that women's reliance upon dominant norms and institutions to make their gender-based claims threatens the little bit of indigenous self-determination that has been achieved. Yet, the version of sovereignty rights that these men defend is also a product of the colonial experience. They believe this construction of post-colonial sovereignty is crucial for cultural survival (or to maintain their traditions). Also, it is important to note how the contradictions of colonialism are related to dilemmas and contradictions that exist in contemporary politics. Painted this way, the legal battles under consideration represent the broader cultural struggle within which indigenous women attempt to carve space for their complicated identities.

It is important to note that these are just three of the cultural narratives that indigenous women draw upon when constructing their political identities and making legal claims. These cultural narratives overlap and are the products of profound historical forces. Once these forces are seen as vectors of power, which can be provisionally deployed to make claims, one can see how indigenous women might exercise power. Examples abound of identity construction within these conflicting forces. In the late sixties in both the US and in Canada, a pan-Indian identity[28] movement emerged, which still informs indigenous politics today. One's affiliation with a particular tribe was less important than the political and cultural solidarity felt across tribes with other indigenous peoples.[29] This shows how oppositional politics sometimes force diverse peoples to band together against a common oppressor. A similar example is when indigenous women (who married out of their tribe and lost their indigenous status) mobilize together, regardless of their band. They might identify with each other more than with their own bands merely because of their similar exclusion.[30] These two types of mobilization are based upon a common lived experience of exclusion or domination. Thus, in cases such as these, political identity is defined by the complex power dynamics at work. One important strand of power that helps define intersectionality is "the law," which is central to the current analysis.

A Constitutive Account of Legal Power: Are Rights Discourses Politically Useful?

Within this diffuse conception of power, how does one conceive of "the law"? Is it appropriate or helpful for indigenous women to fight the double bind of intersectionality using legal tactics such as rights discourses? I focus on legal tactics in this study because of their unique qualities, and because they illustrate how power can coalesce into a structure or institution, while remaining malleable and open for innovative deployment.

There is much debate about whether legal mobilization matters, and the answers that scholars provide depend upon their conception of law. I adopt a constitutive[31] account of law, which assumes that law constitutes and represents social relations and that law and politics are deeply intertwined. Some legal scholars would like "law" to be disassociated from political maneuvering. A constitutive conception of law presumes that legal terrain is inherently political. The institutions and narratives that fall under the broad umbrella called "law" inform political tactics. Legal power includes more than rules, texts, courts and lawyers. It represents and mediates multiple cultural legacies and power relationships.[32] Formal state legal institutions and societal legal narratives are mutually constitutive, making the law more scattered and pandemic in social interactions. Constitutive theorists are also quick to take note of the plurality of law;[33] acknowledging that indigenous communities have practices that are just as "legal" as colonial legal structures. The recognition of the co-existence of multiple legal systems within one state allows one to better understand how political actors can creatively combine various legal norms to make a political claim. These insights help construct a more diffuse conception of law, which echoes the account of power that I described in the previous section. While many socio-legal scholars have attempted systematic analyses of how law constitutes social relations, few have focused on the phenomenon of intersectionality. Once one recognizes the mutually constitutive relationship between culture, politics, and law, it becomes clear that legal discourses help construct the double bind of intersectionality.

Just as there is a debate about how to conceive of law more generally, scholars also disagree about the political efficacy of rights discourses in particular. There are some who believe that justice can be found by demanding legal rights from government, and that as long as groups mobilize these ideals, their promise will eventually become reality.[34] Other scholars are very suspicious of the political efficacy of liberal rights discourses and apply a "false consciousness" rubric[35] to their analysis of rights. Still others focus on the inability of courts as institutions to foster social change or to attain rights ideals.[36] Other theorists, while suspicious of idealistic liberal accounts of rights, still want to acknowledge the unique qualities of legal rights and want to retain space for their provisional power. The strategic deployment of rights has a potentially transformative outcome; reforms which acknowledge previously alienated groups shake existing hierarchies, and eventually transform them in lasting ways.[37] These scholars also focus upon a symbolic value of rights ideals that can have a great deal of mobilizing potential.[38] Some scholars[39] stress that legal tactics can act as catalysts for (as opposed to the "causes" of) change, both within and outside formal legal institutions. These scholars are often the first to acknowledge the internal contradictions of liberal ideals as well as the multiple ideological influences upon the construction of rights. My exploration of legal mobilization at the intersections of power relies upon this much more contingent account of legal tactics.

To better understand the account of rights that informs this study, it is helpful to turn to Karl Marx's "On the Jewish Question."[40] Marx's critique of legal rights is based upon his observation that there is a lack of community in capitalist society. The abstract citizen, which falsely universalizes all experience, is also the foundation for the promise of abstract legal rights. Thus, rights, which are founded upon this conception of the individual, are a fallacy. But, in the name of pragmatism, Marx does not discount the utility of what he calls "political emancipation," for a greater dialectical struggle.

> *Political* emancipation certainly represents a great progress. It is not, indeed, the final form of human emancipation, but it is

the final form of human emancipation *within* the framework of the prevailing social order. It goes without saying that we are speaking here of real, practical emancipation . . . Man emancipates himself *politically* from religion by expelling it from the sphere of public law to that of private law. Religion . . . is no longer the essence of *community*, but the essence of *differentiation*. It has become what it was at the *beginning*, an expression of the fact that man is *separated* from the community, from himself and from other men. It is now only the abstract avowal of an individual folly, a private whim or caprice . . . The division of man into the *public person* and the *private person*, the *displacement* of religion from the state to civil society—all this is not a stage in political emancipation but its consummation. Thus political emancipation does not abolish, and does not even strive to abolish, men's *real* religiosity.[41]

Hence, rights talk and the legal tactics that spring from it bring the liberal state to its ideal form. They do not abolish the atomistic, competitive individualism upon which the state is built. Rather, "equal" rights represent the culmination of the atomistic state. Therefore, one could conclude from Marx's essay that rights talk and legal tactics might be necessary to reveal contradictions that will push the revolution beyond mere political emancipation toward "true" human emancipation.

Human emancipation will only be complete when the real, individual man has absorbed into himself the abstract citizen; when as an individual man, in his everyday life, in his work, and in his relationships, he has become a *species-being*; and when he has recognized and organized his own powers (*forces propres*) as *social* powers so that he no longer separates this social power from himself as *political* power.[42] Rights claims could play a key role in this progression. When Marx stresses the oppressive nature of transitory legal rights, he contrasts immediate victories from the ultimate emancipatory process. His stark language can be misleading. He argues that the retreat into the private sphere, with private rights, will not lead to freedom. Rather, it leads to the destruction of community and the increased atomization of humans. Thus, it seems as though rights, for Marx, do have some provisional utility, but that claim is tempered by his fear that this temporary victory will keep individuals out of touch with their exploitation and diminish their desire for change.

Marx's analysis relies upon an epistemological stance that is very "modern." He sees a correct path to human emancipation, and his dialectical method is based upon a progressive notion of history. Thus, his pragmatic or provisional posture towards rights logics makes sense given his faith in the inevitability of revolution. The account of rights that informs this project relies a bit less on this modernist reading of Marx, using dialectical methodology in a more chaotic and less linear manner.

Wendy Brown offers some helpful insights about Marx's account of rights in "On the Jewish Question." Her interpretation of Marx and her juxtaposition of Marx's and Foucault's methods parallel the notion of rights that informs this project. Brown argues that Marx points out some important paradoxes in rights logics. They are deeply culturally and historically embedded, yet they claim to be ahistorical and acontextual.[43] Thus, there is a paradox between the "universal idiom and the local effects"[44] of rights.

> [This paradox] is expressed . . . in the irony that rights sought by a politically defined *group* are conferred upon depoliticized *individuals*; at the moment a particular 'we' succeeds in obtaining rights, it loses its we-ness and dissolves into individuals . . . When does identity articulated through rights become production and regulation of identity through law and bureaucracy? When does legal recognition become an instrument of regulation, and political recognition become an instrument of subordination?[45]

It is in the moment of universal abstraction that rights represent the most "devious" aspects of state power. "Liberal equality guarantees that the state will regard us all as equally abstracted from the social powers constituting our existence, equally decontextualized from the unequal conditions of our lives."[46] Once context and inequality are considered, the limitations and dominating effects of rights become apparent. Yet, the paradox lies in the fact that any attempt to achieve the promise of rights ideals requires that human experience be contextualized. This is why looking at the intersections of power is so crucial. It involves unveiling the forced abstraction of individuals by revealing their context. The contradictory structures of power that prevent indigenous women from becoming abstracted or universalized citizens uncover the fallacies of rights talk in their current forms.

But can indigenous women, or others suffering from intersectional domination, afford to forgo even the temporary gains of rights? Brown states:

> Being regarded by the state *as if* we were free and equal is an improvement over being treated as if we were naturally subjected and unequal vis-à-vis stratifying social powers . . . (Here, a discerning contemporary eye might see an analysis concerned with the way ideological idealism masks social power slide into one that emphasizes the discursive production of political possibility).[47]

Here, Brown hints at the political possibilities that can be unearthed when one embraces a more contingent account of rights (as discursive power in their idealistic form). Brown also acknowledges that the desire to fulfill rights ideals might help establish the material conditions for them. She states that "political emancipation in the form of civil and political rights can be embraced precisely because it represents a 'stage' of emancipation."[48] As long as rights ideals are seen as a temporary political possibility, subjects will not be marked or injured by their mobilization. Here, Brown adopts a reading of Marx that stresses contingency. The look and feel of emancipation is unspecified, and the next stage of struggle is unclear, but the provisional promise of current rights ideals is important nonetheless.

What is so compelling about Marx's account of power is its focus on struggle. The ability to continue fighting and revealing contradictions becomes central to the account of power that emerges from the juxtaposition of Foucault and Marx. If one exists in a web of power where there are multiple modes of domination, political emancipation becomes all the more difficult to achieve and thus, provisional victories become even more important.

> If, as Marx argued 150 years ago, the democratizing force of rights discourse inheres in its capacity to figure an ideal of equality among persons qua persons, regardless of socially constructed and enforced particularities, then the political potency of rights lies not in their concreteness . . . but in their idealism, in their ideal configuration of an egalitarian social, an ideal contradicted by substantive social inequalities . . .

> [T]he democratic *value* of political emancipation lies partly in its revelation of the *limits* of political emancipation. But where Marx counted on a progressive dialectical process for such revelation, it now becomes a project for a discursive struggle whose parameters are invented rather than secured in advance and whose outcome is never guaranteed.[49]

Brown feels that the moment rights become particular, defined, and concrete they mark identities and lose their democratic potential. When groups are marked as different from the abstract universal equal citizen, that is when they are injured the most.[50] The possibility for resistance lies in the possibility of giving new meaning to rights and applying them to new situations. But those meanings cannot solidify; their lack of specificity is the root of their democratic potential. Thus, the possibilities of resistance lie in new meaning-making opportunities. Brown's final assessment of rights focuses on battle, struggle, and everyday victories.

Antonio Gramsci's[51] related constructions of the organic intellectual and counter-hegemonic movements similarly stress the necessity for continuing struggle and have influenced many legal scholars. Alan Hunt expands upon them to build a theory of law as a "constitutive mode of regulation," which is malleable and mobile. Scholars such as Michel De Certeau[52] and James Scott[53] look to everyday subversive acts to find resistance within oppressive structures of power. These studies find micro-moments of resistance that prevent structures of power from ossifying. All of these scholars imagine law and power as temporally contingent and changing over time. Or as Joan Cocks states, "As soon as the elements of disorder begin to coalesce in a new way, critical theory should reappear in the guise of a gadfly, to agitate on behalf of the exuberance of life against a too-avid fixing and freezing of things."[54] Invoking rights logics in order to reveal their contradictions allows women who occupy the intersections of power to act as the gadfly Cocks refers to. Legal norms remain ever-changing and plural as long as they are asserted by those who occupy the margins of power. Legal meanings become even more contingent when the contradictions of history are explored.

Diverse Colonial Impulses and the Historical Evolution of Rights

Some feel that the democratic possibilities of rights are least accessible to indigenous peoples. Many see rights as a colonial project, and any attempt to summon them on behalf of indigenous peoples is seen as selling out to the "western liberal agenda." This assumes that rights logics are cohesive and predictable and that there is a unitary "western liberal agenda." A brief look at the historical roots of colonialism reveals that multiple and contradictory cultural and economic forces have influenced the contemporary legal form called rights. Once this complicated history is acknowledged, the possibilities for mobilizing rights discourses multiply, and their democratic function becomes accessible even to colonized groups.

Many of the diverse interests that existed during colonial times were incorporated into the legal systems of the US and Canada, rendering them incoherent or even contradictory. In his book *Civic Ideals*, Rogers Smith stresses that, historically, liberal ideals have not been the only ones that informed the evolution of US legal logics. In his study of citizenship laws, he notes the influence of diverse ideologies such as liberalism, civic republicanism and ascriptive, inegalitarian theories. Republicanism stressed the values of consent, representative government, majoritarianism, homogeneity, self-governance, virtue, the agrarian spirit, and community. Liberalism stressed individuality, social compacts, the separation of power, a prosperous commercial economy, property ownership, and more limited government. Ascriptive hierarchies, based upon race, sex, nationalities, and other immutable characteristics, helped rationalize the subordination of Native Americans and Africans. The process of building a "national" American identity involved bringing together a patchwork of competing ideals.

> [F]rom 1776 on, revolutionary leaders were actively promoting conceptions of true Americans as, first, the bearers of new, unique, and precious ascriptive identity; second, the rational social contractors creating governments dedicated to securing individual rights imagined by Lockean liberals, and third, public-spirited republican citizens, spurred by concerns for political liberty and the common good. Despite their

contradictions there was as yet little sense of conflict among these conceptions.[55]

By delineating these three ideological currents, Smith shows that there are many historical components of "rights talk" in the US. These facets of rights discourses provide fodder for contemporary struggles.

In addition to contradicting each other, the ideologies have their own internal contradictions. The resulting legal logics sometimes can't live up to all the facets of the ideals. Thus, rights talk often reflects internal tensions that exist between aspects of liberalism, as well as the other ideologies (such as republicanism and ascriptive norms) that helped construct the US legal system. Smith tends to favor a very egalitarian view of liberal individualism, which leads him to explain the existence of racial and gender hierarchies as the residue of historical ascriptive ideologies. This allows him to construct a pristine account of liberalism, focusing on procedural equality and ignoring the equally important and often contradictory values of liberty and individual property ownership. At times, these three things cannot coexist. Because liberal ideals focus squarely on the individual, the freedom to acquire property often creates a great many societal inequalities. Thus, Smith makes an important argument about the many cultural and ideological influences upon current legal forms, but I would take his points a step further, and not treat these ideologies as internally coherent. This further complicates the web of power that creates opportunities and constraints for indigenous women to mobilize the law.

John Comaroff also offers important insights about how colonialism was never a unitary project, planned and implemented by one party. There were "missionaries and merchants and mining magnates, administrators and agriculturalists, and army men," who all had a particular vision of how to colonize South Africa.[56] Not only were there different parties involved in setting up colonies, they were the bearers of multiple and contested ideologies.

[M]any of the 'civilized' practices exported from Britain to the colonies were anything but uncontested at home—not least rights to property, to fair labor conditions, to the franchise . . . Patently, the imperial frontier was not a place where a mature ideology of rights was presented, fully tried and tested, to premodern Africans. It was a space in which the unfolding

sociolegal and political histories of Britain and Africa met—
there to be made, reciprocally, in relation to each other.[57]

Insights drawn from Comaroff's description of British influence in
South Africa are relevant here for a couple of reasons. First, Britain
was a primary colonial force in the US and Canada, and second, his
points apply to the dynamic of colonialism more broadly than just to
the British experience. Moreover, I would argue that the US and
Canadian governments inherited the complex legacy of British
colonialism, along with its contradictory impulses, continuing some
aspects of it, and re-figuring others.

The colonial cultural encounter creates many different possibilities
for the content of a construct such as rights. It defines and destroys
political identity-making, and it is a unique form of domination, which
breeds new kinds of resistance. Comaroff's account of colonial power
dynamics echoes the Foucauldian network of power that I described
earlier.

> For the colonial process was never monolithic, never merely a
> matter of states and politics. And, far from being an encounter
> between two clearly defined 'sides,' *all* the parties involved
> were as much remade by it as it was by them. In all this,
> moreover, in the building of new identities, of newly imagined
> worlds of possibility and political reality, the discourse of
> rights, rightlessness, even righteousness, loomed increasingly
> large—albeit within complex cultural fields and power
> relations.[58]

Comaroff also echoes Marx's observation about the paradox of rights
and applies it to a colonial context.

> British colonialism . . . was everywhere two-faced,
> everywhere a double gesture. On the one hand, it justified
> itself in terms of difference and inequality: the greater
> enlightenment of the colonizer legitimized his right to rule and
> to civilize. On the other hand, that legitimacy was founded,
> ostensibly, on a commitment to the eventual erasure of
> difference in the name of common humanity and modernity.[59]

Therefore, the forces of colonialism represent aspects of modernity, and the enforcement of an abstract account of citizenship. The process of defining differences upon contact with indigenous peoples, and then trying to remove that difference in order to convert them into abstract citizens, has very real implications for modern day indigenous politics. But it is important to underscore that there was no singular method for this process of imposed abstraction, and there were diverse conceptions of such citizenship.

The diversity of colonial cultural forms and the various possibilities for rights interpretations trickles into the way that contemporary South African identity politics play themselves out. Comaroff delineates two competing "registers within the colonial discourse of rights,"[60] which are "radical individualism," which creates "universal citizens," and "primal sovereignty," which creates "ethnic subjects."[61] He argues that colonialism created contemporary indigenous identities by unifying diverse cultural groupings. These colonially constructed identities form the foundations for modern claims for self-determination. By showing how the colonial dynamic created identities and erased them, Comaroff starkly shows the productive nature of colonial power. The interaction of various definitions of rights, and the competing colonial interests created new groups, who would eventually claim rights from the South African state. This is one way that rights mark difference as injury. Even today, ethnic difference as the basis for rights reinvigorates the existence of primal sovereignty.

> One and all, they were encouraged to embark on the road to modernity, to fashion themselves into citizens of the civilized world. At the same time, as black Africans, they were made into ethnic subjects, ineluctably tied to their fellows, to their primal origins, an to *setswana,* a body of custom that marked them as premodern—and was invoked to deny them the kind of personhood to which they were exhorted to aspire . . . Is it any wonder that resistance to overrule should have taken root in the crevices and contradictions of their colonial experience, on the terrain between its promise and its reality? On that they should have contested European domination sometimes by asserting their universal rights as citizens of empire,

sometimes through carnivals of violence, rites of rebellion, and uprisings that bore the distinctive stamp of *setswana*.[62]

Here, Comaroff's description of African political tactics echoes indigenous peoples' continuing struggles to define themselves, to preserve re-constructed versions of tradition, sometimes embracing some modern legal discourses in order to achieve some self-determination. Comaroff's study shows that the diverse political tactics that contemporary Africans deploy are related to historical colonial struggles. The same could be said about the tactics employed by indigenous people in the Americas. The diversity of forces that created colonialism also left multiple legacies, which might be the seeds for current day resistance.

The creation and interaction of the three cultural forces that I described earlier—pre-colonial tradition, colonized indigenous culture, and dominant colonial culture—rely upon a relationship between what Comaroff labels radical individualism and primal sovereignty. The construction of primal sovereignty is rooted in particular notions of tradition, and this is what constructs colonized indigenous culture and contemporary claims to self-determination. Indigenous women's claims sometimes draw directly from a particular construction of radical individualism. Yet, when one considers indigenous women's place at the intersection between these two ideological strands, the contradictions between them become quite clear. It is not just a matter of sometimes referring to one over the other, but by invoking either, indigenous women expose their unique place in the power matrix of indigenous-colonial relations. Thus, the multiple registers created by conflicting colonial impulses both increase the number of discourses that indigenous women can draw upon and multiply their domination at the intersections of power.

Both Smith and Comaroff point to the multiple and competing forces of colonialism. These competing historical forces form the foundations for competing rights discourses, offering more opportunities for resistance while complicating the forces of domination. Plurality complicates the language of resistance, but it does not necessarily defeat its utility. Rather, it multiplies opportunities for both domination and resistance, rendering them more temporary and contingent.

[T]he language of the law *sui generis* is reducible neither to a brute weapon of control nor simply to an instrument of resistance. The inherently contradictory character of the colonial discourse of rights—its duality of registers and the double consciousness to which it gave rise—ensured that it would be engaged on both sides of the dialectic of domination and defiance. It still does everywhere.[63]

As Comaroff argues, there is a dialectic between domination and resistance, each in constant flux, and the law, or rights discourses, add to the multiplicity of both. The language of domination and resistance might seem quite binary, but once one injects temporal and spatial contingency, both domination and resistance become multiple forces in the web of power that represents social interaction. Looking at the experiences of indigenous women, who occupy the intersections of several power structures, helps emphasize the plurality of domination and resistance.

I argue that an examination of intersectionality underscores the provisional utility of legal "myths"[64] or ideals. Subjugated people can draw upon aspects of the ideals that best serve their immediate interests in order to expose intersectional relations of power. Once rights are viewed as one of many discourses, they can serve as a tool of empowerment and innovation. The tension between multiple hierarchies ultimately forces political actors to have a more provisional notion of rights, acknowledging their usefulness as a mobilizing symbol, yet underscoring their role in continued domination. Despite (or because of) the legal contradictions, the women in the "marrying out" cases had to employ existing legal narratives. I claim that such an invocation of rights ultimately changes their nature because it reconfigures the balance of power and thereby transforms the ideals that inform political tactics and legal decision-making. Thus, the provisional use of rights discourses is a very important form of legal power, where actors can temporarily construct their own (very contingent) legal narrative which might capture their multiple layers of oppression. Indigenous women, by using courts and the UN, aspire to refigure the terrain of identity, tradition, and political action in order to "resist" (and change) dominant legal logics.

Interestingly, some who defend rights talk do so from first-hand experience with the invisibility created by the intersections of power. Those who suffer from dual oppression (such as sexism plus racism) realize that some aspects of the promise of rights can be deployed instrumentally against others to win some temporary political points. Kimberlé Crenshaw notes that the use of rights is especially important for groups that suffer multiple levels of oppression in liberal societies because they have fewer tactical choices.[65] Since rights talk is not the only dominant logic, it becomes useful to counteract other hegemonic structures, such as (colonial) racism or sexism. This is why I argue that legal scholars must look at the intersections of power to better understand the operation of legal mobilization.

The way that indigenous women employ the language of individual rights might illustrate the contested nature of the dominant legal culture, and the contradictory colonial legacies that it represents. Indigenous women use a particular aspect of the dominant ideals in order to contest other aspects of the same system. For instance, they might stress liberal egalitarian values over equally liberal notions of individual acquisition and property-ownership, which are premised upon inequality. Even when indigenous women invoke gender rights, one cannot assume that they wholeheartedly embrace an Anglo conception of feminism, or the abstract ideal of individual rights. At the same time, analysts cannot assume that indigenous women always believe that tribal sovereignty automatically must trump gender equality. Both sets of ideals are contested. The impetus to use dominant legal logics such as civil rights remedies might even have been rooted in indigenous traditions, but rights or feminist discourses might be the most convenient and available frames for resisting particular injustices. Thus, instead of committing a feminist act, these women may be asserting their indigenous identity. Such a hypothetical is a good example of the provisional use of a contradictory legal legacy.

The cases under consideration in this study illustrate how existing law/legal narratives fail to construct a provisional remedy for complex layers of domination. Competing legal narratives articulate conceptions of individual right and collective good that inevitably come to loggerheads. The invocation of individual or sovereignty rights is a double-edged sword for indigenous women. While individual rights might help them win benefits from dominant institutions, they might also further oppress them by undermining the different value structure underlying what they conceive to be their traditional way of life. At the same time, if indigenous women uncritically advocate certain conceptions of sovereignty or tradition, they might entrench gender domination. Such a cumulative effect of power forces one to adopt a more provisional posture toward legal tactics, rather than assuming that they can serve as the ultimate guarantor of justice.

Indigenous women might question sexist membership rules simply because they were denied certain material benefits. Thus, one could read the use of rights less as a statement against sexism, or even against colonial oppression, and more as an act of basic material survival. The point is that when one examines the intersections of race and gender, many conclusions can be drawn from the tactics employed in particular situations. Dominant legal tools can be mobilized instrumentally to resist various spheres of domination, and the fact that such norms are being mobilized should not stand as evidence of "false consciousness." Indigenous women simultaneously resist dominant legal norms, contest their tribe's/band's sexist construction of cultural tradition, and maneuver within contemporary conceptions of sovereignty and individual rights. This dynamic calls for a deeper look at what counts as legal mobilization and political impact.

Legal Mobilization and the Democratic Possibilities of Re-evaluating Rights

> The rhetoric and rules of a society are something a great deal more than sham. In the same moment they may modify, in profound ways, the behaviour of the powerful, and mystify the powerless. They may disguise the true realities of power, but, at the same time, they may curb that power and check its intrusions. [66]

So far I have described the account of power and law that informs this discussion. In brief, legal norms constitute and echo complicated social relations. This account of law will benefit from an examination of the intersections of power. At the intersections of power, legal remedies often exacerbate the "double bind" that indigenous women face when they try to act politically. It becomes clear when one examines intersectionality that legal norms can facilitate both domination and resistance and therefore, legal mobilization happens provisionally. Given the limited choices that exist at the intersections of power, it is often necessary to employ the "master's tools"[67]; playing the contradictions of such tools off of one another to produce a new and different terrain for struggle. Once one realizes that the "master" is also constrained by these imperfect tools, it becomes apparent that the tools themselves are transformed when different parties invoke them.[68] An examination of gender and race together helps reveal the systemic contradictions of dominant legal norms and the possible limitations of rights as they are currently imagined. Not only is domination found in more places, but the possibility of resistance multiplies.[69] I am not simply asking whether the legal system works or not. Instead, I am interested in exploring the dance of domination and resistance that ultimately shakes foundational legal logics and changes them over time.

Looking at how law functions in the lives of indigenous women can shed light on how legal mobilization operates more generally in society. I am not putting forth an account of mobilization that requires a "measurable" impact, as Gerald Rosenberg[70] does, or one that assumes that there is a cohesive legal narrative which can be uniformly invoked in every situation. Instead, I offer an account of legal mobilization that includes moments where law's "catalyst"[71] effect might not even be immediately apparent. In other words, the impact of legal mobilization becomes more diffuse and harder to measure as relations of power multiply. Therefore, to capture how particular legal acts represent moments of simultaneous domination and resistance, impact must be expanded to include "rights re-evaluation."

Two layers of rights re-evaluation are crucial to this study. The first is a meta-theoretical contribution, referring to the position that scholars should take when assessing the utility of rights discourses in political struggles. Much of this chapter has focused on re-conceiving power, and how the law operates in society. For scholars to embrace a more contingent and ever-changing notion of law, it is necessary to re-evaluate what counts as impact of legal mobilization, and how to frame useful questions for studying law and society. By urging legal scholars to look at the intersections of power, I am suggesting that they adopt a new approach to understanding rights. Positive impact of legal mobilization may not be measurable in discrete terms, but should be assessed according to how future participation is spurred by a particular act of mobilization.

The second form of rights re-evaluation that is central to this study pertains to political actors and their opportunities to re-evaluate the meaning of rights in a way that might better describe the effects of intersectional power. These two aspects of rights re-evaluation are very much interrelated. It is necessary to adopt a more provisional scholarly posture toward legal mobilization to find moments where political actors such as indigenous women have the opportunity to re-define and re-evaluate rights.

Revealing legal or ideological inconsistencies should count as an impact of legal mobilization. I consider these acts of resistance because even though they occur within a seemingly overwhelming web of power, they might open up opportunities for future political participation. Therefore, resistance in my framework is based upon the assumption that some groups' (intersectional) experiences are not represented by the ideals embodied in the rhetoric of rights, yet those groups might still invoke the rhetoric to clear space for future political action. They unearth the internal historical contradictions and make use of them to try to rebalance legal power relations. This counts as resistance because such provisional use of rights talk might raise important issues that spur future legal critique. Such resistance sparks changes in the intersubjective knowledge of rights. This can be measured by noting an increased attention to the problematic of intersectionality and the changing opportunities for indigenous women to be able to articulate this double bind. Rights re-evaluation reveals the contradictions that exist within liberal ideals; it notes that the dominant culture or legal structure is merely a patchwork of competing ideals; and it shows how aspects of that patchwork can be mobilized against each other in order to produce new legal meanings.

Rights re-evaluation captures the possibility of bringing two identity strands together to force legal recognition of intersectional power. My attention to intersectionality disrupts and prevents the sedimentation of rights discourses, and helps reinvigorate their democratic potential. The ability to continue to re-evaluate rights and to contest meanings is a very important form of political participation. I use the term re-evaluation to acknowledge the limited degree of agency that political actors have, and the constraints or dominating effects of the legacy of rights. The ability to evaluate whether rights are the best tactic at a particular moment, or the ability to evaluate and re-create the meaning of rights must be considered within an overarching and ever-changing web of power.

Therefore, what emerges is a very humble account of resistance, which acknowledges the small victories in sustaining the movement of politics and in the evaluation and selection of particular tactics. Here, domination and resistance describe the dynamic relationship between identity, strategy, and political interests. How one defines one's political identity and long-term goals is deeply embedded in existing discourses and tactics. As Comaroff and Brown describe, rights discourses simultaneously mark identities and erase them. The legacy of colonialism, and the imposition of certain legal discourses are overwhelming forces of domination, especially when one considers the intersections of hierarchies such as colonialism and sexism. Yet, the ideals expressed by rights provide the seeds for future resistance, for identity-construction, and for setting the terms for new and different struggles. All of this depends upon the acknowledgement of the ever-changing and contingent nature of rights discourses. This allows the contingency of strategies to spill over to the adoption of provisional identities. People who occupy the intersections of power might be able to re-negotiate their interests in terms of either identity strand, all the while remaining aware of the continuing lack of attention to another crucial aspect of their identity. Thus, by looking at the intersections of power, one can see the complex relationship between strategies and identity, and how both are contingent upon the tools and categories that are available at a particular moment.

Justice may never be realized. The remedies/solutions that are available will be inherently contradictory. But the "myth" of justice must be rearticulated and reframed to fit current power dynamics. Uncovering contradictions, silences, and categorical cracks should count as an impact of legal mobilization because it unveils the simultaneity of domination and resistance and it clears space for future political participation. People are conscious of how multiple hierarchies limit their tactical choices, so their only option for change might lie in the incremental reconstruction of existing discourses.[72] This does not mean that they are suffering from false consciousness or unknowingly legitimating coercive legal forms. Even though they might be feeding their domination, the fact that their limited palette of choices is being exposed provides a macro-critique of the overarching power dynamic. The instrumental use of dominant narratives might even yield gains that are more empowering than immediate material pay backs.[73] If one "loses" in court, but shakes the existing power structure (by revealing the double bind of intersectionality), a greater symbolic victory may have been won.

To systematically assess how rights have been re-evaluated in the "marrying out" cases, the following chapters include an in-depth discursive analysis of the legal arguments put forth by all of the parties involved in the two cases. Below I explain the framework that I developed for doing this discursive analysis. The analysis of legal texts provides concrete evidence of how legal mobilization acts as a moment of simultaneous domination and resistance.

Framing the Legal Claims

E.P. Thompson wrote, "The law may be rhetoric, but it need not be empty rhetoric."[74] This study explores the meanings ascribed to legal rhetoric, and how those meanings might be mobilized to improve indigenous women's legal and political status. I focus on legal discourse for several reasons. Given the constitutive account of law that informs this project, and the complex layers of power that are being observed, one way to begin this exploration is to look at the kinds of legal logics and narratives that are employed in the process of describing indigenous women's situation and proposing remedies to the double bind of intersectionality. The documents that I focus on in my analysis are court decisions, amicus briefs, newspaper articles, and interviews with lawyers. While these materials are all bound by formal legal procedures and institutions, they provide an inkling of how legal norms might help frame political claims and facilitate political identity construction.

While many socio-legal scholars argue that it is important to study how legal discourse is invoked in extra-legal settings,[75] my study focuses on legal argumentation in more formal legal venues. I feel that such argumentation, along with an analysis of the kinds of groups that submit amicus briefs, helps provide a window into legal consciousness more broadly. First, my study sets out the predominant frames of argumentation that social movement organizations might capitalize upon in an attempt to win over constituent followers.[76] Second, it is very difficult to get at "consciousness" and whether legal actors actually believe the legal rhetoric that they might invoke. It is more important for my purposes to understand how official legal discourses get constructed in order to force the formal legal institutions (courts and the UN) to acknowledge the double bind of intersectionality.

As demonstrated in the Canadian case, the initial formal articulation of the problem was adopted by a more widespread movement. The frames used in the legal venues are molded, changed, invoked at the grassroots level, and mobilized in legislative contexts. But grassroots legal consciousness is not the focus of this study. Rather, I focus on the multiple legal discourses that had to be molded in order for lawyers[77] to make claims on behalf of indigenous women. Implicit in this study is the assumption that these formal legal arguments do affect extra-legal identity construction and legal consciousness outside of the formal legal institutions. Assumed is the great influence of the "radiating affects of the courts."[78] Therefore, this study provides a discursive analysis that can form the foundation for future research. A subsequent study would take the insights gleaned from this analysis to better understand the extent to which legal arguments constitute indigenous women's political identities at the grassroots level.

Thus, to capture the multiplicity of power and the pluralistic nature of legal norms, I analyze legal arguments within discursive frames. The expression "frame" has many meanings, varying by context. William Gamson states, "A frame typically implies a range of positions, rather than any single one, thus allowing for a degree of controversy among those who share the same package."[79] By placing legal logics into a discursive framework, I acknowledge the multiple meanings that can be assigned to legal norms even in the most formal venues. The way that dominant legal narratives are creatively reconstructed or combined provide new and different ways of presenting claims and constructing political identity. It is in the creative combinations of dominant legal narratives that one can find resistance. As stated earlier, what Marx called political emancipation is possible through the strategic deployment of dominant institutions and ideologies. By understanding the multiple meanings that can be constructed from dominant legal narratives, one can find more sites for political resistance.

In this analysis, frames are conceptual themes, which stem from formal legal texts and institutions, but require an understanding of historical and political context. I present them here to systematize some very messy relationships. Legal ideals are open to divergent interpretations and, therefore, do not necessarily lead to one correct meaning. We should not "assume the coherence and consistency of legal discourse but [we should] . . . search out the resonances of the social economic, and political struggles that reside behind the smooth surface of legal reasoning and judicial utterance."[80] No discourse exists in its pure form because the tangle of discursive elements mutually influence each other a great deal. Crosscutting ideological, economic, political and legal factors mediate all of these frames, which complicates the kinds of legal arguments and political claims that can be made. Thus, I disaggregate overarching legal themes into frames, which help make sense of the multiplicity of meanings that can be ascribed to them.

The six frames that I study are 1) individual civil rights, 2) sovereignty rights, 3) membership standards, 4) the construction of tradition, 5) jurisdiction and the separation of governmental powers, and 6) economic and material forces. I created these frames based upon a first reading of the pertinent documents: court decisions, amicus briefs, law review articles, and interviews with attorneys. These themes are raised repeatedly in all of the documents that I analyzed. After I developed the framework, it quickly became clear that none of these frames had a definitive meaning, but legal argumentation was a process of interpretation and meaning-making. Next I provide a provisional explanation of what set of ideas each frame includes, and how the frames might relate to one another. But it is important to emphasize that these frames are malleable and take on different meanings depending on the context.

Individual civil rights refers broadly to the set of rights that individuals demand from their governments. There is great debate about whether governments should actively prevent injustice or inequality between individuals, or rather merely remove obstacles that individuals face in being productive citizens. Of course, the distinction between these two government roles is not so easy to make. This frame is important to the study of the "marrying out" cases and indigenous women's legal mobilization in general because individual rights form the foundation for both Julia Martinez's and the Canadian women's legal claims. The sex equality claims were about individual women achieving access to the same status as individual men. This contrasts with predominant accounts of indigenous sovereignty rights.

Sovereignty rights, in their most abstract form, refer to the rights of states to full control over their domestic affairs. Sovereign autonomy in the international realm is most basically the freedom from intrusion by other states. Sovereignty rights in the context of indigenous politics are much narrower. They involve the degree of self-government or self-determination that indigenous bands or tribes can exert while existing within the borders of a colonial state. So, the traditional definition of sovereignty does not really exist for indigenous peoples, but this particular word is what indigenous people often invoke in order to strengthen their autonomy claims. In using this term, they point out their loss of sovereignty and can leverage a degree of self-government. Therefore, sovereignty discourses vary wildly depending on the context. Some indigenous peoples argue for complete separation and eventual nationhood, but this is rare. More often, indigenous nations argue for autonomy over tribal/band affairs, with a special institutional relationship with the federal government. The multiple versions of sovereignty that are presented by indigenous peoples point to the destabilizing effect that certain interpretations of this frame can have. Boaventura de Sousa Santos makes this point very well:

> By denouncing the social exclusion and political suppression brought about in the name of false, abstract equivalences between nation, state, and law, the indigenous struggles open the ideological space for a radical revision of the vertical political obligation that underlies the liberal state, and call for new conceptions of sovereignty (dispersed, shared, polyphonic sovereignty).[81]

Individual civil rights and sovereignty rights can be considered "master frames,"[82] which define how the others get constructed. They also represent the intersectional concerns that are central to this study: Individual civil rights broadly correspond to the gender strand of power, while sovereignty loosely represents the race strand. Yet it is important to note that these strands of power and legal discourses are cross-cutting and are invoked in combination. This is part of what it means to occupy the intersections of power.

Membership standards refers to how one determines one's tribe/band affiliation. This frame is particularly important to the cases under consideration in this study, because the codified membership standards instituted the sex-based distinctions that excluded indigenous women from their tribes or bands. Membership standards usually balance cultural and biological factors. Blood quantum was a measurement developed by colonial governments in order to count and dominate various indigenous populations. This colonial influence has created a racial category called "Indian" or "indigenous." But today, biological determinants are often employed by the tribes/bands themselves as a way to exclude outsiders and to assure cultural survival. Some indigenous people feel that cultural affinity should outweigh one's biological connection to a tribe/band in determining membership. If one speaks the language, practices the religion and is generally connected to the community, one should be allowed to remain. This tension between biology and culture plays itself out on many levels and reflects broader cultural struggles that result from colonialism.

Tradition is invoked in many different ways. Simply put, tradition refers to historical practices that supposedly predate colonial conquest. Included in the tradition frame is the method that one uses to authenticate that tradition. Tribes/bands often apply sexist membership standards because they claim that they traditionally followed a patrilineal membership scheme. Oral historians and anthropologists are often asked to vouch for the authenticity of this tradition. The cases analyzed in this book show how contested tradition can be.

Jurisdiction refers to the relationship between various governing bodies. Court decisions often focus on whether the issue falls within the court's power vis-à-vis the legislative and the executive branches of the federal government. The jurisdiction frame also includes the division of power between the federal, state/provincial, and tribal/band governments. Indigenous women's legal claims are affected by jurisdictional decisions because courts sometimes defer either to other branches of the government or to tribal sovereignty, which sometimes render gender-based legal claims moot. In short, jurisdiction sometimes charges institutions with the power to define indigenous and women's rights.

Economic and Material Forces include the effects that a sexist membership rule has upon indigenous women's access to services, reservations, and employment. It also includes the motivation for creating these rules, and their impact upon the ability of tribes/bands and the federal government to provide services to their constituencies. These economic implications are often contested, and different economic claims often inform the presentation of legal arguments.

These discursive frames are very interrelated. They are disaggregated here for the purpose of systematic analysis. For example, an argument that stresses sovereignty rights will be informed by a particular account of tradition, which also determines one's stance on jurisdiction. It is important to realize that different parties sometimes combine these discursive frames in unique ways to try to describe distinct power relations. That is why it is helpful to break legal arguments into their constituent frames. The interaction of the different frames and the various interpretations of each frame provide a window into indigenous women's domination and resistance. Moreover, aspects of specific frames might be used by social movement organizations to rally grassroots support and resources for future mobilization.

I selected the cases in the US and Canada because they both exemplify the puzzle of intersectional power for indigenous women. Both cases are about rules that discriminate against women who married out of their tribe, but there are important differences between them. In Canada, there was continuing legal mobilization, while in the US, the issue was never brought to federal court again after Julia Martinez lost her case. This variation between the cases sets up an interesting comparison for two reasons. One could argue that I have a simple comparison between a "successful" instance of legal mobilization, and one that failed. This would be a very sleek design for a positivist, who looks for simple causality and measurable impacts. Yet, by applying an interpretive discursive analysis, I can show that, despite the variation in outcomes, these two cases have very similar themes in legal argumentation. Although there are important institutional differences between the US and Canada, these cases both exemplify the unique web of power that indigneous women must navigate. My interpretive analysis details these similarities and differences to better illustrate the complexity of legal mobilization.

The following chapters help elucidate how these six frames operate in the US and Canadian cases. Chapter 2 offers a brief history of US-Indigenous relations plus the frame analysis for the *Santa Clara Pueblo v. Martinez* case. Chapter 3 is a brief history of Canadian-Indigenous relations and traces the progression of the legal mobilization surrounding the "marrying out" issue in Canada. There was much more mobilization in Canada than in the US, which makes the analysis of the discursive frames a bit more complicated. Therefore, the analysis of how the six discursive frames evolved during the two decades of legal and political mobilization in Canada is divided between chapters 3 and 4. The second half of chapter 3 includes the analysis of the "master" frames: individual civil rights and sovereignty rights. Chapter 4 analyzes the remaining four discursive frames.

Chapter 5 compares the US and Canadian cases, arguing that while there is more mobilization in Canada, there are great similarities between the way that the discursive frames are constructed in the two countries. This sheds light on the continuing ideological domination and resistance that exists in both contexts. While the Canadian case offers an example of concrete legislative changes that might ultimately alleviate the double bind of intersectionality for indigenous women, it also exemplifies the complicated power relations that intersectionality embodies. How those legislative changes play themselves out might actually reinforce indigenous women's intersectional domination, thereby making future resistance all the more difficult. Chapter 6 attempts to make theoretical sense of this comparative study, revisiting the account of power introduced in this chapter and assessing whether rights re-evaluation can indeed reconstruct the power relations that define intersectionality.

To better understand the workings of legal power, it is necessary to study some "hard cases," where the constraints of legal power are very potent. The cases that I analyze epitomize the dynamic of intersectional power, where indigenous women must navigate multiple hierarchies in order to make political claims. They must re-construct existing legal discourses to carve out space for their unique identities. In indigenous women's dual domination, one can uncover the political possibilities of the ideals of rights discourses. The following chapters present the struggle to give rights new meanings to resist the double bind of intersectionality.

CHAPTER 2

"Marrying Out" in the US

Santa Clara Pueblo v. Martinez Facts

In 1939, The Santa Clara Pueblo amended their (US approved) constitution to stipulate that membership would be extended only to "children born of marriages between members of the Santa Clara Pueblo" and "children born of marriages between male members of the Santa Clara Pueblo and non-members." The ordinance explicitly states that children "born of marriages between female members of the *Santa Clara Pueblo* and non-members shall not be members of the Santa Clara Pueblo."[1] In 1941, Julia Martinez married a Navajo man and subsequently had children with him. Even though these children lived on the Santa Clara Pueblo reservation and and had many ties to the community, they were denied official membership in the tribe. This rule that had been on the books since the 1930s was not enforced until the 1970's when HUD housing was beginning to be limited.[2] Since her children would be evicted from the reservation upon her death, Julia Martinez, along with her daughter Audrey, filed a class action suit under Title I of the Indian Civil Rights Act (ICRA), claiming that the Santa Clara Pueblo tribe's membership rules denied them (and similarly situated women) equal protection of the law.

Despite their non-member status, the Martinez children were allowed to reside on the reservation and to participate in community activities. But they could not vote in tribal elections or hold office. They were also denied medical care (which might have contributed to the death of one daughter).[3] They could not live on the reservation after their mother died nor could they inherit her home or "her possessory interests in the communal lands."[4] The denial of these benefits, along with federally allocated funds that accompany membership in an Indian tribe, prompted Martinez[5] to question the fairness of the membership rule. After Martinez's claim failed to sway the (all male) tribal council, she turned to the federal court system for declaratory and injunctive relief. Given the lack of local support, Martinez was forced to turn to the courts of her tribe's historical oppressor in order to force the tribe to change its discriminatory membership rules.

37

The district court[6] found that it had jurisdiction to rule on Santa Clara Pueblo's membership ordinance. The district court further found that the membership rule did not violate the ICRA because it reflected the Pueblo's traditional practices and because membership was a vital aspect of tribal self-determination, the courts could not overturn such practices. The Court of Appeals for the Tenth Circuit[7] upheld the district court's ruling on jurisdiction, but overturned its ruling on the merits. The appeals court ruled that the membership ordinance was a violation of the ICRA's equal protection clause because it invidiously discriminated against Santa Claran women.

Ultimately, the case reached the US Supreme Court. In an effort to acknowledge that Indian tribes were really sovereign entities, the Court ruled against Martinez. "Indian tribes have long been recognized as possessing the common-law immunity from suit traditionally enjoyed by sovereign powers."[8] Since the ICRA did not explicitly waive this sovereign immunity, the Court found that the tribe was immune to Martinez's suit. At the same time, the Court stressed that Congress retained the plenary power to decide the cases in which tribes are not immune to suit. To show "a proper respect both for tribal sovereignty itself and for the plenary authority of Congress,"[9] the Court thus decided that this case was out of its jurisdiction. It ruled that habeas corpus was the only relief explicitly noted in the ICRA and, therefore, that would be the only area in which the federal courts could intervene.

In the majority opinion, Thurgood Marshall pointed to the ICRA itself to show the federal government's desire to respect tribal self-government. He claimed that the Bill of Rights was not simply extended to the tribes, but rather, the ICRA was catered to the "unique political, cultural and economic needs of tribal governments."[10] The Court acknowledged the competing purposes of this case and the ICRA more generally: Individual tribe members' rights (i.e., protection from the tribe) often clash with tribal self-government/sovereignty. In the end, Julia Martinez's case of individual gender discrimination was overshadowed by the Court's desire to validate tribal self-determination and Congressional plenary power.

One could read this case in many ways. It could be seen as a moment of individual resistance using the ICRA—and all the dominant legal legacies attached to it—against another (colonized indigenous) legal narrative that produced the sexist membership rule. These possible readings must be set against the continuing legal struggle to attain tribal sovereignty, which is a complicated concept that has been integrated into many colonized indigenous cultures. Martinez brought suit using the ICRA in order to maintain her and her children's connection to the tribe. From her perspective, her children's inclusion in the tribe would augment Santa Claran cultural survival, because they were a part of the community and could help maintain tradition.

In this case, not only were Martinez's individual (gender-based) rights being denied, but problematic conceptions of tradition and sovereignty were being reinforced. There has been quite a bit of analysis of this case, yet most of it whittles it down to a dichotomous debate between sovereignty and individual rights. Ultimately, *Santa Clara Pueblo* has served as strong precedent for subsequent sovereignty cases. The historical narrative and discursive analysis that follows show how the dichotomy between individual and sovereignty rights might reinforce the double bind of intersectionality for indigenous women. When the problem is set up as a dichotomy between indigenous self-determination and sex equality, the two cannot coexist, thereby entrenching the dual domination of Julia Martinez's race and gender.

A Brief History of US-Indigenous Relations

To better understand the nuances of the *Santa Clara Pueblo* case, it is necessary to examine the tides of history that led to the establishment of the Santa Clara Pueblo's Constitution and membership ordinance. The federal government forced Indian tribes to codify tribal law and create recognizable legal institutions. Thus, the very concepts "sovereignty" and "membership" were historical constructions resulting from the ongoing US domination of Native American peoples.

In general, US-tribal relations went through phases that emphasized assimilation and tribal self-determination at different times. The US government inherited many tactics from the British crown, and could be termed a colonial power through this legacy. Early on, colonial powers dealt with different tribes according to pressing economic concerns. As the demand for land increased, and the US became a more cohesive state, Indian tribes became a greater obstacle to expansionism. Thus, Indian people were killed or relocated. The Indian Removal Act of 1830 led to the "Trail of Tears," one of the most notable and depressing instances of Native American relocation.

The Cherokees were forced to move from their ancestral lands in Georgia to US-defined "Indian Country" in Oklahoma, and many were killed during the journey. This is just one example of the land robbery and forced assimilation that characterized US-Native American relations.

The Allotment Act of 1887[11] signaled a different kind of colonial coercion. It was an effort to convert Native people into farmers, thereby making them into agrarian citizens idealized by civic republicanism or liberal property-owning individuals.[12] Both of these impulses were efforts to make Native people into abstract citizens, subsumed under the US government (rather than their own tribal governing bodies). To accomplish this end, the US allotted plots of tribal land to individual tribe members in an effort to break communal ties. This flew in the face of many traditional Native practices. Some tribes lacked a notion of ownership altogether, seeing their relationship to the land in completely different terms than the Europeans did. The government also labeled certain Native American lands "surplus," allowing them to be sold off to whites, thereby further diminishing Native American territory. As a result of the allotment policy, Indian (communal) land holdings decreased from 138 million to 48 million acres by 1934.[13]

The Indian Reorganization Act (IRA) of 1934[14] stopped allotment and proclaimed congressional support for Indian self-government. Under the IRA, the Secretary of the Interior could approve tribal constitutions and laws.[15] Most of the tribes that chose to create a constitution did so according to a template provided by the Bureau of Indian Affairs, which included word-for-word excerpts from the US constitution. While there was a great deal of paternalism in the way that tribal governments were fostered, and the governments reflected US norms of governance, this was an important step in the process of increasing tribal self-government.

The Santa Clara Pueblo was one of the tribes that accepted the IRA. It instituted a Constitution in 1935 and amended its membership rules in 1939. The Santa Clara Pueblo could only extend tribal membership to a limited number of people because their federally allocated funds were inadequate. To distribute these scarce resources, the Pueblo chose to determine membership along gender lines. Therefore, membership was extended only to the children of mixed marriages whose father was a member of the Santa Clara Pueblo. The assumption was that a man would be more likely than a woman to teach children the Pueblo's cultural traditions.[16] Hence, the tribe's membership rules were dictated by a patriarchal assumption that women followed their husbands upon marriage more so than vice versa. Since some Santa Clarans feared that in the future, their land might be "allotted" to children who did not identify with the tribe, they instituted this gender-based rule.

Federal Indian policy was geared toward assimilation in the 1940s and 50s, the era of termination. Several policies were instituted in an attempt to discontinue Native Americans' special relationship with the US. Tribes were terminated (or ceased to be recognized), programs were cut, some federal power over Native Americans was transferred to the states, and incentives were given to individual Native Americans to leave the reservations. Eventually, this wave of assimilation policy was followed by some reforms, starting in the 1960s. Much of the states' jurisdiction over Native Americans was transferred back either to the federal government or to the tribes themselves.

It was in this context that the Indian Civil Rights Act (ICRA) was passed in 1968. This is a piece of federal legislation that is crucial for understanding Julia Martinez's claims against her tribe. It extended an abridged version of the Bill of Rights to individual Indians. The ICRA was passed at a time when tribal institutions were being given new power. With increased tribal jurisdiction, the federal government became aware of individual injustices that were perpetrated by tribal institutions. The ICRA was an attempt to respect tribal self-governance while extending civil rights to individual Native Americans. In part, the ICRA states, "No Indian tribe in exercising powers of self-government shall . . . deny any person within its jurisdiction the equal protection of its laws or deprive any person of liberty or property without due process of law."[17] Therefore, the federal government, with the passage of the ICRA, allowed individuals to challenge their own tribal government's structure from within, using federal legal norms and tools. Since the ICRA could potentially pit individual Indians against their tribes, many tribes feared that it would undermine their increasing sovereignty. To assuage some of these fears, Congress passed the Indian Self-Determination and Education Assistance Act of 1975. In part it states,

> The Congress declares its commitment to the maintenance of
> the Federal Government's unique and continuing relationship
> with and responsibility to the Indian people through the
> establishment of a meaningful Indian self-determination
> policy which will permit an orderly transition from Federal
> domination of programs for and services to Indians to
> effective and meaningful participation by the Indian people in
> the planning, conduct, and administration of those programs
> and services.[18]

The passage of the ICRA and the Self-Determination Act in such close
proximity exemplifies the dual policies followed during this era. Native
Americans were simultaneously given a bit more self-governing power
and increased individual civil rights.

In this context Julia Martinez sued her Pueblo in federal court. The
case exemplifies the tensions between individual civil rights and tribal
self-determination. Most tribal leaders were pleased with the outcome
of *Santa Clara Pueblo* because the Court acknowledged that the ICRA
had to be limited in order to prevent individual claims from eroding
tribal sovereignty. The nuances of this conflict have long-term
implications for indigenous women's mobilization at the intersections
of race and gender.

Framing the Legal Claims

What emerges from a close look at the amicus briefs and the court
decisions in the *Santa Clara Pueblo* case is a very complicated
balancing act between Native Americans' individual rights and tribal
self-determination. Each party had a stake in combining the frames in a
particular way. Martinez's attorneys tried to balance tribal autonomy
and individual rights in a way that would allow her version of tradition
to be heard. They hoped that the Supreme Court would interpret the
ICRA in a way that allowed the courts to protect Martinez's individual
right to pass on membership in the Pueblo to her children.

The Pueblo's tribal council wanted to define individual civil rights
without federal intrusion. Thus, they argued for the court to first
establish sovereignty rights, and assumed that individual rights would
fall into place once tribal self-determination had been achieved. The
Pueblo argued for a very narrow interpretation of the ICRA in order to
limit the jurisdiction of the federal courts. This would help prevent the
federal government from ruling on the content of the Pueblo's

traditional practices in the future. The Pueblo also wanted judicial deference because if the courts scrutinized tribal acts, then the tribe would remain vulnerable to future lawsuits coming from its members. Regardless of whether the Court deferred to Congress or to tribal autonomy, in this case, any deference would advantage the Pueblo. Therefore, appealing to federal jurisprudential norms, as well as to federal institutional constraints, had strategic value for the Pueblo.

The courts had to weigh whether to defer to tradition (i.e., letting the Pueblo decide its membership); whether to defer to Congress by ruling very narrowly and interpreting the ICRA very explicitly; or whether to take a more active role in protecting Native American women. Thus, what emerged was not necessarily an act of judicial respect for tribal autonomy, but rather a statement about judicial legitimacy. The reasoning that emerged from this case acknowledged that Congress could ultimately determine which individual rights are compelling enough to limit tribal autonomy, but denied a judicial role in actively protecting those rights.

Frame One: Individual Civil Rights

Julia Martinez had to frame her sex-based claim in terms of the ICRA, which relies upon a very particular conception of individual civil rights. This was the only legal tool available for her to make her claim. Martinez claimed that, as an individual, she was being denied "equal protection of the law" because of her sex. Her lawyers argued:

> These facts reveal two kinds of discrimination: Julia Martinez is denied rights accorded her male counterparts and thus suffers discrimination on the basis of her sex. Audrey Martinez and her four brothers and three sisters suffer ancestry discrimination, being denied rights accorded male-line children otherwise identically situated.[19]

The appeals court, which ruled in Martinez's favor, framed the conflict in a similar manner. "[N]o court has come to grips with the issue of discrimination by a tribe against Indian women. And so we ask the question whether a tribe may extend to men members fundamental rights while simultaneously denying the same rights to its women."[20]

This way of framing the conflict echoes some interpretations of the Fourteenth Amendment equal protection clause. In general, such jurisprudence attempts to identify the fundamental rights that individuals have which cannot be limited by the government. The Supreme Court has attempted to develop some methods for balancing governmental interest against these individual rights. It has also tried to determine how to scrutinize laws that classify groups based upon identity characteristics such as race or gender, in order to distinguish acceptable from invidious discrimination. As with all jurisprudential practices, the standards articulated by the Court are not static, and have changed over time. Often their meanings are fluid and difficult to pin down. Since the Fourteenth Amendment explicitly mentions race, any law that distinguishes people based upon their race is considered to be "suspect," and therefore deserves a greater degree of judicial scrutiny. Since sex is not mentioned explicitly in the Fourteenth Amendment, it is often considered to be a "quasi-suspect" classification, deserving some judicial scrutiny, but not as much as racial classifications. Over time, the jurisprudence that has emerged seems to have set up a hierarchy of rights as well as a hierarchy of groups deserving protection from government intrusion. In other words, being free from sex-based discrimination is often not as fundamental a right as being free from race-based discrimination. Of course, this hierarchy is as solid as the precedent that created it, and new judicial interpretations have varied from this trend. The specific "test" applied to many sex-discrimination cases at the time that the Martinez case reached the Supreme Court has been called "mid-range" scrutiny. The language that the court uses when applying mid-range scrutiny is that a sex-based distinction in a law must be "*substantially related*" to the achievement of an "*important*" government objective in order to be deemed constitutional.

While this logic applies to the Fourteenth Amendment's equal protection clause, in *Santa Clara Pueblo*, the courts were explicitly trying to figure out how to apply equal protection logic to Native American tribes. The clearest expression of this standard is articulated by the appeals court decision, which ruled in favor of Julia Martinez.

> It is conceded that if the validity of the . . . [1939] ordinance were to be measured by the Fourteenth Amendment alone, it would have to be held violative because it draws its classification lines solely on the basis of sex . . . The Fourteenth Amendment standards do not, however, apply with full force. They do, nevertheless, serve as a persuasive guide to the decision. The history and decisions teach us that the

Indian Bill of Rights is modeled after the Constitution of the United States and is to be interpreted in the light of constitutional law decisions.[21]

Even Martinez's lawyers acknowledged the unique balancing act that must apply to Native Americans:

The cases from the 8th and 9th Circuits, as well as those from the 10th, all agree that the tribal interest in cultural autonomy is entitled to consideration in an Indian Civil Rights case; that it is to be weighted against the individual interest involved; and that this creates differences from the application of the 14th Amendment to the States in some cases.[22]

The district court decision also mentions this point:

Plaintiffs do not suggest that the Indian Civil Rights Act should be interpreted in a manner which would impose an Anglo-American equal protection standard on tribes in derogation of their traditional values.[23]

All of these quotes show how equal protection under the ICRA must take tribal sovereignty and tradition concerns into account.

A staunch individual rights advocate would treat tribal governments as any other governmental structure under the US Constitution. If sex was used as the basis for the legislation, it would be subject to mid-range judicial scrutiny. But, the court acknowledged that strict constitutional tests of individual rights (which are contested anyway) cannot apply here. The equal protection provided by the ICRA is not the same as that found in the Bill of Rights. There are several reasons why this is the case. Not all of the enumerated rights that exist in the Bill of Rights were included in the ICRA.

The Act incorporates only selected portions from the federal bill of rights contained in the first ten amendments and subsection (8) contains an edited version of the language of the 14th Amendment. Nowhere are privileges and immunities of citizens mentioned, nor is any mention made in the Act of the right to vote.[24]

There is also no first amendment non-establishment clause in the ICRA. Plus, habeas corpus protections were the only rights explicitly given federal court oversight. All of the briefs submitted for this case explore the legislative history of the ICRA to show how it differs from the Bill of Rights.[25] The appeals court decision explains why traditional Fourteenth Amendment individual rights norms should not apply here:

> Congress actually considered the various rights contained in the Bill of Rights and retained those which it considered essential and eliminated those parts which it deemed to be out of harmony with Indian culture . . . The concern of Congress was to protect against serious deprivations of constitutional rights while giving as much effect as the facts would allow to tribal autonomy.[26]

According to this logic, Native Americans as a group are not considered an insular minority, which deserves equal protection from the federal courts along racial lines because of their unique historical relationship to Congress. Therefore, Congressional plenary power over Native American tribes led the judiciary to reframe its reasoning for this equal protection claim.

These points establish that a strict individual civil rights reading cannot be applied to this case. Since it was established that the ICRA did not provide indigenous women with the same level of protection that other women enjoy under the Fourteenth Amendment, how should the competing interests be weighed? Each side of the dispute preferred a different method. There were several ways of articulating how these conflicting interests should be balanced. Martinez's lawyers argued:

> Where the strict application of traditional equal protection doctrines would significantly impair a tribal practice or alter a custom firmly embedded in Indian culture, *and where the individual injury alleged by the tribal member is, by comparison, not a grievous one,* then the equal protection clause at 25 USC §1302 (8) may be implemented somewhat differently than its constitutional counterpart.[27]

The brief continues:

> Those courts of appeals which have addressed cases arising under the ICRA have unanimously agreed on federal jurisdiction over such cases, provided that internal remedies within the tribal government are first exhausted (as here). The courts have further agreed on the standards to be applied, giving due consideration to a tribe's governmental interest,

which is to be weighted against the individual interest involved. The Court of Appeals in this case applied these settled rules and correctly concluded that the very serious harm to plaintiffs could not be justified by the 'incongruous and unreasonable' tribal interest claimed.[28]

Alan Taradash[29], Julia Martinez's attorney, made a strong argument for deferring to tribal practices, in order to respect tribal sovereignty. He wanted the federal court to make sure that tribal remedies had been exhausted prior to stepping in to protect individual tribal members. "And so they were putting an Indian blanket . . . around the Civil Rights Act, which was the decent thing to do . . . So you can have discrimination based upon tribal rules or customs or traditions—perfectly valid."[30] All of these quotes show that even the party who would benefit most from a pure individual rights reading of the ICRA tempered that position with a due concern for tribal autonomy and the authority of tradition. These dual interests exemplify indigenous women's intersectional identities. They must simultaneously consider the implications of certain legal arguments for each facet of their identity. Taradash's points show that tradition and tribal autonomy are just as important to indigenous women as gender equity.

The Pueblo (and the amicus briefs submitted in its favor), on the other hand, wanted much less judicial scrutiny than is described by Martinez's lawyers. Deferring to tribal remedies would require the court to determine if they had been truly exhausted, which the Pueblo thought would be too much interference. The Pueblo's advocates even went so far as to apply the minimum scrutiny ("rational relations") test, implying that the heightened scrutiny that the federal judiciary normally used for sex discrimination was inappropriate under the ICRA. They wrote:

> The inquiry under this test is the legitimate state interest the classification promotes balanced against the fundamental personal right the classification might endanger. The Supreme Court has required that a statutory classification bear some rational relationship to a legitimate state purpose.[31]

The Pueblo went on to propose a pure "fairness" argument.

It is undisputed that the Santa Clara enrollment rule was
applied uniformly to all and that there has been no exception
to the rule since it was codified in 1939. So long as there are
no exceptions and identical rules and laws are applied to all
members with either an even hand, or in a fair manner, then
such action is within the safeguard intended and proper.[32]

Similarly, many of the amicus briefs argue that the ICRA standard of
equal protection should be on procedural rather than substantive
grounds. According to this logic, "Under the ICRA, courts are
mandated only to ensure that these [membership] criteria, whatever
they may be, are applied fairly and equally."[33] This shows how they
chose to appeal to the individual rights sensibilities that exist in federal
jurisprudence. Yet, they did not ponder the fairness across sex, or the
differential treatment of men and women. Rather, the rule had to be
applied "uniformly"[34] to all similarly situated women to pass muster
under the ICRA. In its argument, the Pueblo also noted that the appeals
court's analysis in favor of Martinez did not offer a clear principle for
balancing individual civil rights and tribal autonomy.[35] The Pueblo also
argued that if the federal courts were going to interfere, they should at
least provide clear guidance for future cases.

It is rare to find a "pure" individual civil rights argument in any of
the briefs.[36] Instead, even Martinez's attorneys used cultural bases to
question the membership rule on cultural grounds to show respect for
tribal autonomy. Thus, in the process of making an individual rights
argument, issues of sovereignty and tradition inevitably came up. A
pure individual rights argument was avoided because they did not want
to re-inscribe colonial domination on both an ideological and legal
level. As the above discussion shows, more conventional notions of
Fourteenth Amendment individual civil rights do not really apply to
indigenous women. Individual rights must be considered alongside
sovereignty rights. The discussion below will show how sovereignty
rights do not really exist in a pure form either.

Frame Two: Sovereignty Rights

Historical conceptions of sovereignty play a very important role in the
arguments presented in this case. Santa Clara Pueblo felt that the ICRA
was a direct assault on tribal sovereignty. Allowing individuals to sue

tribes in federal court is a serious infringement of tribal self-determination. The Pueblo wrote:

> It must always be remembered that the various Indian tribes were once independent and sovereign nations and that their claim to sovereignty long predates that of our own Government . . . They were, and always have been, regarded has having a semi-independent position when they preserved their tribal relations; not as States, not as nations, not as possessed of the full attributes of sovereignty, but as a separate people, with the power of regulating their internal and social relations, and thus far not brought under the laws of the Union of or the State within whose limits they resided.[37]

A staunch sovereignty rights advocate would say that the federal government must bow out of this dispute entirely, regardless of the traditions involved and regardless of the "proper" judicial role vis-à-vis Congress. Individual rights, according to this view, must be authorized and respected at the tribal level, if at all.

> Tribal sovereignty is about cultural survival and the ability to shape the tribe's make up and practices for time immemorial. The Governor of the Pueblo explained the probable effect of not enforcing the 1939 ordinance: "It would tend to destroy the Pueblo as a whole . . . Without it we would have an influx of people that we don't know who they are. They would come in from all directions; Indians and non-Indians alike. So it would be a destruction on the Santa Clara Indian culture."[38] In the context of this case, the most important aspect of sovereignty is the ability to exclude "outsiders." "The most basic and fundamental sovereign right of any Indian tribe is its complete and absolute authority to determine all questions of its own membership as a political entity."[39] Sovereignty also brings immunity from suit by individual tribal members, and the denial of tribal immunity to suit would have very debilitating economic effects.

In addition to not being subject to federal law, many argued that tribes should be free from ideological domination. This means that tribal institutions should not have to mimic western forms of government or ideologies. The tribe also should have the right to construct its own version of individual civil rights norms or reject them altogether. The Pueblo's attorney stated, "above all, courts must avoid the unconscious tendency to bring missionary zeal to the task of extending the blessings of our philosophy of individual liberties to Indian tribes and tribal members."[40] Many tribes testified in Congressional hearings against the ICRA. The appeals court decision says, "It is significant that the Pueblos opposed the legislation in question [the ICRA]. They regarded it as an effort to import into the tribal government the standards of United States constitutional law. The effect of this would, of course, be to undermine tribal law."[41] One interesting example of an argument to counter such intrusion is found in the amicus brief of the Pueblo de Conchita et. al. In order to acknowledge the heterogeneity of different tribes' legal systems, they suggested that Fourteenth Amendment standards should not be applied uniformly to all tribes. Instead, they suggested the following distinctions:

> The closer a tribe has developed rules similar to that of the anglo-saxon legal and political system, the closer the ICRA equal protection clause will be construed as being consistent with Fourteenth Amendment standards. Conversely, tribal customs alien to the anglo-saxon legal tradition will not be viewed in light of Fourteenth Amendment requirements, but instead viewed in the tribal cultural context.[42]

This suggestion assumes that someone can judge the level of similarity between a tribe's customs and Anglo-Saxon legal norms prior to deciding what level of federal scrutiny should apply. Again, this is a prime example of how individual civil rights are not being dismissed by the tribes themselves. Instead, they wish to construct some culturally sensitive way of arbitrating individual rights claims in order to acknowledge tribal sovereignty.

In this case, one finds that even the Pueblo deferred to the Congress a bit more than would be expected from a staunch sovereignty advocate. There are many instances in the briefs where they explicitly acknowledge Congressional plenary power over their sovereignty. The Pueblo found value in the individual civil rights norms that are at the root of the ICRA. They just wanted the tribal government to be the venue for such individual rights protection. The

National Tribal Chairmen's Association argued, "It is ethnocentric in the extreme to assume that federal courts are the only tribunals capable of protecting those individual rights guaranteed by the ICRA."[43] So, according to the arguments offered by the Pueblo and the amicus curiae, sovereignty must come before individual rights, but not necessarily at their expense. The Pueblo's attorneys wrote:

> Congress in order to protect civil rights of members of Indian tribes decided to strengthen tribal governments and tribal institutions. Testimony before the Ervin Committee indicated that Indian tribes lacked certain civil rights protections, many not having constitutions or other formal governments.[44]

Thus, according to the tribe, the best way to protect civil rights of individual members is to strengthen tribal governments. It is important to note that US government structures form the foundation for these "strengthened" tribal institutions. So, even if the federal courts were to wholeheartedly defer to the tribal institutions (which they haven't), one must recognize the historical influence that the federal system has had upon tribal institutions and ideologies. Even with this constructed view of sovereignty, the Pueblo was convinced that the federal government (or at least the courts) should not intrude on membership decisions. According to them, membership is the bedrock of cultural survival. The Pueblo's attorneys quoted the trial court decision on this point:

> In deciding who is and who is not a member, the Pueblo decides what it is that makes its members unique, what distinguishes a Santa Clara Indian from everyone else in the United States. If its ability to do this is limited or restricted by an external authority, then a new definition of what it is to be a Santa Claran is imposed and the culture of Santa Clara is inevitably changed.[45]

Compare this to the appeals court's account:

> The interest of the Tribe in maintaining its integrity and in retaining its tribal cultures is entitled due consideration . . . And where the tribal tradition is deep-seated and the individual injury is relatively insignificant, courts should be

and have been reluctant to order the tribal authority to give way[46]

The appeals court decision balanced the individual injury more than the Pueblo would like, but it also acknowledged the tribal interests. The ACLU suggested that the "standard of review under the ICRA should be identical to the Fourteenth Amendment standard with one major difference: the concept of Indian sovereignty serves as a 'backdrop' against which the tribal action should be viewed."[47] So even in the briefs and decisions in favor of Martinez, sovereignty was mentioned and given due consideration.

Both sides agreed that determining membership is integral to indigenous cultural survival. Martinez argued that the tribe was not following tradition. So, if the federal government deferred to the current tribal council's position, it would be deferring to an inauthentic tradition. Therefore, Martinez wanted sovereignty to be maintained, but she disputed the tribal authority's interpretation of tradition and felt that the federal courts could legitimately arbitrate such a dispute about tradition. Martinez's brief states that "the trial court's refusal to judge the cultural evidence was in error."[48] The appeals court also thought it would be appropriate for a federal body to judge the impact of a tribal action upon cultural survival. In contrast, the Pueblo felt that the trial court was correct when it found that the ICRA does not "require or authorize this Court to determine which traditional values will promote cultural survival."[49]

In addition to disputing the impact of the federal venue, both sides disagreed about the effect that the norms embodied in the ICRA would have upon tribal sovereignty. Martinez thought that continuing with the inauthentic tradition found in the membership ordinance ultimately would have a more detrimental effect than forcing the tribe to bend to individual civil rights norms. The Pueblo believed that the influence of the civil rights norms themselves would destroy the Santa Clara traditions.

So far, this analysis of the first two frames—individual civil rights and sovereignty rights—show that this dispute over sexist membership standards is embedded in a larger cultural and legal context. While neither individual civil rights norms nor sovereignty rights norms exist in any "pure" form (that is, disentangled from colonial relations, or even divorced from each other), they both serve as lenses for analyzing the other discursive frames. Thus, these two frames qualify as "master" frames, because they guide most of the other kinds of legal arguments.

As discussed in chapter 1, individual and sovereignty rights echo John Comaroff's discussion of the competing registers in colonial liberal discourse. The first parallels what he labels radical individualism, while the second is similar to his conception of primal sovereignty.[50] The colonial legacy of the simultaneous construction and erasure of indigenous identity influences the interpretation of these master frames in the *Santa Clara Pueblo* case. The fact that neither side advocates a pure version of either individual civil rights or sovereignty rights is a testament to the complicated history that constructed these frames. Additionally, the simultaneous construction and erasure of indigenous identity and their unique legal status comes through clearly in the legal arguments presented by each side. Julia Martinez's position at the intersection of race and gender power is reflected in these complicated legal arguments, as are her apparent dual loyalties to tribal self-determination and gender equity. The other frames also echo these complicated forces.

Frame Three: Membership Standards

There are many ways that tribal membership can be determined, but it is important to note that all of the different standards are colored by the colonial experience. The contest over membership standards is a product of the complicated web of power that affects indigenous women's lives. One way to determine membership in a Native American tribe is by looking at blood quantum (i.e., the percent of one's biological lineage that can be traced to a particular tribe). This is the method that was created by the US government in an effort to dominate Native Americans. Another membership scheme relies upon affinity to the tribe through cultural, religious, and linguistic practices. At first, the fight over membership standards seems to be based upon a straightforward distinction between biological and cultural connections to the tribe. Ultimately, the two streams are combined and the standards that emerge are difficult to disentangle. As I show in the discussion of the tradition frame, the conflict between biology and affinity measures is central to the debate about whether the 1939 membership rule is "authentic" tradition.

The Pueblo emphasized its historical reliance upon biology to determine membership. Beyond that, it stressed the value of a biological connection to a male tribe member. The district court decision echoes this point, stating that "the criteria employed in classifying children of mixed marriage as members or non-members are rooted in certain traditional values. It appears that Santa Clara was traditionally patrilineal and patrilocal . . . "[51] This traditional practice is stressed in the amicus brief submitted by the Pueblo de Conchita et. al., attached to which were the membership standards of nine Pueblos that had "male-dominance rules."[52]

Martinez pointed to the historical practice of naturalization into the tribe as evidence of her perspective. Anyone who lived and practiced Santa Clara culture could eventually become Santa Claran (despite biological lineage). Martinez claimed that since naturalization existed both before and after blood-quantum standards were imposed, the cultural affinity standard must be the tribe's authentic traditional practice. Naturalization was discontinued in 1939 (at the same time that the sexist rule was adopted) because of economic pressures (see the economic/material forces frame for further discussion about this dynamic).

Martinez's brief suggests a process by which membership standards could be developed that would balance individual and tribal rights.

> Tribes should have the opportunity to show that a particular individual right should be viewed as less important in the tribal context, and individuals should have a chance to show the opposite. Tribes should also be able to show that denial of very important rights is justified as incompatible with their separate political status. Racial affinity to a tribe is a justifiable tribal classification, while tribal rules favoring whites over blacks would not be.[53]

The last sentence makes an interesting distinction. One can have racial affinity to a tribe, hinting that affinity to a tribe is more than just in cultural practices, but includes biological affinity as well. This muddles the biology-culture debate even further.

The District and Appeals courts offered a somewhat similar construction of affinity: "The facts about the Martinez children led the district court to conclude that they 'are culturally, for all practical purposes, Santa Clara Indians."[54] To clarify this point, they offered the following facts: The Martinez children were lifelong Pueblo residents, they spoke and understood Tewa, practiced traditional customs, and they were accepted into the ancient religion of the Pueblo. But the courts also looked to the blood quantum standard to show that the Martinez children had a biological connection to the tribe by pointing to the children's 100 percent Indian ancestry and 50 percent Santa Clara ancestry.[55]

Martinez also argued that rather than making rigid and arbitrary distinctions, the Pueblo traditionally dealt with membership on a case by case basis. This is an argument about the procedure for determining membership (as opposed to the standards themselves), which dovetails nicely with Martinez's larger cultural affinity argument. The district court decision says:

> Before 1939 mixed marriages were relatively rare in the Pueblo, and consequently there was no need for a hard and fast rule concerning membership; rather, the Council considered each case separately. In that sense, the establishment of any rule must be seen as a break with tradition.[56]

Martinez's lawyers also looked at the practices of other tribes to explain how rigid membership rules contradict traditional practices.

> While the claim is made that a few other tribes have male-line or female-line traditions, there is no showing that any other tribe applies a rigid rule of this kind to expel cultural insiders. For example, the Navajos and western Pueblos have very strong female-line traditions, but these have no bearing on tribal membership.[57]

Martinez also pointed out that the arbitrary rule actually admitted members who had little affinity to the tribe. "By contrast the 1939 Ordinance requires membership of male-line children, even if they are only half Indian or less; even if they have never lived at the Pueblo, and even if they know nothing of its language or religion."[58] Also, membership was given to children who were born to single mothers. Martinez noted that this rule emphasizes marital status and parental membership over either the degree of Santa Claran ancestry or affinity to the Pueblo.

Both Martinez and the Pueblo proposed particular standards of membership. The Pueblo favored biological lineage while Martinez stressed cultural affinity. Yet, neither side made strict biological or cultural arguments. The two sometimes are combined to such and extent that they become indistinguishable. Each side pointed to historical practices to validate the standards for membership that they suggested. In the process, each side argued that the other's account of tradition was inaccurate. This points to a larger issue of how one makes sense of competing views about a tribe's traditional practices.

Frame Four: Tradition

Since each side had to present its version of tribal tradition, the debate hinged on the proper method for determining a tradition's authenticity as much as it did on the cultural practices themselves. Who are the "correct" voices of "true" tradition? The Pueblo presented expert witnesses who were anthropologists, while Martinez offered the accounts of the Elder members of the Pueblo. Some of the amicus briefs also chimed in with their own expert anthropologists.[59] It is important to note that the colonial experience created this need to validate a tribe's traditions. The federal government required proof of authenticity in order to categorize and recognize Native American tribes. The Pueblo argued:

> Santa Clara Pueblo has consistently taken the position that the 1939 Ordinance is simply a written embodiment of a preexisting unwritten rule of membership that has been in existence from time immemorial . . . [T]he said Ordinance is essential to the cultural and religious heritage that is vital to the Tribe's existence.[60]

Proving that something was tradition entailed proving that it existed prior to colonial contact.

The district court, which ruled in favor of the Pueblo, pointed to the amalgam of colonial influence and Native tradition. The decision states:

> Since 1680 the Pueblo has existed as a conquered people, identifiable as a group but surrounded by an alien culture, first Spanish and later American. From a practical political

standpoint, the result has been a tension in the life of the Pueblo between traditional Pueblo customs and values and the 'modern' customs and values of Anglo-American society. As noted above, this tension was once so acute that the Pueblo became divided against itself. The differences were eventually resolved by the adoption of the Constitution, which drew upon both traditional Pueblo and modern Anglo-American institutions, synthesizing them into a unique structure neither wholly traditional nor wholly modern.[61]

With such an explicit acknowledgement of colonial domination, it becomes implausible to expect a clear indication of "true" pre-contact traditional practices. Therefore, with the history of colonial domination, tradition is dynamic, inconsistent, and constructed over time. Thus, that tradition must change in order to adapt to new economic and political pressures from the outside.

Martinez disputed the Pueblo's claim that the membership rule represented authentic tradition. The appeals court decision articulates some of her reasoning:

> The contention is that the culture is patrilineal, patrilocal, or patricultural. These, however, are conclusory characterizations. What is the history? The ordinance was passed in 1939 to deal with an unprecedented phenomenon, namely, mixed marriages on a relatively wide scale which resulted from Indians of different tribes meeting and encountering one another in Indian schools. An added element was Indians becoming acquainted while employed off the reservation. They met not only Indians from other tribes, but Anglos as well. Traditionally the Santa Clara female moved to the house of the Santa Clara husband and undoubtedly the Santa Clara male played a large role in educating the children in the Pueblo's traditions. This is the strongest argument in favor of the Tribe, but it falls short of justifying sex discrimination since there could have been a solution without discrimination. It is important to note also that prior to the adoption . . . of this ordinance the mixed marriage problem was dealt with on an individual case basis. The evidence shows that under this policy there were situations in which the

offspring of a Santa Clara woman were admitted to the Pueblo
and so historically the 1939 ordinance cannot be said to
represent the Santa Clara tradition.[62]

Ultimately, the appeals court looked at when the rule was adopted as
proof that it was not representative of Santa Clara tradition. "The
instant tribe policy is of relatively recent origin and so it does not merit
the force that would be attributable to a venerable tradition."[63] While
colonial domination might have been acknowledged, it is not clear that
the federal courts were willing to admit that tradition changed over
time. Looking at how recently the ordinance was passed is probably
not the best way to judge whether it is authentic tradition. On the one
hand, the court acknowledged that tradition changes over time and is
affected by colonial intrusion. On the other hand, it was not possible
that a recently adopted policy could be authentic tradition.

Thus, the conception of tradition that informed this decision is
"timeless." The only way to prove authenticity is to show that
colonialism did not change it. Yet, the court itself admitted that most
traditions did not survive this intrusion unscathed. To this the
Shoshone and Arapahoe tribes responded, "Tribes, like other
governments, must have the power to adapt policy to changing
circumstances."[64] Thus, their version of tradition could change over
time and remain an authentic exercise of tribal autonomy.

Martinez pointed to the tribal constitution to find another aspect of
tradition.

> [P]etitioners contended that the 1939 ordinance is essential to
> the traditional pueblo religion, but the district court expressly
> found to the contrary . . . Petitioners also contended that the
> 1939 Ordinance merely codified an ancient rule. However, the
> Pueblo's written constitution of 1935 states that membership
> for children of mixed marriages would be dealt with on a case
> by case basis; no discrimination is mentioned.[65]

This turn to the constitution shows very clearly the strategic evidence
that was offered to determine authentic tradition. Martinez wanted
membership to be determined on a case by case basis, which she felt
was more in line with traditional practices. But, her document of
verification—the Santa Clara Pueblo constitution—is a direct product
of colonial intrusion.

In addition to differing in what they believed to be the "true" traditions of the Pueblo, each side pointed to their own "experts" to provide evidence for their arguments. The Pueblo's expert witness was Florence Hawley Ellis, a professor of Anthropology, who said, ". . . because of the importance of men in connection with the carrying on of the culture, the training of the children in the socio-religious situation *the culture eventually would break down and be lost* [if the ordinance was over-turned]."[66] Alan Taradash, Martinez's lawyer, doubted Hawley Ellis's ability to authenticate Santa Clara tradition. In Taradash's view, not only did she contradict herself, but the authorities that she cited were not necessarily legitimate. Taradash said:

> [Hawley Ellis] said, 'Well the definitive statement on it is this unpublished paper that a student of mine did years ago. Edward P. Dozier's paper. It says it is neolocal, meaning that unlike Navajo, where it's a matrilocal system you go to live where your wife's family lives. Neolocal means either one . . .' It means neither, there's no particular pattern. And that was the traditional rule. And she's claiming that this guy because he's from there and her student is a pre-eminent authority.[67]

Taradash went on to say that this pre-eminent authority (Dozier) was actually a member of the Pueblo because his mother (not his father) was a member. Taradash also said that during that deposition, Hawley Ellis went so far as to invent a term "patricultural," which is not an "accepted" anthropological concept. Needless to say, Taradash believed that Hawley Ellis was inventing tradition in order to bolster the Pueblo's position.

To counter Hawley Ellis's account, Taradash offered the testimony of a Santa Clara religious leader named Alcario Tafoya, who said that the sexist membership rule was "'not the way we do things traditionally.' And he [Tafoya] was very much opposed to what, in his view as a religious leader, to what these non-traditional people [the members of the tribal council] were doing."[68] Here is a terrific example of two "authorities" directly contradicting one another in the process of determining the authentic tradition of a Native American tribe. The anthropologist's "scientific" analysis conflicts with the tribe elders' account of tradition. These two kinds of expert knowledge pit "insiders" against "outsiders." What does it mean that the Pueblo relied upon an anthropologist who was not a member of the tribe to validate its account of tradition? I asked Taradash: "So, do you think that any of the tribal council members felt that it [the 1939 ordinance] was true tradition?" And he answered, "They all knew that it wasn't, they knew. They all knew that what they had done was not tradition. They knew that. That's why they were so eager to hide behind something. Patricultural shit."[69] Similarly, the ACLU finds that the possibility that the ordinance represents ancient tradition a "dubious assertion."[70]

Anthropological expert knowledge is pit against elder expert knowledge; codified law is countered by oral history. The conflict is about more than what traditional practices entail, but also how one determines the authenticity of those practices. Much of this dispute is about the process of determining tradition and deciding which players can voice their account of traditional practices. Thus, *where* the final decision is made has a great impact on how this process will play out. This is why jurisdiction is key to this case.

Frame Five: Jurisdiction

By ruling that it did not have jurisdiction to invalidate the Santa Claran membership ordinance, the Supreme Court chose not to consider the authentic tradition question. It ultimately agreed with the Pueblo that it is not for the federal courts to decide the tribe's authentic traditions or the proper standard for tribal membership. Thus, while not making a statement about what the Pueblo's traditional practices were, the Court made a statement about the appropriate venue for determining authentic tradition. As was discussed under the first frame, much of this decision (as in most legal decisions) involved balancing various government branch interests, where the tribal governments were but one addition to this institutional stew. The historical relationship between the federal government and the tribal government explains some of the intricacies of this decision.

> The essential problem that confronts the Congress in this field is whether or not it is possible to establish a relationship with our other levels of government for the reservation Indians in a way that will harmonize with our levels of government and yet at the same time preserve for them such necessary local self-government as would seem to best serve their interest.[71]

Since the federal government historically flip-flopped in determining the extent of tribal jurisdiction, it is unclear whether the division of labor between the levels of government can ever be so harmonious.

There are several important aspects of the jurisdictional frame that must be considered. First there is the separation of powers between the federal judiciary and Congress. This is important in this decision because there is an underlying assumption that the Court must defer to Congressional plenary power over Native American tribes. Thus, in an effort to defer to Congress, and to uphold its own legitimacy, the judiciary used very literal methods of interpreting the ICRA. The unique jurisdictional dynamic that exists for Native Americans helps to explain why the same level of equal protection scrutiny is not applied to Native American women as to other women in the US.

If the same level of judicial scrutiny was applied to indigenous women under the ICRA, then the Court would have to protect them against acts of Congress as well as against the tribal governments. It would also have to seriously change the precedent that has relatively consistently dictated that the judiciary should defer to Congressional plenary power over Native Americans. If the judiciary stepped in, another layer of colonial domination would be created. It is unclear whether Native American women would benefit from judicial rather than congressional intrusion.

The final decision in *Santa Clara Pueblo* really did not critique or review Congressional plenary power. Much of the Supreme Court's decision was based upon a very narrow and literal reading of the ICRA and deference to Congress. According to the Court's decision, only legislation could determine jurisdiction and only an "express" Congressional act could waive a tribe's immunity to suit. In its briefs, the Pueblo (and all of the amicus curiae in its favor) pushed for this kind of reasoning. The Pueblo wrote, "Plenary authority over the tribal relations of the Indians has been exercised by Congress from the beginning, and the power has always been deemed a political one, not subject to be controlled by the judicial department of the government."[72] During the ICRA hearings, Senator Ervin pointed out that the Congress attempted to take tribes' jurisdictional concerns into account when crafting the legislation. He stated, "This bill does not provide for the federal courts to review all the decisions of the Indian courts. In fact, provision for federal review was in there originally, and at the request of a number of tribes we eliminated that entirely."[73] In a way, there was an assumption that Congress was either looking out for the best interests of tribes, or attempting to "represent" the tribes in creating legislation after conducting hearings. The judiciary deferred to a very loaded relationship between Congress and the Pueblo.

Yet, the Pueblo realized that deference to the plenary power of Congress in this case was going to benefit the status quo, which would allow their rule to stand. The long-term consequences of this reasoning would favor tribal self-determination. Therefore, the Pueblo favored one branch of the federal government over another to preserve its autonomy. It was important to the Pueblo that Congress act explicitly in vesting the judiciary with any oversight of the tribes.

> When the entire Act is viewed against the backdrop of tribal sovereignty, it becomes completely clear that Congress chose in the Act to proceed in a limited fashion by strengthening tribal governments, encouraging tribal self-determination and yet at the same time preserving the civil rights of tribal members. Congress acted knowing full well that it retained plenary jurisdiction over Indian tribes and that if tribal courts in civil and criminal matters, tribal councils in executive and legislative matters failed to protect the civil rights of tribal members, then Congress could take the more drastic step of vesting the federal courts with additional jurisdiction.[74]

The Pueblo even pointed to the history of colonial domination to justify its position about explicit Congressional acts. Their brief states, "In view of the fact that Congress has acted in the area of tribal membership before, it seems even clearer that had Congress intended to destroy tribal sovereignty it would have done so in an affirmative fashion and not by implication."[75] Thus, according to this logic, Congress gave the tribes their sovereignty and the judiciary should not interfere. On top of deferring to Congress, the National Tribal Chairmen's Association recommended that the Secretary of the Interior bear the final judgement about compliance to the ICRA.[76] Either way, the judiciary should interpret the ICRA narrowly and defer to the other branches of the federal government.

In contrast, in the appeals court ruling in favor of Martinez, one can see a looser interpretation of the ICRA, one that augments the power of the federal judiciary.

> We have previously considered these arguments and have ruled that jurisdiction exists . . . We also held that to the extent that the Indian Civil Rights Act applies, tribal immunity is thereby limited . . . On the question of jurisdiction we said that 28 USC Section 1343(4) which provides for district court jurisdiction over actions brought under 'any Act of Congress providing for the protection of civil rights' constituted an appropriate jurisdictional basis for actions under the Indian Civil Rights Act. Finally, since this Act of Congress was designed to provide protection against tribal authority, the intention of Congress to allow suits against the tribe was an essential aspect. Otherwise, it would constitute a mere unenforceable declaration of principles.[77]

Martinez wanted this kind of broad reading of the ICRA in order to assure that tribal immunity would never be waived in civil rights cases. Martinez wanted the federal courts to protect her against both Congress and tribal institutions. So, her lawyers argued that the ICRA "is an exception to tribal immunity from suit and abrogates that immunity in cases where the Act applies."[78]

Each side in this case favored a particular branch of the federal government to have jurisdiction in order to get a positive ruling. Neither side argued that the federal government should completely remove itself from the situation. Instead, each side strategically argued for the interpretation of the ICRA and the jurisdiction that would best serve that side's desired result. The strategic use of legal norms and institutions does set precedent and has symbolic effect. Norms guiding civil rights for indigenous people and sovereignty rights for tribes are molded by these strategic arguments. But the strategic use of certain branches of the federal government affects more than mere symbolism. That is why it is important to consider the material motivations and consequences involved in this case.

Frame Six: Economic and Material Forces

As has been hinted at throughout the discussion of the other frames, legal and political arguments are often motivated by an actor's material context: the need for land on the reservation, services from the federal government that come with membership in an indigenous tribe, or the ability to participate in tribal politics in order to have a voice in allocating funds. Thus, a particular legal interpretation has direct material consequences on the various parties. Therefore, it is important to consider how material forces are invoked in the various arguments, and how they might influence the interpretation of particular legal discourses.

There are many competing economic forces at play in this case. First, the membership rule left Martinez's children economically vulnerable because they could be evicted from the reservation and "they could be denied benefits in the future, since benefits are often tied to tribal membership."[79] The district court decision states:

> [I]n families such as the Martinez family, where the children are not members of the Pueblo, the land use rights cannot be passed on to succeeding generations . . . members may rent or sell their use rights, but again, only to other members . . . Other material benefits and privileges include the right to hunt and fish on the land, the use of irrigation water, and an equal share in any pecuniary benefits made by the Pueblo, or any other programs, present or future, under-taken by the Pueblo for the benefit of its members.[80]

So, non-members were usually allowed to hunt, gather firewood but they could not "inherit their mother's home."[81] Non-members were not allowed to vote in Pueblo elections and they were not allowed to hold office as secular officials of Santa Clara Pueblo.[82] This lack of political power affected their say in the distribution of resources.

There was some disagreement about the extent of the economic impact caused by lack of membership in the tribe. The Pueblo argued that "[t]he denial of tribal membership does not in any way affect the Martinez's entitlement to participate in federal benefits accorded Indians generally."[83] The district court decision points out that the Martinez children were not limited in their "participation in the religious life of the Pueblo."[84] That same decision goes on to assert that all of the Martinez children had received federal benefits (including medical treatment and education benefits) since 1968. The Pueblo's attorney argued that the "Martinez children have all the material rights that full members of the Santa Clara Pueblo have . . . Even Mr. Martinez, a Navajo, has all the privileges that members have, such as irrigation water, farming, wood-hauling, fishing and hunting."[85] According to the district court opinion, only purely "internal, secular, rights and privileges"[86] were affected by lack of membership. Obviously, the Pueblo wanted to downplay the material effect that the membership ordinance had upon the Martinez children because this would lessen the likelihood that it would be deemed a civil rights violation. Martinez wanted to play these material burdens up in order to strengthen her argument.

Another economic concern that was raised was that the Pueblo would be vulnerable to the constant threat of lawsuits if it did not maintain its immunity to suit. "It is especially dangerous to the continued existence of tribal governments for federal courts to attempt to read 25 USC §1302 in conjunction with 28 USC §1343 (4) in such manner as to throw open the floodgates of litigation against Indian tribal governments."[87] They believed that such vulnerability would decrease tribal autonomy because the cost of litigation would take resources away from maintaining an infrastructure for traditional practices. In order to limit the possible economic burden on tribes, the Shoshone and Arapahoe tribes went so far as to suggest that waiving the tribe's immunity to suit should "be limited to tribal officers—not the Tribe itself."[88] Thus, as a last resort, if someone was going to get sued, it should not put the tribal resources into jeopardy.

The economic concerns for the tribe went well beyond the immediate outcome of this case. Membership standards directly affect a tribe's economic status because they determine the distribution of scarce tribal resources. The district court decision states:

> [T]he adoption of the 1939 Ordinance was in response to a sudden increase in mixed marriages, which had resulted in a proportionate strain on the economic resources of the Pueblo. Plaintiffs argue that economic integrity of the Pueblo is less important than cultural autonomy. The difficulty with this position is that the two are not easily separable. The ability of the Pueblo to control the use and distribution of its resources enhances its ability to maintain its cultural autonomy.[89]

Cultural and economic survival are intertwined. A tribe needs a population in order to continue existing but that tribe cannot let just anyone in because the "authenticity" of the practices would be questioned or diluted. At the same time, if membership standards become too strict, the culture will die out based upon sheer numbers. Plus, limited tribal resources will quickly run out if membership standards are too lax. Thus, the 1939 rule was adopted to balance all of these pressures.

But the appeals court saw a different way to deal with these issues without being sexist:

> There is evidence that the ordinance was the product of economics and pragmatics. It appeared to the governing body of the Tribe that the offspring of mixed marriages threatened to swell the population of the Pueblo and diminished individual shares of the property. If this were the pressing problem it could have been solved without resorting to discrimination—by simply excluding the offspring of both sexes where the parent, either male or female, married outside the Pueblo . . . It is also clear that the reasons for this new rule were economic, to reduce the claimants to Pueblo land and money.[90]

According to some, if something was economically motivated (such as the membership rule), then it cannot be "authentic" tradition. The Solicitor General wrote, "Nor can the ordinance be explained as the embodiment of a long-standing Pueblo custom or tradition; rather, it was enacted to solve an economic problem facing the Pueblo in 1939."[91] Again, the vision of tradition that this portrays is unchangeable, regardless of external pressures. The Pueblo disputed the economic motive for adopting the rule in order to strengthen its argument that it was a traditional practice:

> The Court of Appeals found that the enrollment rule is strictly the result of economics. This finding is inconsistent with the facts and simply answered by showing that the group of people in the class represented by Audrey Martinez has never been asked to leave the Pueblo, notwithstanding the fact that there are some one hundred people in that category, or almost ten percent of the entire population . . . Also of relevance is the fact that illegitimate children born to a Santa Clara tribal member woman are granted full rights and cared for by the Pueblo . . .[92]

At the same time, the cause of the economic situation (namely, colonialism and domination by the US government) was not considered when deciding whether the federal courts should have jurisdiction. One could argue that the colonial history leading up to the adoption of the sexist membership rule caused the changes in the tribal economy that were responsible for the adoption of the rule. Put simply, intermarriage increased the tribal population, which not only placed an economic burden upon the tribe, but some thought that it posed a direct threat to cultural survival. Intermarriage increased after Native Americans were forced to attend boarding schools off the reservation, and to serve in the US army.[93] These trends transformed the tribes' economic situation, while changing their conception of Native American identity.[94] Thus, by not considering its own role in the adoption of the rule, the US federal government was able to extricate itself from a role in the discrimination against Julia Martinez and her children.[95]

The relationship between cultural autonomy and economic pressures further complicates the kinds of legal arguments that were presented in this case. What originally spurred the suit was a material need—Martinez's children were afraid of losing their home on the reserve (among other things). But, the cultural importance of official membership in the tribe raises important issues about tradition, autonomy, and self-identification. At the same time, some saw the tribes' economic motivation for adopting the membership rule as proof that the practice was inauthentic. Yet, those same judges did not deem Martinez's own economic motivation to be suspect. The others, who favored tribal autonomy, diminished the seriousness of the Martinez's material claims. All of this shows that material welfare plays a huge role in legal mobilization. In addition to sparking the mobilization, it also influences the courts' legal reasoning.

Conclusion: Intersectionality and Rights Re-evaluation

The object of this study is to examine how legal arguments either reinforce and reproduce the indigenous women's dual domination at the intersections of power, or how they might represent creative instances of rights re-evaluation. Again, the double bind of intersectionality is manifest when a woman of color must choose between her race or her gender in order to make a political claim. Often the two dimensions of identity negate each other, exacerbating domination, and making resistance all the more difficult. This case illustrates this dynamic because Julia Martinez had to use individual civil rights norms against her tribe in federal court. While the outcome of this case did not favor Martinez's gender claim, and it foreclosed the possibility of future resistance for indigenous women, it did serve as powerful precedent for tribal sovereignty claims. Unfortunately, this victory was won at the expense of any kind of real alleviation of intersectional concerns.

It is necessary to look at the arguments offered by each side as well as the court decisions to determine whether the discursive frames provide any openings for future legal mobilization. There were moments where legal arguments were presented creatively, in ways that might help indigenous women re-evaluate the predominant rights discourses in order to capture the double bind of intersectionality.

The individual and sovereignty rights frames were combined in a way that attempted to refigure both in a less zero-sum way. Both sides and most of the amicus briefs argued for a different level of scrutiny than would apply to a sex discrimination case under the Fourteenth Amendment, thereby acknowledging indigenous people's unique status. This may be a place where the intersection of race and gender could be integrated in future legal claims. Not having Fourteenth Amendment equal protection standards apply to indigenous women does not necessarily mean that they deserve *less* protection than other women. The Pueblo asserted that only strengthened tribal institutions could assure members' individual civil rights. In order to prevent federal intrusion, the Pueblo made individual civil rights contingent upon increased autonomy. There might be a way for indigenous women to call the Pueblo on this claim and demand greater gender equity. They could also make their individual rights seem crucial for maintaining tribal autonomy in order to gain a voice in their local institutions. Rights re-evaluation would be apparent if unique forms of individual rights or gender equity were actively developed at the tribal level, without prompting from the federal government.

Sovereignty rights prevailed in the Supreme Court decision. *Santa Clara Pueblo v. Martinez* is still used as an important precedent to assert Native American sovereignty rights, or at least tribal immunity from suit.[96] Authenticating tradition is a complicated process, and the Supreme Court's decision assures that this battle should be waged and resolved at the tribal level. One could argue that, since the Supreme Court deferred as much to Congress as it deferred to tribal sovereignty, old patterns of colonial domination are alive and well. Given the current state of tribal institutions, it is important to show how federal deference actually invigorated indigenous women's intersectional domination because, in the short term, it gave no relief for Martinez's gender claim.

Indigenous women could attempt to pressure tribes to codify the tribal remedies to which the federal courts must defer. I can imagine legal arguments being made that would emphasize the significance of the "Indian Blanket" or "sovereignty backdrop." One interesting point made by Taradash is that some of the tribes have been making preemptive moves to provide tribal remedies (in torts and other legal areas) so that they would not be exhausted so quickly, which would avoid a federal battle. But this does not seem like it will do much to help indigenous women unless they are explicitly brought into the process of determining remedies that gibe with traditional practices.

In the course of assessing whether the 1939 ordinance was authentic Santa Clara tradition, there was an interesting and explicit discussion of colonial influences on tradition. While ultimately this debate was not concluded in the Supreme Court, it was substantial in the lower courts and in the briefs. The arguments that tribal traditions are malleable and influenced by colonialism (both ideologically and materially), are based upon a very complicated account of history. Some even argued that gender inequity was a result of either ideological or economic colonial domination. This argument might serve indigenous women well in future legal mobilization aimed at the double bind of intersectionality. Once the constructed nature of tradition is called into question, modern ordinances that supposedly derive from tradition are more easily challenged. If colonialism is increasingly explored as a cause for certain kinds of traditions, the federal government might have to redraw the line at which it will defer to the tribes. While this re-negotiation of federal-tribal relations is likely to further entrench colonial domination, it might also allow indigenous women to re-frame gender-based claims to get some protection from Congress or the courts.

Overall, this case provides very little room for indigenous women's future resistance or future political participation in the form of rights re-evaluation. While there are a few creative combinations of the prevalent rights discourses, none are actively re-evaluated by indigenous women. There is a superficial bow to sovereignty, but this does not accomplish much for women who are being discriminated against by the "sovereign" tribe. One might argue that this is not the proper role for the federal courts because it would replicate colonial relations. But this ignores the role that the federal government played in constructing contemporary tribal institutions that are oppressive to women. If the tribal institutions were strengthened in a way that would allow them to withstand debate over "authentic" tradition, one could argue that indigenous women might gain a greater voice. It is unclear what role the federal government can play in confronting the double bind of intersectionality. This case is an instance where an indigenous woman strategically used dominant norms and institutions in order to articulate her version of her identity. Unfortunately, the ultimate outcome was not in her favor. Most of Julia Martinez's children have moved away from the reservation, and there have been no other challenges to the Santa Clara Pueblo's membership ordinance

CHAPTER 3

"Marrying Out" in Canada: Part I

A Brief History of Canadian-Indigenous Relations

In Canada, the sexist membership rule originated in the Indian Act, the federal law in which the Canadian Indian Act government defined who was "Indian." The debate about this raises many important themes. What began as overt colonial domination evolved into a more subtle account of protection of indigenous land and culture. Thus, those who "benefited" from Indian status sometimes rallied around the sexist aspects of the Indian Act in order to preserve this "protection." After the passage of the Charter of Rights and Freedoms, a new discursive theme of "Aboriginal rights" emerged, which displaced (but did not replace) this account of colonialism as protection. The following historical narrative will help delineate the discursive transition from the federal protection of indigenous peoples to aboriginal rights, and how each interacts with indigenous women's competing individual rights claims. What emerges is an evolving account of sovereignty that does not shed the history of colonial domination, but only further complicates indigenous women's drive for equality.

Dominating and "Protecting" Indigenous Peoples

In 1763, in response to a rebellion led by Chief Pontiac, a Royal Proclamation first codified the terms of colonial settlement. According to this proclamation, Indians who ceded land to the Crown could expect to have exclusive control over the land that was reserved for them (later known as "reserves") and to receive annual payments. After 1763, written treaties and agreements marked indigenous peoples' loss of their land, and the "extinguishment" of their aboriginal (pre-contact) rights. The Royal Proclamation was the beginning of the "trust" relationship and the attached fiduciary obligation that British/Canadian colonial government had with indigenous peoples. While this proclamation and the subsequent treaties are the texts that represent a history of colonial oppression, they also form the bedrock for many contemporary claims for indigenous rights in Canada.

Section 91(24) of the Constitution Act, 1867 (also known as the British North America Act) granted the federal government exclusive jurisdiction over Indians and the lands reserved to them. Subsequently, in 1876, the government consolidated all of its previous policies toward indigenous peoples into one encompassing Indian Act. It is in this Act that one finds the articulation of how Canada proposed to dominate and "protect" indigenous people. Much of the Indian Act was geared to assimilating indigenous peoples into Canadian society. For example, the Act foisted European conceptions of property ownership onto indigenous people, and also set up strict criteria for who could attain "Indian" status. The Indian Act applied to all individuals that Canada deemed to be "Indians."[1] It was revised numerous times, and 1951 marked the last significant revision prior to the first case under scrutiny in this study, *A.G. of Canada v. Lavell—Isaac et. al. v. Bedard* (1973).

Section 12(1)(b) of the 1951 Indian Act[2] states, "The following persons are not entitled to be registered [as an Indian:] . . . a woman who married a person who is not an Indian, unless that woman is subsequently the wife or widow of [an Indian]."[3] Thus, the Indian Act excluded women who married non-Indians (or non-status Indians) from band membership (which allows residence on reserves and confers shares of band annuities) and Indian "status" (which includes economic benefits from the federal government). At the same time, non-Indian women who married Indian men attained Indian status and the accompanying benefits. "Indian status thus depended on Indian descent or marriage to a male Indian"[4] regardless of band traditions. As a result, between 1955 and 1975 more than 8,500 women lost their Indian status under section 12(1)(b) of the Indian Act.[5]

Prior to 1960, indigenous people who wanted to vote, earn a university degree, or be a doctor, lawyer, or Christian minister had to be "enfranchised."[6] They had to give up their treaty rights and access to their Native identity in order to be considered Canadian citizens. This choice was very difficult for many indigenous people, who did not want the "benefits" of Canadian citizenship, but needed them to attain some political and economic power.

In 1960, Canada passed the Canadian Bill of Rights, which, among other things, promised due process and equal protection of the law regardless of a person's "race, national origin, colour, religion or sex."[7] In 1969, in *Regina v. Drybones*[8] a divided Supreme Court invalidated a section of the Indian Act that imposed a harsher punishment on indigenous people than other Canadians for public drunkenness. The majority opinion says that "an individual is denied equality before the law if it is made an offence punishable at law, on account of his race, for him to do something which his fellow Canadians are free to do without having committed any offense or having been made subject to any penalty."[9] This was considered a major ruling that exposed the Indian Act to judicial scrutiny under the Bill of Rights.

The passage of the Bill of Rights, the *Drybones* ruling, and the increased awareness of sex equality norms, led indigenous women to protest 12(1)(b). In 1968, thirty Mohawk women presented a brief to the Royal Commission on the Status of Women which argued for the reversal of the sexist policy found in 12(1)(b). In 1969, Mary Two Axe Early, who had lost her status after she married out of her band and eventually became a national symbol for the plight of indigenous women, formed a group called Equal Rights for Indian Women. This group's primary agenda was to fight 12(1)(b).

That same year, Prime Minister Pierre Elliott Trudeau presented the "White Paper on Indian Policy" which proposed a termination of special status for Indians, and sparked a great deal of indigenous rights mobilization.

> [Trudeau] analyzed the 'Indian problem' as one of Canadian racism. He assumed Canadian racism towards Indians would halt if Indians became 'Canadians as all other Canadians.' From this assumption, he proceeded logically to his 'solution': deracializing Indians by eliminating their aboriginal and treaty rights—in effect, denying their historical claim to inherent nationhood.[10]

The outcry in reaction to this policy led to its retraction in 1971. Many of the status Indians' actions against indigenous women's mobilization were driven by the fear roused by the ideology represented in the white paper. Therefore, the 1970s saw a great deal of political and legal mobilization on two fronts. Indigenous women fought to achieve the sex equality promised in the Bill of Rights, while indigenous peoples more generally struggled to maintain their ethnic identity and possibly achieve a greater degree of self-government.

In 1971, Jeannette Lavell went to federal court to challenge 12(1)(b), using the sex equality clause of the Bill of Rights. She lost at the trial level, but the appeals court ruled in her favor. A similar case was brought by Yvonne Bedard in the Ontario Courts, which, drawing upon the appeals court decision in *Lavell*, ruled in her favor. In response to these two rulings, Jean Chrétien, minister of Indian Affairs, announced that the Department of Indian Affairs and Northern Development (DIAND) would support any status Indian organization wanting to appeal this decision. DIAND did not want Indian policy to be subject to judicial scrutiny under the Bill of Rights. Thus, this federal ministry in charge of Indian Affairs was a sponsor of the status Indians' resistance to changing the Indian Act's sexist membership rule. Ultimately, the *Lavell* and *Bedard* cases were consolidated and heard by the Supreme Court in 1973. As a result of Chrétien's sponsorship and the subsequent publicity, hundreds of groups appeared at the Supreme Court hearing.

Status Indian organizations came out against Lavell and Bedard because they feared that the whole Indian Act, and the "special status" that it conferred on indigenous peoples, would be vulnerable on grounds of racial discrimination if the Bill of Rights were able to overrule any part of the Act. Status Indians feared that a weakened Indian Act would offer them no protection. Protections that they did not want to lose included treaty rights and the policy of not allowing white men to live on reserves and become status Indians by marrying indigenous women. The latter possibility was particularly threatening to status Indian groups.

> Richard Isaac, the chief of the Six Nations, state[d] that with the Lavell ruling 'the reserves will eventually be dissolved' . . . Harold Cardinal, leader of the Indian Association of Alberta, [said] that unless the federal court decision of 1971 [was] overturned, 'it could destroy any chance of our survival in this country as a distinct cultural unit'.[11]

Some saw the sexism in the Indian Act as a way of preventing too much intermarriage, which would eventually lead to assimilation through the "whitening" of Indian blood. Some argued that white men would have a great economic effect on reserves if they had access to Indian status through marriage. Others feared changes to Indian Act so much that they even defended it as representing not only their immediate interests, but historical indigenous tradition.

> [A] tactic employed by the IAA (Indian Association of Alberta) was to use the tasteless reasoning that

enfranchisement was in keeping with Indian culture, and that subservience to the male was a time-honored tradition. They ignored the historical fact that enfranchisement was a clause entered into the Indian Act to eventually assimilate all Indians.[12]

This thinking transforms the Indian Act from a mere tool of colonial protection to the guarantor of authentic tradition.

In 1972, the National Committee on Indian Rights for Indian Women (IRIW) was founded to fight 12(1)(b) and to present an alternative voice to the status Indian organizations. They argued, among other things, that

> most of the women fighting the case were married to Metis and non-status Indians . . . NIB (National Indian Brotherhood) under its president, George Manuel, is a male-dominated status organization purported to represent Canada's 250,000 registered Indians. Since before they fought the Lavell case on behalf of the department of Indian affairs, they have consistently attempted to scuttle any moves by non-status Indians to amend the invidious legislation that separates Canada's native population.[13]

According to this view, 12(1)(b) was not merely about limiting white men's access to Indian reserves, but it was meant to diminish the ranks of status Indians and to divide indigenous peoples against each other. These women felt that status Indians were trying to limit the number of members who had access to the limited land and funds allocated to reserves. They pointed out that 12(1)(b) was actually a Canadian assimilation tactic, because it forced women to renounce their indigenous identity upon marrying non-status Indians or non-Indians. Thus, indigenous women refuted DIAND's and the status Indian establishment's contention that 12(1)(b), and the Indian Act more generally, were about the protection of Indian culture and land. Each side offered a unique analysis of what would be more threatening, assimilation through intermarriage or assimilation through limiting band numbers and dictating membership standards. Because of this divergent view of the Indian Act,

Lavell pitted the interests of Indigenous Women against those of a male dominated national organization for status Indians. Ever since, the issue of sex discrimination in the Indian Act has been characterized as a conflict between collective (Aboriginal) rights and individual human rights (sex equality rights).[14]

This dichotomy evolves, but continues in some form throughout all the cases that that are analyzed here. Presenting the interests of indigenous women as a dichotomy between collective and human rights, or aboriginal versus sex equality rights epitomizes the bind of intersectional power. The two identity strands counteract each other to completely negate the complexity of indigenous women's identities.

The Supreme Court ultimately ruled against Lavell and Bedard, saying that the Bill of Rights could not render the Indian Act inoperative. The majority claimed that the Court could only override legislation that "offends against one of the rights specifically guaranteed" in the Bill of Rights.[15] Additionally, the Canadian Supreme Court found that the Bill of Rights only applied to those laws before the "ordinary courts of the land."[16] In essence, The Indian Act would have to be amended by Parliament to remove the sexist status rule. Thus, the Canadian Supreme Court was reluctant to use the Bill of Rights to interfere with Parliament's power to "protect" indigenous peoples with the Indian Act.

The *Lavell/Bedard* ruling helped publicize the 12(1)(b) problem and sparked increased mobilization, both of indigenous women and status Indians who wanted to retain the provisions of 12(1)(b). In 1975, at the International Women's Conference in Mexico, women from all over the world protested against the Canadian government's treatment of indigenous women. This protest exemplifies how the Indian Act roused international attention, which was amplified when it became the subject of international adjudication at the UN.

In 1977 Sandra Lovelace, a Maliseet Indian from the Tobique reserve in New Brunswick (with the help of the New Brunswick Human Rights Commission) filed a complaint against Canada with the United Nations Human Rights Committee (UN HRC)[17] on the grounds that 12(1)(b) denied her sex-based equality. At that time, there was a great deal of activity on the Tobique reserve.[18] Women occupied the band council office for four months; two women—Juanita Perley and Cheryl Bear—took over houses that were not allotted to them; and

Sandra Lovelace was living in a tent on the reserve to protest her loss of status. Both sides threatened violence and there was a great deal of tension on the reserve that drew national attention.

In 1979, while the UN was considering Lovelace's case, approximately 200 Tobique women and children walked 160 kilometers to Ottawa to gain the attention of the Minister of Indian Affairs. They managed to meet with Prime Minister Joe Clark, who said that

> [T]he Conservative government [would] remove discriminatory sections from the Indian Act, with or without acceptance by Indian leaders. But . . . he would prefer that the National Indian Brotherhood . . . take the initial action . . . The brotherhood said in a statement recently that it supports the women but that the band councils who run reserves must maintain the right of having the final say of who is an Indian . . . The prime minister said the Government 'would prefer to have the (Indian Act) amendments come from the NIB because there would be broader acceptance by the Indian community and also because that would indicate our respect for the very special place the document has as a law for the Indian people.[19]

This deference to status Indians went on for years, and was used as an excuse for inaction in Canada's submissions to the UN. Since the status organizations wanted control over band membership, they preferred the known entity of the Indian Act over unknown changes in favor of sex equality, which might have a detrimental effect upon the sovereignty fight. This point became crucial to the amendments to the Indian Act that eventually did get implemented. Lovelace commented on this dynamic:

> Even if the UN decides in my favor, it's still up to the government. All along they've been saying they don't want to impose their will on the Indian people. But that's been their excuse not to do anything. They told the brotherhood to rewrite the Act but they can't agree on anything. I don't blame the chiefs. I blame the government for everything. They made the Act. Let them change it.[20]

Lovelace was highly suspicious when the Canadian government claimed to be respecting indigenous peoples' desires. As reflected in the above passage, her hesitance to blame the band chiefs reveals her dual loyalties. She understood why the band councils and status organizations reacted the way that they had (despite the violence on her own reserve), because she had first hand experience of the domination of the Canadian government. Sandra Lovelace's position at the intersections of multiple power strands (namely as a colonized indigenous woman) allowed her to see the complex historical forces at work in this struggle. This unique perspective provided her with a more nuanced account of who were "enemies" and "allies."

In 1981, the UN Human Rights Committee ruled that the Indian Act violated article 27 of the International Covenant on Civil and Political Rights, which requires that ethnic, religious, and linguistic minorities be able to practice their culture, reside with their community, and speak their language. The UN HRC did not rule based upon sex-discrimination because Lovelace had lost her status before Canada had signed onto the covenant. Instead, the ruling was based upon Lovelace's perpetual lack of contact with her "minority" culture. Thus, it was on cultural grounds that the UN determined that the Indian Act violated Lovelace's human rights.

The Canadian government continued to consult with and defer to status Indian organizations for four more years before the sex discrimination was eliminated from the Indian Act. First, bands were asked to voluntarily ignore 12(1)(b).

> Last month, the federal Government moved to allow Indian women in bands that requested it to be allowed to retain their native status when they marry non-Indians. But Indian women say this is a tiny concession because only a handful of Canada's 568 bands have requested the exemption from the Indian Act, and most band councils are dominated by men opposed to the change.[21]

The bands, fearing an influx of new members, demanded more federal resources in the wake of reforming the Indian Act. Del "Riley, president of the 300,000-member National Indian Brotherhood, said Ottawa should correct economic and social conditions on reserves before giving Indian status—and the right to live on reserves—back to an estimated 65,000 women and children."[22]

Joe Stacey, president of the Confederation of Indians of Quebec, pointed out that the proposed changes to the Indian Act were probably more about responding to the international embarrassment from the UN decision, than out of interest in protecting indigenous peoples' needs. Moreover, he thought that removing 12(1)(b) was another tactic to assimilate indigenous peoples. He said:

> 'It isn't our act. It was forced on us 30 years ago by the federal Government. They made the Indian male the status carrier. We had no imput [sic] into that act.' Mr. Stacey said Ottawa's second objective [in reforming the Indian Act] is 'to dilute the Indian race and lead us to assimilation by slowly reducing the blood quantum' . . . Two years after they marry Indian women, these men come with proposals of mass development of the reserve.[23]

This quote illustrates the general fear of intermarriage and the status Indians' tendency to be more threatened by non-Indian men than non-Indian women on the reserves. Thus, these opponents of reform wished to hang on to the protection found in 12(1)(b).

From Protection to Aboriginal Rights: Where do Indigenous Women Stand?

In addition to the UN HRC's ruling, Canada faced additional pressure from the impending passage of the Charter of Rights and Freedoms in 1982. This Charter was part of an overhaul of the Canadian Constitution and guaranteed an expanded set of individual fundamental rights. Once the Charter came into effect, 12(1)(b) would be subject to greater judicial scrutiny than under the weaker Canadian Bill of Rights. The probability of such Charter-based judicial scrutiny, on top of the 1981 reprimand from the UN, prompted the Canadian government to actively revise the Indian Act.

Finally, in 1985, the Canadian Parliament passed Bill C-31, which amended the Indian Act, eliminating the "more obvious aspects of sex discrimination and introduced a degree of band control over band membership."[24] Women who had previously lost status due to 12(1)(b) were eligible to apply for reinstatement and women who married non-Indians no longer lost Indian status. As of 1995, there were 101,428 new registrants under C-31. "By 31 August 1995 the status Indian population had risen from its 1985 level of 360,241 to 586,580. This is an overall 61.4% increase, 27% of which is from new [C-31] registrations."[25] The impact of C-31 was very significant, in terms of the number of new status Indians, and also in less quantifiable ways.

The reinstatement process was quite complicated, because C-31 delineated two levels of "Indianness:" Federal Indian Status and Band Membership. Status was restored for most women who applied for reinstatement, and unless bands adopted membership rules that were different from federal status requirements, those same women gained band membership too. If the band did develop band membership criteria that differed from federal status requirements, it was possible, if not probable, that women and their children would gain status but not band membership. This distinction allowed women to receive education and health benefits from the federal government, but they were unable to live on the reserve, or take part in band politics. "Reinstated persons who wish to assert their rights as band members therefore c[a]me into conflict with reserve communities refusing to accept their reinstatement or without the resources to accommodate them."[26] Thus, C-31 removed most of the federal-level sexism found in 12(1)(b), but, by expanding band autonomy (in membership decisions), not all sex discrimination was eliminated.

C-31 also included a "second generation cut off" or "half descent" rule, which terminated Indian status for persons with fewer than two "Indian" grandparents.[27] In the revised Indian Act, section 6(1)[28] allows women who married out to be reinstated. Section 6(2) allows children with one status Indian parent (i.e. a mother who got reinstated under section 6(1)) to be registered. This was meant to "terminate status after two successive generations of intermarriage between Indians and non-Indians."[29] But, there was residual sex discrimination as status extended to the children of intermarriages.

Since a non-Indian woman who married an Indian man gained Indian status prior to C-31 (equivalent to 6(1) status), she could pass the benefits of (6(1)) status onto her children (since they were considered to have two Indian parents). Even if those children married out of the band, they could pass status on to their children (under 6(2)). The same could not be said for a non-Indian man who married an Indian woman under the amended Act, because they would pass down 6(2) status to their children, who, if they married out, could not pass any form of status onto their children. In addition to perpetuating sex discrimination, this section 6(1) versus section 6(2) distinction further bifurcated indigenous identity. People's identities were divided into many subsections and distinctions: federal status, band membership, 6(1), 6(2), among other things. These distinctions created a great deal of divisiveness within indigenous communities. People began to label others "reinstatees" or "C-31s," implying that they were not "true" band members. Cliques formed, and local services were sometimes meted out according to these federally created delineations.

It is important to stress that C-31 had two objectives. The first goal was to eliminate the sexism found in the Indian Act. Second, in order to acknowledge the bands' concerns about reform, C-31 significantly expanded band power. Thus, the two-tiered status system (status and band membership) was created in order to acknowledge band autonomy. "As of September 1995, 240 of 608 bands had assumed control of band membership."[30] As noted above, this band power sometimes had a deleterious effect on indigenous women's access to their natal bands. The tension between band rights and indigenous women's rights found in C-31 reflects the dual mobilization that happened during the 1970s.

The passage of the Charter of Rights and Freedoms was also quite significant for the expansion of indigenous self-determination. In addition to enumerating a more exhaustive list of individual civil rights protections, the Charter included three sections that acknowledged and expanded aboriginal and treaty rights.[31] Thus, changes to 12(1)(b) were going to be considered in light of these expanded aboriginal rights. It is unclear whether the simultaneous expansion of individual equality rights and aboriginal rights would provide opportunities for indigenous women to express their dual domination.

There were other developments on the indigenous rights front that complicated indigenous women's equality claims. Examples include: In 1982, the Penner Report, which was produced by the Special Committee of the House of Commons on Indian Self-Government suggested that First Nations be recognized as a distinct government body within the Canadian Federation. In 1984, as part of a land claims agreement, the Indian Act no longer applied to the Cree and Naskapi bands. In 1986, the First Self-Government Act was passed by Parliament. In 1993, the Nunavut Land Claims Agreement Act passed and on April 1, 1999, Nunavut became a territory with a majority of Inuit residents. The government of Nunavut has almost as much authority as a Province.

In addition to mobilization around land and self-government issues, a very important sign of broadened indigenous rights was their increasingly visible presence in the Constitutional reform process. In 1983, the 1982 Constitution Act was amended to ensure that aboriginal people were included in subsequent Constitutional conferences. In 1990, the Meech Lake Accord, which had excluded aboriginal peoples from the Constitutional reforms, was defeated. "Elijah Harper, lone Indian member of the Manitoba legislature, used procedural tactics to block Manitoba's ratification of the Meech Lake Accord. Because the Accord required the ratification of all ten provincial legislatures, Harper single-handedly killed the Accord."[32] In 1992, the Charlottetown Accord included Aboriginal organizations and recognized their inherent right of self-government. This Accord ultimately failed to pass in a national referendum in 1995, but its inclusion of (some) indigenous voices, and its recognition of self-government had huge symbolic power.

The desire to be included in constitutional considerations is very interesting because it simultaneously provides a way to expand indigenous self-government (by having rights written into the Constitution), and acknowledges the extent of Canadian power to grant such autonomy. An added wrinkle to an indigenous presence at constitutional conventions is the lack of representation of indigenous women. In 1994, the Supreme Court ruled in *Native Women's Association of Canada v. Canada*[33] that Canada did not have to fund Native women's groups' participation in the Charlottetown Accord because the funded indigenous groups could act as their representatives. This exclusion pit Native women against the mainstream indigenous groups yet again and diminished their political clout. One important difference in position between the women's groups and the status First Nations groups is that the former argued that the equality provisions found in the Charter should apply to all band acts, while the latter wanted Aboriginal rights to trump equality provisions. Native women recognized that their only refuge in the expansion of band power was the sex-equality protections found in the Charter.

In June 1995, the Canadian Human Rights Commission ordered the Montagnais du Lac-Saint-Jean band council to pay damages to four women who had regained their status under Bill C-31. Prior to the passage of the bill, the band council placed a moratorium on various rights and services for reinstated members until a membership code was in place. While the moratorium was later lifted, the Commission ruled that the women had been discriminated against.[34]

This example shows that in the process of asserting their newfound self-determination, bands in Canada are still answerable to human rights norms. The federal courts are still in the process of deciding how much leeway they will give to bands in making distinctions between male and female members.

The last case that I analyze, *Sawridge v. Canada,*[35] presents some of the tensions surrounding the implementation of C-31 and the passage of the Charter. The Sawridge Band and others challenged C-31 based upon the Charter's promise of aboriginal rights. To argue that the remedies for sex-discrimination found in C-31 were a violation of aboriginal rights, the plaintiff bands maintained that the pre–C-31 Indian Act embodied authentic pre-contact aboriginal practices. Specifically, the bands asserted that there was an aboriginal tradition called "the woman follows the man" upon marriage. Given that this was a tradition that predated colonial contact, they claimed that Parliament was out of line when it amended the Indian Act to eliminate sex discrimination. The bands did not prevail at the trial court level, but the case was appealed. Eventually a retrial was ordered because the trial court judge was deemed to be biased against status Indians' "special benefits." The retrial still has not occurred and the plaintiff bands seem to be pursuing other avenues for their claim. I will limit my analysis to the original trial court proceedings, because the discourse it presents is so fascinating. In many ways, the conceptions of tradition and the methods of legitimating such tradition parallel the arguments presented in the *Santa Clara Pueblo v. Martinez* case. Comparing these cases will yield some interesting conclusions about US and Canadian legal institutions and norms vis-à-vis indigenous women.

Aspects of the cultural "protection" found in the Indian Act was replaced with the (ill-defined) Aboriginal rights rhetoric found in the Charter. This, along with the expanded sex equality found in C-31 and in the Charter (which may or may not apply to the bands), complicates the intersectional struggle that indigenous women face. The next few sections of this chapter and chapter 4 examine the discursive transition from protection to aboriginal rights in the sphere of membership, and will explore how these discourses complicate indigenous women's claims to sex equality. What was presented in this summary as a binary opposition between aboriginal rights and sex equality will be expanded and complicated. An examination of the legal arguments presented under the discursive frames will provide a more nuanced assessment of whether the Charter's simultaneous expansion of sex equality and aboriginal rights helped women better articulate their political claims at the intersections of power.

Framing the Legal Claims: The Master Frames

The Canadian case is comprised of three different instances of legal mobilization (including one at the UN) and several important legislative acts. Thus, the analysis of the discursive frames is quite a bit more complicated than it was for the US case. In order to capture the multifaceted nature of continuing mobilization, I analyze both government implementation reports and legal documents. The temporal trajectory of each discursive frame shows how legal arguments evolve with each new case. The Charter of Rights and Freedoms and the amendments to the Indian Act expand the universe of legal arguments. Therefore, depending upon the party and the stage at which the legal argument is being made, some frames are emphasized over others. As legal mobilization progresses, rights discourse is re-evaluated in order to capture the competing strands of power that affect indigenous women's lives. The evolving and malleable nature of these discursive frames show the changing relationships between the Canadian government, indigenous women, and the bands.

The discursive frames, again, are: 1) Individual Civil Rights, 2) Sovereignty Rights, 3) Membership Standards, 4) Tradition, 5) Jurisdiction, and 6) Economic and Material Forces. As found in the US case, these discursive frames are intertwined. I have disaggregated them here in order to offer a more systematic analysis of the legal arguments presented in each case. The cases that I will examine are: *A. G. of Canada v. Lavell—Isaac v. Bedard*,[36] *Lovelace v. Canada*,[37] and *Sawridge Band v. Canada*.[38] Throughout these cases, individual civil rights claims form the foundation for indigenous women's equality arguments. They employ the language of sex discrimination to regain access to their natal bands. The individual civil rights logic that they use is found in the Canadian Bill of Rights, The International Covenant on Civil and Political Rights and The Canadian Charter of Rights and Freedoms. The Bill of Rights provided a weaker version of sex equality that was unable to invalidate the sexist membership rule found in 12(1)(b) of the Indian Act. In contrast, the Charter was created in response to the UN's ruling in *Lovelace* and other pressures for Canada to improve its human rights record. The Charter strengthened individual civil rights logic while introducing aboriginal rights. The account of aboriginal rights that began to emerge was rooted in individual civil rights logics, reflecting an ideological dialectic that results from colonialism. Thus, women's individual civil rights claims simultaneously compete with and define aboriginal rights.

As mentioned earlier, sovereignty was first invoked in the context of the Indian Act's protection of indigenous culture and land. Since sovereignty depends upon cultural survival, it is important to consider how bands wanted to maintain federal protection as a way to continue existing as a distinct cultural entity. This was not a statement about nationalistic separation. Rather, most indigenous constructions of sovereignty are premised upon a long history of federal protection. After the passage of C-31 and the Charter, there is discursive shift from sovereignty as federal protection of cultural survival to sovereignty found in aboriginal rights. This shift causes the relationship between sovereignty and sex equality to become more nuanced and complicated. This dynamic is reflected in how the other frames (membership standards, tradition, jurisdiction, and economic and material forces) are presented over time.

With the transition from federal protection of indigenous peoples to aboriginal rights, and the accompanying expansion of rights discourses, "Indianness" becomes increasingly multi-layered. Various membership standards are developed for federal status and band membership, each offering different kinds of benefits. As the cases progressed, legal arguments invoked pre-contact tradition more than ever. Additionally, there was a shift in jurisdictional arguments, because as bands asserted their sovereignty, the federal institutions realigned their jurisdictional reach. The resulting distribution of power was confusing and many programs fell through jurisdictional cracks. Finally, the economic consequences of the changing status of indigenous women were rather complex. With the process of reinstatement, women were confronted with a new set of economic challenges that did not exist when they were simply excluded from their bands. Moreover, band resources were taxed with an influx of new members at the same time that the Canadian government withdrew some crucial funding for Indian programs. The evolving legal arguments reflect these economic shifts.

The analysis of these discursive frames will show the subtle effects of ongoing legal mobilization. As new legislation was passed, legal arguments were re-framed to reflect and respond to the complexity of indigenous women's changing legal status. As discussed in chapter 1, new legal strategies often help re-define political identity and goals. Groups often re-assess and re-present their identities to fit the available political tools at a particular time. In this case, rights were re-evaluated over time, and new legal arguments became available, but this change in the available tools did not necessarily alleviate or acknowledge the double bind of intersectional power. In fact, sometimes this double bind was exacerbated by the reforms found in the Charter and C-31.

The remainder of this chapter analyzes the two prominent frames: individual civil rights and sovereignty rights. The various arguments presented under these two "master" frames guide the interpretation of the other discursive frames (which are analyzed in chapter 4). The discussion of each discursive frame is presented in four phases of legal argumentation: Phase one discusses the *Lavell/Bedard* case; phase two analyzes the *Lovelace* case; phase three is about the implementation of the Charter and C-31; and phase four covers the *Sawridge* case.

Frame One: Individual Civil Rights

Phase One: Lavell/Bedard: Will Non-Discrimination Lead to Equality?

The *Lavell* and *Bedard* cases forced the courts to consider whether the guarantees in the Canadian Bill of Rights invalidated part or all of the Indian Act. The individual freedoms promised by the Bill of Rights (1960) are "the right of the individual to life, liberty, security of the person and enjoyment of property, and the right not to be deprived thereof except by due process of law; [and] the right of the individual to equality before the law and the protection of the law . . . "[39] and they "exist without discrimination by reason of race, national origin, colour, religion or sex." In these cases, the Canadian courts had to consider the meaning of "equality." Presumably, legislation that offends this principle of equality should be repealed. From the court decision and the arguments presented in this case, it becomes clear that equality under the Bill of Rights is limited to not invidiously discriminating against individuals.

The individual civil rights at stake in this case depended upon who demanded those rights. Some felt that since the Indian Act differentiated between people according to both their race and their sex, if it were deemed sexist, it would also eventually be deemed racist, which would require that the entire Act be repealed. The lower court decisions in *Lavell/Bedard* tried to discern if invidious discrimination happened. If it did, it would be along race or sex lines. The courts had to decide just how much differentiation qualifies as illegal discrimination.

Thus, the trial court in *Re Lavell and Attorney-General of Canada*[40] had to decide what kind of individual Lavell *was* in order to decide who she should be equal to. Judge Grossberg discovered a new "status" for Lavell, as a Canadian married female:

> The marriage of the appellant has created a status . . . The appellant entered into a voluntary marriage which gave her the status and all the rights enjoyed by all other Canadian married females . . . I am unable to conclude in enacting the Canadian Bill of Rights it was contemplated that, as a general or inflexible principle, inequality within a group or class itself, by reason of sex is necessarily offensive to the Canadian Bill of Rights. In my view, in this case, the equality which should be sought and assured to the appellant upon her marriage is equality with all other Canadian married females. The appellant has such equality. The appellant has not been deprived of any human rights or freedoms contemplated by the Canadian Bill of Rights.[41]

Here, Grossberg compares married women to each other, instead of comparing married women to married men. In so doing, he concentrated on possible racial discrimination, avoided considering the sex-based claim, and certainly did not contemplate the two identity strands simultaneously. Interestingly, despite Grossberg's focus on race, he did not question the existence of the Indian Act, nor did he discuss how non-indigenous Canadian women's individual civil rights might change based upon who they marry. They became "Indian" when they married Indian men and they did not lose their Canadian citizenship to boot. Thus, if Grossberg had truly explored the equality between married indigenous and Canadian women, he would have grappled with this asymmetry. Grossberg failed to see much of the racism inherent in the Indian Act and he completely overlooked the sexism of section 12(1)(b). All of this maneuvering allowed him to conclude that there was no violation of the equality standards found in the Bill of Rights, which in turn, allowed the Indian Act to stand. After this ruling, Jeannette Lavell said, "[Grossberg] believed I was better off marrying a white man. In fact according to his readings this was the thinking of all intelligent native people." [42] She felt the denial of her sex discrimination claim was an effort to further assimilate Native people.

In the Federal Court of Appeals, Judge Thurlow[43], who ruled in favor of Lavell, stated that " . . . the apparent effect of the legislation is . . . to discriminate by reason of sex." [44] By focusing solely on the sex discrimination claim, Thurlow did not consider the racist premises of the Indian Act or the narrow instance of race-based discrimination against indigenous married women. He compared Indian women to Indian men and concluded, "These provisions are thus laws which abrogate, abridge, and infringe the right of an individual Indian woman to equality with other Indians before the law."[45] While Thurlow's ruling was favorable to Lavell, he still ignored one component of her identity in order to give meaning to the equality found in the Bill of Rights. By ruling this narrowly, the rest of the Indian Act could stand and Thurlow could focus on 12(1)(b).

Even though these two decisions relied on a different identity strand to decide whether discrimination happened, they both focused narrowly on individual instances of illegal discrimination, rather than asking deeper questions about the structure of inequality. While they could identify categories by which one might be discriminated against, they were unable to consider the groups that those categories represent, nor did they consider the historical and structural domination experienced by those groups. Thus, the civil rights jurisprudence that emerged identified individual moments of discrimination rather than developing the deeper meaning of equality. The juxtaposition of these two lower court decisions shows how the intersection of race and gender is not considered. As will be seen in the Canadian Supreme Court decision, sometimes the two identity strands cancel each other out, yielding a ruling against indigenous women.

When judges try to look at both race and sex, the resulting reasoning reveals a great deal of discomfort. In the ruling that favored Bedard, Justice Osler[46] of the Ontario High Court tried to look at both sex and race-based discrimination. Osler even went so far as to mention the structural racism inherent in the Indian Act. But, his ultimate ruling rested solely on the grounds of sex discrimination. He realized that the courts should probably defer to Parliament on the larger question of the entire Indian Act (more on this under the jurisdiction frame) and, therefore, he narrowly ruled that individuals should be free from sex-based discrimination. He wrote:

> Regardless of the larger question of whether virtually the entire Indian Act, which is plainly based upon a distinction of race and has no other reason for its existence, may be said to be a valid exercise of the powers of Parliament and may remain in force despite the Canadian Bill of Rights, it is abundantly clear that under various provisions of the Act there . . . is plainly discrimination by reason of sex with respect to the rights of an individual to the enjoyment of property. Indeed, the whole status of such a person as an Indian is completely altered.[47]

The conception of private property that underlies this decision echoes the foundation for liberal rights. It is a strange construction of this problem, given that the property that Osler refers to is reserve property, which is held in trust for bands as communal entities. Osler superimposes liberal conceptions of individual property ownership on Bedard's complaint. Given this underlying logic, it makes sense that Osler ruled narrowly on the sex discrimination claim because it allowed him to find an individual moment of invidious discrimination, without having to interrogate the structural inequalities inherent in the Indian Act.

Ultimately, in *A. G. of Canada v. Lavell—Isaac v. Bedard*,[48] the Canadian Supreme Court ruled against Lavell and Bedard. Lavell and Bedard presented their arguments using similar language as Osler's above. They argued that "the Respondent has . . . been denied her right to equality before the law and the protection of the law without discrimination by reason of race and sex contrary to the Canadian Bill of Rights."[49] Their sex-based claim was based upon the fact that only females lost their status upon marriage to a non-Indian. The race-based claim was based upon the following:

> (a) Only *Indian* women are subject to the particular disabilities which fall upon marriage to non-Indians, whereas

non-Indian women suffer no such disability upon marrying
non-Indians; (b) The decision as to what her status is to be
following marriage and the decision as to whether or not she
ceases to be an Indian is a decision based solely upon the *race*
of her husband. The tendency of such legislation can only be
to create and deepen divisions between racial groups.[50]

An Indian woman did not have the same freedom as a non-Indian
woman to marry whomever she wanted because she had to consider
how the race of her husband would affect her own identity. While
Lavell and Bedard argued against racial inequality, they still viewed
the race-based distinctions found in the Indian Act as a viable method
for protecting Indian culture. In their factum, they referred to both
identity strands, but they did not argue that the entire Indian Act should
be overturned based upon ongoing colonial domination. Lavell and
Bedard wished to be treated equally as Indians under the Indian Act.
Thus, Lavell and Bedard wanted to maintain some racial distinctions.

The Alberta Committee on Indian Rights for Indian Women
(IRIW) urged the court to follow the precedent of *Drybones* and argued
that if "the word 'sex' [was] substituted for 'race,'" then 12(1)(b) could
be deemed inoperative.[51] Later in the same factum, the Alberta IRIW
argued that since no other woman in Canada lost her citizenship or
legal status as a result of marriage, 12(1)(b) was an instance of race
discrimination against Native women.[52] In order to make both a race-
based and a sex-based claim, Indian women had to be compared to
both Indian men and Canadian women, because they did not have the
same kind of autonomy in making personal decisions. These kinds of
arguments show how Lavell, Bedard, and the interveners on their
behalf based their arguments mostly upon conceptions of individuality
that informed the interpretation of the Canadian Bill of Rights and
Canadian jurisprudence in general.[53] They attempted to fit their
intersectional identity into the liberal framework provided by Canadian
legal norms. This did not lead them to argue for strict equality, but
merely for non-discrimination.

The Attorney General wrote, "For a woman, her release from the
provisions of the Indian Act is entirely a matter of free choice."[54]
Individual Indian women who "chose" to marry outside their tribe
"chose" to lose the benefits of being a status Indian, but also "gained"
the benefits enjoyed by any other female Canadian. This is the starkest
account of individual rights found in the legal arguments presented in

these cases because it relies on a very abstract conception of an unencumbered citizen, who makes choices freely regardless of the context.[55] The consequences of these choices run deep: according to the Indian Act, such choices completely redefine one's ethnic identity. Lavell's factum describes the extent of this loss. "A free choice of spouse by the respondent necessarily entails what is in fact a penalty: the compulsory loss of Indian status."[56] Thus, Lavell framed the issue in terms of human rights, and focused on the deprivation of the "dignity and worth of the human person" because she felt that "the classification scheme treat[ed] one such group more harshly than another."[57]

Both Lavell and the Attorney General felt that deciding whether 12(1)(b) illegally discriminated in any way required proving that some individuals (namely indigenous women) were treated more harshly than others. The Indian Association of Alberta claimed that "[t]he loss of status means the loss of the positive rights available to Indians by the Indian Act, but not harsher treatment than the general Canadian population."[58] To prove that the loss of Indian status was not harsh treatment, the Attorney General and interveners contended that the status rights lost were replaced by new rights that were guaranteed to all Canadian citizens. Whether or not these different rights are of equal weight should not require a consideration of equality, or so the argument goes.

The Attorney General's factum states that "the determination of the present issue . . . requires no further probing of the content of the expression 'equality before the law.' As in the *Drybones* case, it is not necessary and probably not desirable to attempt any exhaustive definition of the expression."[59] The Attorney General feared that the Bill of Rights would apply to

> all classes of legal rights [which would require that] the Bill must demand complete uniformity of rights of individuals under the laws of Canada, regardless of the group or class of persons to which an individual may belong . . . It is submitted that there can be no true equality under the law unless the law recognizes and makes reasonable provision for those fundamental differences that are frequently discernible in those who are subject to it.[60]

The US Supreme Court Case *Reed v. Reed*[61] was even cited to show that the Fourteenth Amendment in the US did not require "uniformity of rights among different classes of persons."[62] A requirement for uniform rights would certainly preclude the protective policies found in the Indian Act. The argument claims that while the rights promised under the Indian Act may be different, they are not necessarily unequal to the rights of Canadian citizens, and therefore they require no court scrutiny. For both the Attorney General and Lavell and Bedard, strict equality was not desired. Lavell and Bedard wanted to maintain some race-based distinctions (i.e., allow the Indian Act to stand) while eliminating sex-based distinctions. The Attorney General was in favor of maintaining all distinctions, fearing that an elimination of sex-based distinctions would empower the court to scrutinize all distinctions, and possibly weakening the Indian Act's provisions. The Attorney General's primary concern was to prevent the court from being the venue where the meaning of equality was defined and enforced.

In the Supreme Court's majority opinion, Justice Ritchie concluded that discrimination under the Bill of Rights only includes a denial of enumerated rights, and because this particular instance of unequal treatment did not involve an enumerated right it was not a violation of the Canadian Bill of Rights. Moreover, Ritchie implies that the Bill of Rights and the precedent of *Drybones* only apply to race-based discrimination, not sex-based discrimination.

> The fundamental distinction between the present case and that of *Drybones*, however, appears to me to be that the impugned section in the latter case could not be enforced without denying equality of treatment in the administration and enforcement of the law before the ordinary courts of the land to a racial group, whereas no such inequality of treatment between Indian men and women flow as a result of the application of s. 12(1)(b) of the Indian Act.[63]

Here, Ritchie relies on a very narrow reading of precedent to rule against the sex-based argument. Ritchie seems to be saying that the judiciary would only be able to act in this case if race-based discrimination had occurred between Indian men and Indian women. It is quite clear that Ritchie does not think that the Indian Act should be overturned by the judiciary. This is the most limited account of equal rights that emerges from this case. According to this view, only the most egregious distinctions are invidiously discriminatory and there is no systematic analysis of either racial or gender inequality.

In contrast, the dissent by Justice Laskin couples race-based and sex-based discrimination and acknowledges that the effect of the Indian Act is not merely about the discrimination against individuals.

> It appears to me that the contention that a differentiation on the basis of sex is not offensive to the Canadian Bill of Rights where that differentiation operates only among Indians under the Indian Act is one that compounds racial inequality even beyond that which the *Drybones* case found unacceptable.[64]

Not only did Laskin feel that *Drybones* should apply to this case, he framed the problem in terms of racial inequality rather than race-based discrimination. Laskin actually tied the moment of sex-based discrimination to enduring racial domination. This is probably the most macro or structural analysis of the problem found in this case.

The majority of the Court found that there was discrimination by reason of sex, but ruled that the Bill of Rights could not render the Indian Act inoperative. The swing vote, Justice Pigeon, stated that "if discrimination by reason of race makes certain statutory provisions inoperative, the same result must follow as to statutory provisions which exhibit discrimination by reason of sex."[65] Pigeon's and the majority opinion focused less on equality than on individual moments of discrimination. Although Pigeon disliked the sex discrimination in 12(1)(b), his conception of the proper role of the judiciary ultimately led him to agree with the majority ruling that the court could not override the Indian Act. This very close decision represents a greater struggle about the strength of the Bill of Rights. In the end, the *Lavell/Bedard* case is often cited as proof of the inability of the Canadian judiciary to check Parliamentary infringements of individual freedoms (more on this later, under the jurisdiction frame).

The version of individual civil rights that emerges from the *Lavell/Bedard* decisions is all about who should be free from discrimination. The prevailing view relegates individuals to certain identity characteristics in order to decide whether discrimination has occurred. Thus, according to the majority opinion, the Canadian Bill of Rights could only prevent race- or sex-based discrimination, but not both, and certainly not both simultaneously. Ritchie's reading of precedent allowed the court to prevent only very explicit instances of race-based discrimination, while preserving the more pervasive sexism and racism in the Indian Act. Lavell, Bedard, some interveners, and the dissenting opinions pointed out that both identity characteristics must be acknowledged in order to establish equal individual civil rights for indigenous women *qua* indigenous women. Some even went so far as to point out that individual civil rights are deeply intertwined with the historical inequality that forms the foundation for the Indian Act. Yet, even the arguments and opinions that coupled race and sex-based discrimination did so somewhat superficially. In fact, none really questioned the entire Indian Act. Lavell and Bedard wished to retain the protections of that Act. Thus, they did not really attempt to offer a unique legal analysis that acknowledged the cumulative effect of such dual discrimination. Instead, they were reluctant to dig too deep because they felt that doing so would shake any existing foundations for protecting indigenous peoples. The "protections" of the Indian Act were important enough that legal arguments focused on individual moments of invidious discrimination instead of trying to construct a meaningful notion of equality. If the latter were emphasized, surely the Indian Act would fall. The *Lavell/Bedard* case shows how individual civil rights claims dominate Canadian legal norms. Thus, the overarching issue was whether individuals should have equal access to the "protections" of the Indian Act.

Phase Two: Lovelace v. Canada: Cultural Rights as Human Rights

While *Lovelace v. Canada* took place in a different venue—before the United Nations Human Rights Committee (UN HRC)—much of the underlying logic was similar to that employed in *Lavell/Bedard*. Sandra Lovelace argued that Canada had breached "the right to equal protection before the law" because it treated women who choose to marry non-Indians differently from men who do the same.[66] Additionally, Lovelace listed other rights enumerated in the International Covenant on Civil and Political Rights that apply to her case: the right to marry and the protection of the family. She also mentioned Article 27, which says that in states where "ethnic, religious, or linguistic minorities exist, persons shall not be denied the right, in community with the other members of their group, to enjoy their own culture, to profess their own religion, or to use their own language." About this particular article, she argued:

> On first glance, it might appear that this Article can be used as a defense against a charge of inequality; one might say, for example, that the loss of certain rights for women marrying outside their Indian culture is an attempt to protect both the Indian minority and its reservation lands from outsiders. The intent may be laudable, but one cannot condone the method of protection which has been devised in this instance, because . . . it is done in a discriminatory manner . . . In short, if the Indians, as a minority group, are to be protected, then the government must revise its method of protecting them. The Parliament of Canada must adopt a formula for their protection that does not involve discrimination between males and females.[67]

Thus the only reason Lovelace mentioned minority rights was to say that those cannot be used to justify the Indian Act's protection of Indians' rights in a sexist manner.

Canada argued that Lovelace, as a Canadian citizen, had all the individual civil rights that other Canadians had. The argument reveals Canada's inability to acknowledge all of Lovelace's identity characteristics. The government's submission states, "Mrs. Lovelace is no longer a member of the Tobique band and no longer an Indian under the terms of the Indian Act. She, however, is enjoying all the rights recognized in the Covenant, in the same way as any other individual within the territory of Canada and subject to its jurisdiction."[68] Note the similarities between this argument and the analysis found in *Lavell* that focused on the rights that married indigenous women gained when they became Canadians. The underlying logic of such arguments is that individuals deserve certain governmental services, and as long as all individuals have access to some such benefits, their rights are not being violated. But, access to one's ethnic community and the survival of that community are not important components of these rights.

The UN HRC ruled that since Sandra Lovelace got married before the Covenant applied to Canada, they could not apply Article 3's sex equality provision[69] to the Indian Act. But the opinion focused on Article 27 (minority rights), concluding that "[t]he major loss to a person ceasing to be an Indian is the loss of the cultural benefits of living in an Indian community, the emotional ties to home, family, friends and neighbors and the loss of identity.[70] The UN HRC ruled that an individual has the right to foster a relationship with his/her natal community, and practice its culture and language. The decision states that " . . . the right of Sandra Lovelace, to access her native culture and language 'in community with the other members' of her group, has in fact been, and continues to be interfered with, because there is no place outside the Tobique Reserve where such a community exists."[71] Cultural distinctiveness is important to the UN Human Rights Committee only insofar as individuals can choose to take part in it or to foster it. The crux of this ruling is that individuals have a right to access their ethnic community. Interestingly, the majority opinion focuses on the very article that Lovelace feared would strengthen Canada's power to "protect" indigenous cultural practices. But the Committee interprets that article in a way that benefits Lovelace.

While the majority opinion of the UN HRC focuses on an individual's lack of cultural contact, the opinion of Nejib Bouziri states that "[t]he [Indian] Act is still in force and, even though the Lovelace case arose before the date on which the Covenant became applicable in Canada, Mrs. Lovelace is still suffering from adverse discriminatory effect of the Act in matters other than that covered by article 27."[72] Bouziri notices that there is continuing sex discrimination against Lovelace and similarly situated women. His conception of individual civil rights uses a more sophisticated account of historical sex discrimination than the primary ruling of the committee. The latter focuses on a very literal micro-moment of sex discrimination, which happened before Canada signed on to the Covenant. The UN HRC's inability to see the structural sex-based inequality faced by Lovelace or similarly situated women shows the exclusive focus on individual civil rights. Similar to the arguments presented in *Lavell/Bedard,* here individual moments of clear-cut invidious discrimination are most likely to get a favorable ruling.

Interestingly, the UN HRC's decision never really mentions the racism that is inherent in the Indian Act. This is significant because it underscores how human rights law focuses on individuals rather than on minority communities and, even when the international community attempts to prevent cultural destruction, it can only do so on a case-by-case basis. This methodology can only deal with discrete acts of race-based discrimination, and, therefore, cannot rule on the structural racism represented by the Indian Act.

After the UN HRC's ruling, to show a good faith effort to deal with the denial of individual civil rights and the denial of indigenous people's autonomy, the Canadian government reported that it was in the process of reforming the Indian Act and that it was about to pass The Canadian Charter of Rights and Freedoms. The government felt that these reforms would provide a "domestic remedy in Canada for persons who feel they have been discriminated against on the basis of sex by federal laws."[73] At the same time, Canada pointed out that "other sections of the charter reflect Canada's respect for ethnic and aboriginal rights."[74] Canada argued that the Charter would serve a dual purpose, protecting both aboriginal rights and sex-based civil rights. But this dual purpose ultimately sets up a tension between two kinds of rights, which inevitably spurs future legal mobilization. It is unclear whether aboriginal rights will be protected in a manner similar to the UN HRC's version of minority rights as individual human rights, or if the Canadian government will try to develop a group-based version of aboriginal rights.

Phase Three: C-31 and the Charter of Rights and Freedoms: Can Individual and Aboriginal Rights Coexist?

After the UN HRC decision and with the amendment of the Indian Act (C-31 in 1985) and the passage of The Charter of Rights and Freedoms (1982), Canada removed the most obvious sex-based discrimination from the Indian Act and simultaneously bolstered aboriginal rights.[75] Individual civil rights claims became even more complicated because the government had to protect individual equality without trampling aboriginal rights.

In this context, how could the individual civil rights of indigenous women be protected? "The QNWA [Quebec Native Women's Association] argue[d] that membership rules developed by bands ought to be consistent with section 15 of the Canadian Charter of Rights and Freedoms . . . the WNWA [Winnipeg Native Women's Association] maintain[ed] that any government, whether it be a band government or the federal government, must protect the right of the individual."[76] Hence, some of the pressing questions in the wake of reforming the Indian Act were: Should the membership rules developed by the bands be subject to sex equality provisions in the Charter? Is it necessary or proper to foist norms of sex equality (or at least non-discrimination) upon the bands as they are being given expanded self-government power? If so, it is ideological domination and if not, it is leaving Native women high and dry. Either way, the dichotomy between aboriginal and individual rights seems to exacerbate indigenous women's dual domination. Neither construction takes the intersections of these two forms of power into account. These questions are central to the *Sawridge* case and others.

Another problem that emerged as C-31 was being implemented was the second generation cut-off rule, where the grandchildren of reinstated women faced the residual effects of 12(1)(b)'s sex-based membership rules.

> The sexual discrimination that was to be redressed through Bill C-31 continues to be felt. There remains unequal treatment of male and female siblings. Women who lost status through marriage cannot pass status along through successive generations in the same way as their brothers who married non-Indian women prior to 1985. The brothers, their non-Indian spouses and children are automatically considered band members while their sisters' children can only acquire status. The children of the female line have conditional entitlement to band membership.[77]

Therefore, the "second generation cut-off clause has served to create new classes of aboriginal people and sexual discrimination has simply been hidden in the legislation."[78] With this continued residual sex discrimination, it is clear that the flaws of the jurisprudence mentioned earlier under *Lavell/Bedard* seep into the legislation that is meant to create sex equality. Sex discrimination in a very narrow sense might be eliminated by C-31, but sex inequality endures and remains an unintended consequence of some seemingly benign statutory distinctions.

With the new distinctions between Indian status and band membership, individual civil rights become even more complicated. Indian status is conferred with sex equality in mind. But when a band denies a reinstated woman band membership, it is very difficult for her to reintegrate into her community. Thus, the intended effect of giving women who married out of their bands access to their ethnic identity does not always come to fruition.

The minority rights language presented in Lovelace is reiterated in a C-31 implementation report. Celina Minoose-Ritter, a woman who was reinstated to the Cold Lake First Nation, states:

> All the women reinstated under Bill C-31 from the Cold Lake First Nations reserve have been refused their treaty monies . . . We are being denied our right to practice our cultural heritage on the reserve level and are being treated like second class citizens by our own people, and now we are nomads in our own land because we chose to marry who we wanted to. And that is a basic right practiced worldwide by humans from every other ethnic group.[79]

Minoose-Ritter states that it is an individual's human right to marry whomever she wants, and also to practice her cultural heritage. Thus, heritage and culture are practiced on an individual basis, as a result of individual choice, rather than being a group-based creation. This logic comes from the UN HRC's ruling in *Lovelace*.

> The problems associated with discriminatory clauses contained in the old Indian Act still exist. Once people learned to accept the government's term of status and non-status Indians, the problems of discrimination began. This was, and continues to be, a social dilemma not only for Bill C-31 natives, but for the entire native community as well. Because the old legislation divided our people, everyone lost something in the process. What we all lost was equality, the ability to treat each other as equals and, therefore, the ability to work together cooperatively to ease our transition into modern multicultural society.[80]

According to this quote, equality was lost with the passage of the first Indian Act. Now, the best aboriginal people can hope for is less discrimination and an easy transition to multi-cultural society. This goal is a uniquely modern one. All that is needed is for individuals to respect each other's differences and to coexist. The goal of a multicultural society is very different than the indigenous desire for autonomy or sovereignty. It is ultimately based upon the concept of individuality that informs Canadian legal norms.[81]

As the *Sawridge* case will illustrate, Native women who were reinstated tended to rely on the individual civil rights frame as they mobilized the law, while bands tended to embrace the language of aboriginal (sovereignty) rights in their counter-arguments. But, the arguments set forth in *Sawridge* also show that Native bands explicitly acknowledged the liberal individualist bias of Canadian legal norms. They felt that this bias had deleterious effects on self-determination, but nonetheless, they tried to eke out a bit of band autonomy within the individual civil rights rubric.

Phase Four: Sawridge v. Canada: Band Membership and the Freedom of Association

As stated earlier, it is unclear whether the explicit prohibition of sex discrimination found in The Charter of Rights and Freedoms will be applied to the expanding power of indigenous bands. The arguments presented in *Sawridge v. Canada* exemplify the tensions between band autonomy and sex equality because the bands question the viability of C-31 based upon the promise of aboriginal rights found in the Charter, the very document that promises individual civil rights. The bands spent a great deal of time trying to prove that their traditional practices included the practice of "the woman follows the man" upon marriage (more on this under the sovereignty and tradition frames). Additionally, the plaintiff bands were very explicit about their strategic use of the Charter, offering a very interesting back-up argument based upon the freedom to associate. The plaintiff's statement of claim says that with C-31,

> Parliament attempted unilaterally to require Indian bands to admit certain persons to membership. The 1985 Amendment imposes members on a band without the necessity of consent by the council of the band of the members of the band itself and, indeed, imposes such persons on the band even if the council of the band or the membership objects to the inclusion of such persons in the band.[82]

This claim relies very heavily on a particular conception of consent, which they argue should be found at a group level. The band, as an entity (represented by the council), should have the right to reject and accept members. But the plaintiffs acknowledged that the Canadian legal system might not be able to conceive of these rights as existing at the group level.

Therefore, this freedom of association argument was used as "an alternative position," according to the Plaintiffs[83], which only arises

> at all if you [Judge Muldoon] determine . . . that the aboriginal right was either an individual right and not a collective right, which runs counter to everything that the law says, or if you determine that 35(4) transformed aboriginal rights into individual rights for all purposes, then only in that context would this argument come to bear . . . But in that circumstance we were dealing on a plane of individual rights and competing individual interests only, which I submit we could not be but if we were . . . you could have to reconcile any disposition in that respect with section 2(d)[freedom of association] for we say in effect that that would mean that reserves were in effect consensual associations, and we say that the freedom to associate must clearly include the freedom not to associate . . . We say that argument properly doesn't arise . . . because it can't arise unless you've already made a determination which is at odds . . . I say you couldn't do this, only the Supreme Court could do it and it would involve a change in the law and you would have to make a determination at odds with the very nature of what an aboriginal right is.[84]

In essence, this backup argument presented by the bands acknowledges the prevalence of individual civil rights logic in the Charter and attempts to assert some tribal autonomy within it. The bands preferred for the courts to acknowledge their collective rights to sovereignty, but realized that the discourse was stacked against them. Therefore, they explicitly said that the only reason the argument would be pertinent is if the aboriginal rights found in the Charter were individually based. Such an explicit argument shows that the aboriginal rights found in the Charter are underdeveloped and conflict with the promised individual rights.

How does one conceive of aboriginal rights as individual rights? This harkens back to the UN conception of minority rights, which focuses upon an individual's access to culture, rather than cultural autonomy. According to this construction, individuals have a right to aboriginal practices (as long as those practices do not conflict with Canadian law). Sawridge et. al. raised a very interesting and plausible reading of the aboriginal rights promised in the Charter. Since the overwhelming goal of the Charter is to assure individual civil rights, aboriginal rights might be construed as a subset of individual rights.

In response to the bands' claim to freedom of association, one of the interveners in the case, the

> Native Council of Canada [said], yes, there is a freedom of association but not a freedom of association to exclude one's kin from statutory benefits, from Charter protection . . . [D]iscrimination is often cross-cultural and for a discriminating minority to discriminate further and internally against a small minority within itself it's still discrimination. Even if self-regulated. And even if done under the approval of freedom of association.[85]

Thus, the Native Council of Canada did not disagree with the freedom to associate in principle, but did not want it to be enforced by the band. They felt that the individual right to be free from sex discrimination was more important than the band's claim to associational rights.

The court ruling in this case rejected the band's aboriginal rights claim to determine membership. Judge Muldoon, wrote that "[Subsection 35(4) of the Constitution Act, 1982] exacts equality of rights between male and female persons, no matter what rights or responsibilities may have pertained in earlier times."[86] Muldoon asserted that aboriginal rights claims were answerable to the norms of sex equality found in the Charter. Thus, Muldoon ruled that when individual civil rights and band sovereignty claims came directly into conflict, individual civil rights should always win out. He did not comment on whether aboriginal rights were individually or communally based.

The Evolution of the Individual Civil Rights Frame

The individual civil rights arguments evolve from *Lavell/Bedard* through *Sawridge* in many ways. The primary reasons for the different arguments are the changing venues and the different legislative bases for the decisions. *Lavell/Bedard* invoked the Bill of Rights before a conservative court, which was unlikely to overturn significant Parliamentary acts. This court ultimately wanted Parliament to retain the right to "protect" Indians and therefore deferred to that branch of government. Lovelace relied on the UN Covenant on Civil and Political Rights, and the UN Human Rights Committee was unable to base its decision on sex discrimination because the timing of the events muddled its jurisdictional reach. But the Committee did manage to rule in Lovelace's favor by using Article 27 (minority rights) to construct an individual's right to continuing cultural access. The ruling was different from Lovelace's and Canada's interpretations of that same article. By ruling this way, the Committee prevented the possibility that Canada might use minority rights as a justification for preserving 12(1)(b) on grounds that it protected indigenous people. *Sawridge* used The Charter of Rights and Freedoms to assert that bands' aboriginal rights render the sex-discrimination remedies found in C-31 inoperative. Sawridge et. al. explicitly acknowledged the individual/collective rights conundrum. To cover all bases, the plaintiff bands offered a version of aboriginal rights based upon an individual's right to associate freely. These arguments all show that Canadian legal norms and international human rights law are biased in favor of individual rights, which often exacerbates the unique domination of indigenous women. As long as rights are conceived as either individual or collective, or as sex or race-based, the dual domination at the intersections of power continues. As time goes by, the forms of this debate change a bit, and in some places it becomes more explicit, but virtually no arguments presented critique the double bind that indigenous women face.

Prior to the passage of C-31, the individual civil rights claims were strictly about how federal legislation discriminated on the basis of sex or race. Sometimes, the parties involved pondered historical and group-based discrimination, but more often than not, there was a narrow focus on one individual's denial of rights based upon an identifiable identity characteristic. The rulings in favor of indigenous women were so narrow that they failed to construct a coherent vision of equality, which might have revealed the complexities of intersectional power. After the passage of C-31 and the Charter, the sex-based claim became more complicated and an explicit competing argument—aboriginal rights—emerged. It is unclear whether aboriginal rights would be individually or band-based, but they became the basis of band sovereignty claims. What follows is a consideration of the development of this discursive frame.

Frame Two: Sovereignty Rights

Phase One: Lavell/Bedard: The Federal Protection of Cultural Survival

The *Lavell/Bedard* case rested primarily on a conflict between the Bill of Rights and the Indian Act. In order to maintain Indian "special status," some band leaders staunchly defended the sexism found in the Indian Act. The possibility that the courts might overturn the Indian Act put benefits and reserves into jeopardy. The arguments that were put forth in defense of the Indian Act were more about federal protection of indigenous cultural and economic survival than they were about sovereignty or autonomy. Lavell and Bedard did not refute this protection narrative. Lavell's factum states:

> The Indian Act is particularly a law for the 'protection' of Indians and is intended to operate for the welfare of the Indian peoples of Canada . . . It is submitted that the respondent is entitled by force of the Bill of Rights to have the protections of the Indian Act extend to her without discrimination by reason of her sex.[87]

Thus, the Indian Act embodied the "benevolent" protection of Indian people. Their position was that denying women membership was not a valid way to protect indigenous culture and land.

Sometimes interveners and others phrased this argument for protection in terms of cultural survival and future sovereignty. This set up a fascinating strategic relationship between band sovereignty and federal protection. In many ways, from the status Indians' perspective, the *Lavell/Bedard* case embodied the dilemma over which federal legislation (the Indian Act or the Bill of Rights) and which federal institution (parliament or the judiciary) was more likely to protect their interests (more on this under jurisdiction). Some thought that cultural survival depended upon maintaining the status quo. Judge Grossberg wrote:

> There are divided views among Indians themselves . . . as to
> the desirability of continuing s. 12(1)(b) of the Indian Act . . .
> It has been submitted that many Indians wish to retain s.
> 12(1)(b) so that peace, harmony and good will among Indians
> on the reserve will not be unduly endangered by permitting
> Indian bands to be infiltrated with non-Indians.[88]

While this statement says nothing about band autonomy or sovereignty, it does focus on cultural survival, which is a necessary prerequisite for sovereignty or self-determination. It also illustrates the perspective that the Indian Act can be a guarantor of harmony and cultural survival. According to this view, by keeping (especially male) outsiders off of the reserves, Indians are given the cultural space to maintain their traditions.

Some argued that federal protection of cultural survival was, by definition, a form of cultural destruction. In this context, the greatest statement about sovereignty was found in those arguments against having the Bill of Rights apply to Indians on reserves. Mostly, the fear was that legal norms of sex equality would be forced upon the bands. This is an argument against further ideological and institutional intrusion on the reserves. Many proponents of this view felt that at least the Indian Act was a known entity.

Another inadvertent statement about sovereignty came from Indian Rights for Indian Women. IRIW feared that Indian women who married out of their tribes were not guaranteed Canadian citizenship and therefore were possibly rendered "stateless."[89] This was probably the strongest statement of sovereignty coming from women who wished to be reinstated, because it relies on an assumption that without Canadian citizenship or Indian status, one ceased to be a citizen of any state. This implies that bands had state status. By arguing in favor of this level of sovereignty for bands, the group that was fighting so hard for sex equality was showing that it was informed by a complex critique of colonial power. Such a critique is a direct result of indigenous women's intersectional identity.

At the time of *Lavell/Bedard*, nominal band sovereignty existed in the informal ability to allow women who married out to unofficially stay on the reserves. This was not so much about autonomy as it was about subversively resisting the federal edicts. Some felt that since there was a huge statutory framework which was meant to assure cultural survival, any account of sovereignty should have a clear statutory basis. Thus, in his dissenting opinion, Laskin concludes:

> Isaac stated that the Band Council 'has at all times assumed jurisdiction to grant, refuse and revoke permission for persons who are not members of the Six Nations Band to reside upon or occupy property upon the Six Nations Reserve.' The record does not disclose any statutory basis for this assumption of authority which was exercised against Mrs. Bedard by various resolutions already referred to.[90]

Laskin thought that authority could only derive from a federal grant of power. The converse argument emerges in *Sawridge*, which looks for band power where there is a federal legislative gap. Both arguments stress the crucial role that the federal government plays in determining band sovereignty. The federal government's action or inaction forms the foundation for band autonomy. Thus, the arguments in *Lavell/Bedard* focused primarily on the federal protection of cultural survival, but in a few instances, more substantive accounts of sovereignty were unearthed by both sides of the debate. The arguments presented in *Lovelace* reveal a similar dynamic.

Phase Two: Lovelace v. Canada: An Individual's Right to Cultural Survival

The Lovelace case focused on an individual's denied rights. As stated earlier, Lovelace did not want to base her argument on Article 27's minority rights, because that could be read as a justification for federal protection of Indians. Canada would have liked such an argument to stick so that the Indian Act could stand (at least in the short term). Hence, Canada argued:

> Indians are a minority in Canada and the [Indian] Act enhances their ability and opportunity 'to enjoy their own culture . . . (and) to use their own language'. Needless to say, a domestic law such as this could not be effectively made in Canada unless there was also legislative authority to define who is and who is not an Indian and how Indian status is acquired and lost . . . As the Government was seen to protect Indian land, it was also seen as protecting Indian culture.[91]

Lovelace responded: "This excuse has been used for ages but the intent of the Indian Act was to assimilate [sic] the native people in CANADIAN SOCIETY. This is a Red herring."[92] These two quotes illustrate the fundamental issue at stake here: Does Canada have the authority to protect minority cultures, or is such "protection" merely another tactic used to assimilate indigenous peoples into the dominant culture?

Even while most of her argument rests upon individual civil rights claims, Lovelace makes a fascinating statement about her citizenship. This exemplifies her multiple identity allegiances because it rests on one kind of Indian sovereignty argument.

> As she was born in Canada, Sandra Lovelace is technically a Canadian citizen under Canadian law . . . However, a large number of North American Indians who were born either in the Dominion of Canada or the Republic of the United States of America refuse to accept the citizenship designation of either country . . . Indian people argue that, as their original territories were not bound by the present national borders that divide Canada and the United States of America, and as their many treaty agreements granted them various rights and privileges, their status is one which permits them to move freely between the American/Canadian border unencumbered by the limitations which might be placed by either of those nations upon citizens seeking access or egress from one of those countries to the other. Many Indians believe that they need not be considered citizens *per se* of either state. Accordingly, Sandra Lovelace did not declare, in her Communication, that she was a Canadian citizen.[93]

This quote is more about denying Canada's authority than asserting band sovereignty. But, Lovelace implies that there is Indian sovereignty because bands were parties to treaties. Obviously, Lovelace did not want to wholeheartedly embrace a Canadian identity because the crux of her claim was to maintain her band affiliation. But, while she based most of her legal arguments on Canadian legal norms, she renounced Canadian citizenship. While this is not an argument for band sovereignty (in fact, much of Lovelace's case rests on denying bands the ability to exclude her from membership), it illustrates the complicated notions of citizenship held by indigenous women in a colonial state. This argument is similar to fears expressed by IRIW in *Lavell/Bedard* about women being rendered "stateless" under 12(1)(b) because both treat bands as states. Of course, the simultaneous embrace of the Indian Act's protections and the assertion of band statehood seems laden with contradictions (or at least represents the competing identity loyalties which manifest themselves as contradictions).

Lovelace also suggested alternative membership standards to show "that the Indian people and their lands [could] be protected without violating human rights."[94] This is another example of Lovelace's complicated relationship to band sovereignty. While she knew that band control over membership standards would probably ultimately hurt her cause, she also felt that Canada was not a great ally for maintaining her indigenous identity. Accordingly, she suggested "objective" standards to determine membership and assure Indian cultural protection. How those standards would be determined is unclear (this will be discussed in detail under the membership standards frame). It is also unclear *who* exactly would protect Indian peoples and their land.

The UN HRC was also suspicious of the Canadian government protecting indigenous culture. The decision states, "Whatever may be the merits of the Indian Act in other respects, it does not seem to the committee that to deny Sandra Lovelace the right to reside on the reserve is reasonable or necessary to preserve the identity of the tribe."[95] The committee did not deny that Canada might play a role in preserving Indian identity. But the UN HRC implied that a line should be drawn that delineates which kinds of federal "protection" would be inappropriate.

Interestingly, Article 1, Section 1 of the UN Covenant on Civil and Political Rights reads: "All peoples have the right of self-determination. By virtue of that right they freely determine their political status and freely pursue their economic, social and cultural development." This Article was never used by Lovelace to justify her position. She wanted to preserve the special status "protections" and benefits that Indians have in Canada, and arguing for self-determination would make her sex discrimination argument even weaker (given that many bands were against repealing 12(1)(b)). Lovelace preferred to find conflicts between federal norms of sex equality and the Indian Act rather than arguing for greater autonomy for her band.

The UN HRC inquired about the extent of band power in its interim decision. It asked:

> What is the legal basis of a prohibition to live on a reserve? Is it a direct result of the loss of Indian status or does it derive from a discretionary decision of the Council of the community concerned? . . . What reasons are adduced to justify the denial of the right of abode on a reserve?[96]

These questions show that the committee thought that the bands might have retained some discretionary power in determining band membership. Canada stated that women who lost their status could remain on the reserve with the approval of the band council. This band power was very informal, and women who wanted to stay on the reserve were vulnerable to the capriciousness of a particular band council. Moreover, those women who did not have official Indian status could not receive any material benefits.

Canada took this point even further, trying to blame the bands for expelling Lovelace. In order for Lovelace to obtain a reserve house, Canada noted that

> she ha[d] to apply to the Band Council. Housing on reserves [was] provided with money set aside by Parliament for the benefit of registered Indians. The Council ha[d] not agreed to provide Mrs. Lovelace with a new house. It consider[ed] that in the provision of such housing priority [was] to be given to registered Indians.[97]

The band council had to balance a complicated set of interests in executing this informal authority. Unregistered Indians (such as Lovelace) could not be included in tallies that determined the federal funding levels for the band. This and other concerns led bands to deny women reserve housing. Lovelace stated that "[s]he [was] able to remain on the reserve because dissident members of the tribe who support[ed] her cause . . . threatened to resort to physical violence in her defense [had] the authorities attempt[ed] to remove her."[98] Thus, Lovelace herself did not benefit from this informal band power, and was living proof of the vulnerability that unregistered women felt. The Indian Act was the source of their vulnerability because it took away their status and benefits and gave bands incentives for implementing its rules.

In Canada's response to the UN HRC's final decision, one sees the emerging dual interests of individual and aboriginal rights.

> Canada is committed to the removal from the Indian Act of any provisions which discriminate on the basis of sex or in some other way offend against human rights; it is also desirous that the Indian community have a significant role to play in determining what new provisions on Indian status the Indian Act should contain.[99]

Canada was trying simultaneously to bolster indigenous peoples' political voice and to reform the Indian Act to remove the sexist membership rule. The government established a Parliamentary Sub-Committee on Indian Women and the Indian Act on 4 August 1982, which conducted hearings with 41 witnesses (mostly Indian people).[100] Canada's response to the UN's decision indicates the beginning of the gradual shift away from federal protection of cultural survival to granting a greater degree of self-determination to bands. It is unclear just how autonomous the bands would become.

Also, in its response to the UN HRC's decision, as evidence of its increased respect for band authority, Canada pointed to sections 25, 27, 28, and 35 of the Constitution Act, 1982 (of which the Charter is Part I):[101]

> 25. The guarantee in this Charter of certain rights and freedoms shall not be construed so as to abrogate or derogate from any aboriginal, treaty or other rights or freedoms that pertain to the aboriginal peoples of Canada including (a) Any rights or freedoms that have been recognized by the Royal Proclamation of October 7, 1763, (b) Any rights or freedoms that may be acquired by the aboriginal peoples of Canada by way of land claim settlement.

27. This Charter shall be interpreted in a manner consistent with the preservation and enhancement of the multicultural heritage of Canadians.

28. Notwithstanding anything in the Charter, the rights and freedoms referred to in it are guaranteed equally to male and female persons.

[Part II of the Constitution Act, 1982] 35(1) The existing aboriginal and treaty rights of the aboriginal peoples of Canada are hereby recognized and affirmed. (2) In this Act, 'aboriginal peoples of Canada' includes the Indian, Inuit, and Metis peoples of Canada . . . 35(4) Notwithstanding any other provision of this act, the aboriginal and treaty rights referred to in subsection (1) are guaranteed equally to male and female persons.

These sections juxtapose sex equality and aboriginal rights. It seems as though bands would always be required to assure sex equality regardless of how much their sovereignty grew. Much of this conflict rests upon the meaning given to the word "notwithstanding."

As a result of the UN HRC's Lovelace ruling, Canada asserted its interest in expanding indigenous peoples' voice in the political process, increasing band autonomy, and assuring indigenous cultural survival. Thus, cultural survival became increasingly linked with sovereignty and self-determination, rather than falling solely under the purview of federal protection. The implications of such a shift for indigenous women were unclear. As band power increased, it was quite possible that they would continue (or even worsen) sexist membership policies. As C-31 and the Charter were implemented, the discursive strategies of both the bands and indigenous women multiplied.

Phase Three: C-31 and the Charter: An Aboriginal Right to Sovereignty?

C-31 was informed by three fundamental principles: "[O]ne, that all discrimination be removed from the Indian Act; two, that Indian status within the meaning of the Indian Act and band membership rights be restored to persons who lost them; and three; that Indian bands have the right to control their own membership."[102] These principles show

how Canada balanced competing interests while revising the Indian Act. The process of removing sex discrimination became extremely intertwined with increasing band sovereignty. Bands feared that changing the Indian Act would diminish federal benefits to indigenous peoples (loss of reserve lands, social programs, etc.). The Canadian government chose to allay those fears by expanding band by-law and administrative powers while changing the Indian Act. With the changes to the Indian Act, bands could develop their own membership criteria. The C-31 implementation report notes that this newfound power was very limited and subject to DIAND approval. Sharon Venne, legal counsel for Chiefs of Northeast Alberta states:

> First the band must vote according to the department's rules and regulations. Secondly the band council must submit a resolution requesting that the Minister of Indian Affairs recognize the [membership] code. Thirdly the Minister of Indian Affairs accepts or rejects the codes. We view this process as a relinquishment of our right to determine citizenship. In other words, we would be consenting to come under the laws of Canada [that relate to] citizenship. This is not something that the treaty indigenous nations can agree to do.[103]

Thus, the process by which bands were supposed to develop membership standards was intrusive and hence contrary to typical accounts of sovereignty. "In order for a band to gain control, there is a requirement for approval of 50% plus one of their electors; a requirement which the Nuu Chah Nulth Tribal Council of B.C., among others, find paternalistic and patronizing."[104] Some bands argued that this form of election was also contrary to their traditions.

In addition to intrusive guidelines, the new band "powers" were limited to increased administrative authority, which in many cases came with diminished resources. Therefore, many band populations felt that their councils were not doing a good job of administering the nominal increase in their power. Ultimately, in many places, band councils encountered a legitimacy crisis.

> Finally, band councils are often seen as powerless entities with respect to Bill C-31 issues. These perceptions lead to a lack of confidence in the governing body on the reserve. On

the other hand, reinstated members often view band councils as obstructionist, using what little power they have to limit access to services and other benefits.[105]

With this perceived lack of power and the ongoing procedural intrusion upon band policy on top of diminishing funds, bands were far from achieving any meaningful sovereignty. Yet, the legislative move to expand aboriginal rights provided a more tangible foundation for bands' legal mobilization and sovereignty claims.

Many bands thought that the source of their sovereignty came from the treaties, not from contemporary federal proclamations. Sharon Venne stated that bands' "treaty right is not for sale. No amount of force or intimidation practiced by the bureaucrats will have the legislation imposed on our people."[106] Therefore, some bands refused to implement and actively resisted C-31 (e.g. the Kahnawake Mohawks, who are discussed in chapter 4).

> [D]etermining who is an Indian and who should be a member of a nation or band is a sovereign right that was never relinquished. This right was recognized by the Canadian government when they entered into treaty negotiations with the Indian nations. The treaty-making process also protected and kept intact the collective rights of Indian nations. It did not weigh in favour of individual rights. This was a reflection of the unique ideologies and special relationship Indian nations held and intended to protect.[107]

In contrast to *Lavell/Bedard* and *Lovelace*, where claims to citizenship and connections to states hint at a desire for band sovereignty, the above quote exemplifies a much more explicit statement about sovereignty. The unfulfilled promises of aboriginal rights are probably responsible for the emergence of the *Sawridge* case. The arguments presented in *Sawridge* reflect a desire for a new level of band control over membership criteria and use the newfound (but ill-defined) discourse of aboriginal rights. The *Sawridge* case is an example of how a stark dichotomy between individual civil rights and sovereignty rights can entrench the dominating effects of intersectional power.

Phase Four: Sawridge v. Canada: An Aboriginal Right to Residual Traditions

The *Sawridge* case shows how history can be re-framed in order to serve modern sovereignty claims. Sovereignty was presented as a complicated mix of pre-contact aboriginal rights and treaty rights. Treaty rights extinguished some aboriginal rights, and some treaty rights were extinguished by federal legislative acts. The Sawridge band et. al. tried to establish that the power to determine band membership was their pre-contact aboriginal right. But to prove this, not only did they need to offer evidence of authentic tradition, they also needed to prove that no treaty or legislative act ever extinguished this right. Treaty rights and tradition were invoked simultaneously in order to prove that membership fell under the undeniable control of the bands.

The bands argued that C-31 was

> inconsistent with s. 35 of the Constitution Act 1982 . . . [because it infringed] . . . the right of Indian bands to determine their own membership . . . The plaintiffs maintained that their right to control membership stems from an Aboriginal and treaty right to practice their marital custom which permits an Indian husband to bring his non-Indian wife into residence on reserve but which does not permit an Indian wife to bring her non-Indian husband into residence on reserve.[108]

In addition to membership being a pre-contact right, it was, according to the plaintiff bands, reinforced by treaties which did not include any explicit statements to the contrary.[109] The Attorney General responded that the plaintiffs'

> allegations . . . [were] not substantiated by and are inconsistent with the ethnological and historical literature and documents produced and/or filed by the parties . . . if the aboriginal right alleged by the plaintiffs ever existed it was: i) extinguished by the said treaties and by successive Indian Acts commencing in 1876; and ii) replaced by a statutory scheme which provided for Indian Status, band membership based on Indian Status, exhaustive membership provisions and executive decisions made within the framework of this statutory scheme.[110]

The existence of the Indian Acts and their prescriptions for Indian status served as proof of legislative destruction of any traditional right to set membership standards.

The Native Council of Canada (Alberta) agreed with Canada that

statutes of Parliament . . . violated the rights of Indians by stripping aboriginal peoples of their statutory Indian status and membership in the Bands, while in other cases extending statutory Indian status and Band membership to individuals who were not aboriginal people.[111]

The Non-Status Indian Association of Alberta also agreed and stated that

the historical record does not support: A. the allegation that there was no imposition of members upon an Indian band without consent; B. the difference in treatment of men and women as an aboriginal right; C. the difference in treatment of men and women as a treaty right.[112]

The arguments presented in this case were largely about whether federal actions ever infringed upon the Native right to accept or deny members. The interveners representing those without status argued that band membership was not a traditional right of the bands.

Sawridge et. al. even went so far as to argue that the Indian Act embodied historical indigenous custom. According the bands, only with the new amendments (C-31) did the Canadian government infringe upon this historical right. But the Native Council of Canada (Alberta) stated "that by the 1985 Amendment, Parliament attempted to correct injustices and wrongs resulting from the application of the Indian Act prior to the 1985 Amendment, and at the same time to enable Indian Bands to practice a greater degree of self-government."[113] This disagreement centers on which federal action, the early Indian Act or C-31, was the true infringement on sovereignty.

Therefore, in this case, sovereignty became the residue of what was not explicitly usurped by Canada. Much of *Sawridge's* argument was an attempt to prove that membership control was never extinguished. This kind of argument emerged because the Charter's conception of aboriginal rights was underdeveloped. One could argue that by guaranteeing aboriginal rights without adding any substance to that phrase's meaning, the Charter begs for strategic arguments which point to traditional pre-contact practices in order to preserve aboriginal rights.

After extensively quoting various historical documents and treaty texts, Judge Muldoon concluded, "Taken all-in-all with the Act and the negotiations, no treaty right of Indians to control their band and reserve membership can be discerned."[114] He went on to say:

> The plaintiffs assert that the marital regime, for which they contend is an Aboriginal right; and that Aboriginal rights are collective rights. Surely, however, the notion of 'woman follows man,' and is unable to confer her status upon her non-Indian husband, represent a collective right only for men.[115]

Muldoon's language shows his lack of interest in establishing the meaning of aboriginal rights and his overarching bias in favor of individual civil rights. His reading of the evidence was ultimately deemed to be biased because he was very much against the "benefits" that came with Indian status. He wrote:

> If the band could still control its own membership, and if the Government were, as it is, obliged to make payments and confer all of today's further benefits on all members, then notionally, bands could bring the taxpayers to their knees by expanding membership exponentially, without the limits even of Bill C-31 . . . Whoever pays the piper call the tune. The taxpayers are the eternal payers and the government, at least somewhat on their behalf, has since treaty-time called the tune of absolute, all-extinguishing control of band membership, and of who is an Indian entitled to the payments and other benefits.[116]

Muldoon even goes so far to say that band control over membership would be a form of apartheid. He stated:

> It is surely apparent that it is not eternal dependence with apartheid, but equal self-reliance, (including Canada's so-called 'social safety net' for such as it is and will be) which promote the equal human dignity of all Canadians. It is difficult to understand why the Courts in recent years have promoted dependence.[117]

This not only shows his bias against benefits associated with Indian status and his distaste for band control over membership, but it also reveals Muldoon's overall individualist bias and repugnance for government services.

The appeals court declared the case a mistrial. This recognition of Muldoon's bias shows that at least some judges and legal actors wanted to give meaning and respect to aboriginal rights (and not just merely force individual Indians to be treated like every other citizen). Therefore, the unresolved status of the *Sawridge* case shows that the Canadian judiciary is still in the process of establishing the meaning of aboriginal rights.

The Evolution of the Sovereignty Rights Frame

The sovereignty frame developed over time. There was little discussion of self-determination early on because the focus was on cultural survival. Federal protection seemed to be the best route to indigenous cultural survival, and so band autonomy was not emphasized. Because the Charter promised Aboriginal rights, the discourse after its passage focused a bit more on sovereignty. But the same Charter was also the foundation of expanded individual civil rights. Thus, over time, the conflict between individual civil rights and sovereignty rights was exacerbated. The dual promises of the C-31 amendments and the Charter encouraged bands to delve back into history and find the traditions that were not extinguished by parliamentary legislation or by treaties. In order to assert an aboriginal right to determine band membership, bands had to prove that a legitimate tradition existed before colonial contact. In the process of asserting an aboriginal right to define membership, the bands offered their version of what standards should be applied. The contest over defining membership standards becomes the focus of the litigation and political action as the Indian Act falls under greater critical scrutiny. This contest represents the area where indigenous women's participation in the political process is most important. If they are unable to help define the meaning of membership and tradition, then they are not full participants in their community. This might exacerbate the dual domination at the intersections of power because it would force them to make all of their political claims at the federal level, further undermining band autonomy and denying an important aspect of their identity.

Conclusion: Understanding the Master Frames

Individual civil rights and sovereignty rights are considered master frames for several reasons. The former corresponds roughly with the kinds of arguments that indigenous women made in order to gain access to their bands after they married out (although there are quite a few exceptions). The latter, sovereignty, corresponds to the prominent arguments presented by the bands. They also correspond to John Comaroff's account of radical individualism and the primal sovereignty, which are discussed in chapter 1. These two master frames inherited the contradictory colonial legacy that simultaneously created and destroyed indigenous identities. The interaction between these two frames underscores how a colonial legacy trickles into contemporary conceptions of legal rights and sets up contradictory logics that are difficult to resolve. Contemporary conceptions of individual and sovereignty rights reflect historical struggles and the ideological contradictions that are built into most legal systems.

Moreover, indigenous women's unique position at the intersections of race and gender hierarchies are reflected in these master frames. As long as band sovereignty and individual rights are considered dichotomous opposites, there is little promise in alleviating intersectional power. Yet, in a few instances, these two frames were combined in creative ways, acting as a subversive form of rights re-evaluation, which might ultimately help reveal the power relations that affect indigenous women's lives.

These two frames are master frames because they guide the interpretation of and argumentation within the other discursive frames (membership standards, tradition, jurisdiction, and economic and material forces). Chapter 4 discusses these remaining discursive frames and considers how they reflect the complicated power relations at play in the marrying out case.

CHAPTER 4

"Marrying Out" In Canada: Part II

Introduction

This chapter analyzes the kinds of arguments that were presented in Canada under the four remaining discursive frames: membership standards, tradition, jurisdiction, and economic and material forces. As discussed in the previous chapter, particular interpretations of the master frames, individual civil rights and sovereignty rights, usually guide the interpretation of these frames. Indigenous women's position at the intersection of race and gender hierarchies gives them a unique perspective on band tradition and what standards should determine band membership. The power dynamics that define indigenous women's experience also have a direct effect on what institutions they think should have jurisdiction over their cases. And finally, indigenous women's intersectional identities place unique economic and material constraints on their ability to make political claims. All in all, the analysis of the discursive frames reveals the provisional arguments that indigenous women use to try to alleviate the double bind of intersectionality. Over time, the Canadian cases provide opportunities for rights re-evaluation, which might augment indigenous women's future political participation and their ability to better describe the intersections of power that constrain them.

Frame Three: Membership Standards

Balancing Biology and Cultural Affinity

As discussed in chapter 2, there is a tension between the use of biological and cultural affinity standards to determine band membership and federal Indian status. The Act of August 30, 1851 defined for Lower Canada who was an Indian:

> Firstly, All persons of Indian blood, reputed to belong to the particular Tribe or Body of Indians interested in such lands or immovable property and their descendants. All persons residing among such Indians, whose parents were or are, or

either of them was or is, descended on either side from
Indians, or an Indian reputed to belong to the particular Tribe
or Body of Indians interested in such lands or immovable
property, and the descendants of all such persons: And
Thirdly, All women, now or hereafter to be lawfully married
to any of the persons included in the several classes herein
before designated; the children issue of such marriages, and
their descendants.[1]

Female Indian status required being related (through marriage or
lineage) to a male Indian. The passage above makes fascinating
connections between property, blood, and marriage. The 1876 Indian
Act uses a similar combination of blood quantum and marital standards
for determining membership in a band.[2] In fact, 12(1)(b)[3] couples the
blood quantum standard with patriarchy. These are the membership
standards that Canada imposed upon indigenous people. The particular
combination of biological and marital standards reflected European
conceptions of lineage and was the most efficient way to economically
and culturally control indigenous people. Membership became a
codified colonial construct and Indian status was something that
Canada "gave" to indigenous peoples.

*Phase One: Lavell/Bedard: Realigning Biology and Affinity to Include
All Mixed-Marriages*

In the *Lavell/Bedard* case, the standards put forth in 12(1)(b) were
challenged using the Bill of Rights. Lavell and Bedard's basic
argument was that sex discrimination should not be the basis for
deciding who is Indian. They focused on whether the Indian Act should
be accountable to the Bill of Rights. Most importantly, the construction
of status found in the Indian Act was not questioned as an instance of
colonial domination. Instead, Lavell and Bedard hoped to maintain
their status regardless of who they married. In arguing against the sex
discrimination of 12(1)(b) they offered alternative ways to limit band
membership. They argued, "If the object is to restrict the protection of
the Indian Act to those who really need it, this can be accomplished by
a classification that is not sex-based, either by using such concepts as
residency on a reserve, connection with band activity, or alternatively,
by applying the marriage to a non-Indian standard to male and female
alike."[4] Lavell and Bedard wanted to maintain a connection to their

natal band, and since they wanted to be able to pass their status down to their children, their argument was informed by a conception of biological lineage. At the same time, their tolerance of mixed-marriage reflects the affinity component of their desired membership standards. Therefore, Lavell and Bedard's position is premised on a particular balance of biological and affinity standards that is different from those found in the Indian Act.

In order to justify the classification found in 12(1)(b), the status Indian organization, Indian Association of Alberta stated:

> It is reasonable to suggest that the system was an attempt to focus on the way of life of the family and therefore employed kinship or family factors rather than any arbitrary rule of blood percentage. The selection of such factors represents a rational and reasonable legislative decision and one which, for that reason, does not offend the Canadian Bill of Rights.[5]

Here, a particular conception of the male-led family informs their reading of membership standards. The Attorney General wanted to maintain the status quo, so there is no discussion of alternative membership standards. Thus, each side in *Lavell/Bedard* defended the balance between affinity and biology that best suited their desired outcome .

Phase Two: Lovelace v. Canada: Proposing Objective Standards

In *Lovelace v. Canada,* Lovelace also wanted to maintain her federal Indian status. She offered an alternative vision for how to determine status without the sex discrimination, which was even more intricate than *Lavell/Bedard's.* Her submission to the UN HRC states, "Instead of determining Indian status according to the present method, status could be determined according to a combination of factors: sanguinity, affinity and cultural preference."[6] Not only did Lovelace argue that all Indians born into a band should be included in the band, but she was also willing to expand membership to non-Indian spouses (of either sex) and their children. They could be granted membership only if they "embrace[d] Indian society and culture." Therefore, Lovelace wanted to rebalance the Indian Act's combination of affinity and biology standards to include more members based purely on affinity. Whether one displayed the requisite affinity should be determined by "objective" standards. What makes these standards objective is unclear.

Additionally, one who was born Indian could only be denied membership if s/he voluntarily moved away or requested a status change. Lovelace wanted these "objective" standards to place a premium on individual choice, because that would best serve her situation. These proposed standards are steeped with liberal notions of consent, voluntarism, and individual affinity to a culture. Additionally, while Lovelace did not indicate who should apply these objective standards, she certainly did not want the band council to have such power. She said:

> The view which states there should be an objective criteria for determining Indian status is necessary because of the fact that band Councils discriminate again [sic] Certain individual [sic] and if they were in a position to determine who should or should not be an Indian, then it is possible that Sandra Nicholas Lovelace, and others who have rebelled publically [sic] will not stand a Chance when it Comes to being returned to the band list.[7]

Lovelace felt that her activism alienated the Maliseet band council enough that if they had the final say, they would stick by the standards laid out in the Indian Act and deny her band membership. The membership standards suggested by Lovelace acknowledge the competing political interests of the band elites, the federal government, and indigenous women. She seemed to favor an amended version of the federal standards because they were more susceptible to those international human rights norms that would promise equal rights.

While the UN HRC's decision does not describe any alternative membership standards, its account of "ethnicity" sheds light on its stance on the biology-affinity continuum. The decision states:

> Persons born and brought up on a reserve who have kept ties with their community and wish to maintain those ties must normally be considered as belonging to that minority within the meaning of the Covenant. Since Sandra Lovelace is ethnically a Maliseet Indian and has only been absent from her home reserve for a few years during the existence of her marriage, she is . . . entitled to be regarded as 'belonging' to this minority and to claim the benefits of article 27 of the Covenant.[8]

This notion of ethnicity relies upon some biological relation ("persons born and brought up") but, in deciding whether Lovelace deserves ongoing contact, the committee ultimately focuses on the choice to maintain contact with one's natal culture ("kept ties . . . wish to maintain ties . . . "). Therefore, the UN HRC had a particular combination of biological and affinity standards in mind when rendering its decision. Lovelace and the UN HRC combined biology and affinity in similar ways when they described how band membership should be determined. Of course, this combination is different from that found in the Indian Act because both wanted to eliminate sex as a factor in membership standards.

Phase Three: C-31 and the Charter: Indian Status vs. Band Membership

Due to the competing rights that emerged from the Charter and C-31, "Indianness" was divided into two component parts: Federal Indian status and band membership. Evelyn Ballantyne, the President of Opasquiak Aboriginal Women said:

> Bill C-31 has created a number of political and therefore social divisions between: one, those with both status and band membership; two, those with status but who have only conditional band membership; three, those who are band members but who do not have the right to status; and four, those who are not entitled to status and band membership. To put it more simply, Bill C-31 has created further division within the native community.[9]

These distinctions exacerbated conflicts between indigenous women and their bands. The standards for Indian status were laid out in C-31 and bands could choose to apply the same standards to band membership, or they could choose to develop their own standards. If they chose the latter, their rules would be subject to a referendum in which a majority of band members had to approve the new standards. Also, the Department of Indian Affairs and Northern Development (DIAND) was supposed to oversee and fund the process of creating band membership standards and had to approve the final result.

In order to be reinstated and to attain federal Indian status, one had to prove Indian lineage. Under C-31, the process of reinstatement might have actually reinvigorated blood quantum requirements. The

1990, C-31 implementation report states: "What DIAND now requires of applicants is that they prove—uncontrovertibly and with full documentation—their relationship to the ancestor who lost status. In many cases this involves a full-scale genealogical search back as far as the mid-nineteenth century."[10] Such documentation could include written missionary church and Hudson's Bay Company records, but not traditional oral histories. "[T]hose people who did not want to embrace the foreign religion were not added to the church's register"[11] and so there was no written record of their membership in a band. Thus, in the reinstatement process, while the sexist standards supposedly were removed, the federal requirements for proving lineage were rather complicated and stringent and weighed down by historic colonial power relations.

The slicing and dicing of status and membership created confusion, distrust and resentment in Native communities. The C-31 implementation report states:

> There are already too many obstacles acting against the successful integration of reinstated persons back into their First Nations [communities] without DIAND insisting that these persons be constantly identified and treated in a manner different than other citizens of the First Nation.[12]

Many felt that these new standards were just the latest attempts to assimilate them into Canadian society.

Moreover, not all sex discrimination was removed from C-31. The second generation cut-off rule is a very good example of a persisting standard based upon paternal lineage. While women who married out of their tribe might have been reinstated, their status was different from a woman who never lost her status (as discussed in chapter 3). This difference became apparent when she attempted to pass that status down to her grandchildren. Not only did Indian identity become more complicated with the emergence of a two-tiered system, but the biology and affinity standards also were re-balanced. In addition to the new federal standards, various bands asserted their new authority and created unique band membership standards.

> A review of the 236 codes adopted by First nations from June 1985 to May 1992 identified four main types: 1) [38% of the 236 codes use] one-parent descent rules, whereby a person is eligible for membership based on the membership or

eligibility of one parent; 2) [28% of the codes use] two parent descent rules . . . 3) [13% of the codes use] blood quantum rules, which base eligibility on the amount of Indian blood a person possesses (typically 50%); and 4) [21% of the codes use] Indian Act rules, which base membership on sections 6(1) and 6(2) of the Indian Act.[13]

One example is discussed in *Heeding the Voices of Our Ancestors,* where Gerald R. Alfred describes the Kahnawake Mohawk's efforts to resist federal intrusion in setting membership standards. Alfred states that, historically, Kahnawake was "extremely receptive to the integration of outsiders."[14] But, in response to the passage of C-31, the Kahnawake Mohawk developed strict blood quantum measurements[15] for band membership, evicted non-Indians from the reserve, and placed a moratorium mixed marriages.[16] Also, in an effort to resist imposed sex equality and the reinstatement of additional members, the Kahnawake chose to create band membership rules that would ban anyone who was the child of a mixed marriage.

> Kahnawake's rejection of Bill C-31 and the conception of rights embedded in the Canadian constitution are understandable given the Mohawk view that the Canadian Charter of Rights and Freedoms is another culturally specific Euro-American ideal imposed upon Native communities. The fact that Indians did not in the pre-contact era determine membership by racialist criteria is irrelevant; Native cultures evolve like any other in response to changes in the social and political environment. For generations, race has formed one of the central bases for defining boundaries in Indian communities.[17]

The experience of the Kahnawake Mohawk shows how the passage of C-31 and the Charter expanded the field of membership criteria. With increased band authority in setting membership standards, it was inevitable that bands would become more restrictive when developing their own codes. Whether this perpetuated the sex discrimination or not became dependent on the band context.

Phase Four: Sawridge v. Canada: The Woman Follows her Husband: Biology or Affinity?

In *Sawridge v. Canada*, the plaintiffs pointed to the use of both blood quantum and affinity practices in the past, but the crux of their argument had more to do with who controls membership than the standards that should be applied in determining membership. They argued that:

> the reserving of tracts of land for the exclusive use, occupation and benefit of Indian bands, must mean that such bands can control whomever they will permit to come on their land: and that means . . . that they enjoy an unextinguished right to control their own membership.[18]

In order to establish band control over membership standards, Sawridge et. al. had to prove that "the woman follows the man" was a band tradition. This "ancient" practice combined biology and affinity standards. Women, through marriage, could be construed to be joining the band of their "choice," but a child's status is determined by that child's paternal lineage. According to this scheme, women should gain their husband's band membership, but they would be unable to pass down their natal band membership.

As will be discussed in more detail under the tradition frame, a great deal of contradictory evidence was offered as the plaintiff bands tried to prove which membership standards were true traditions. They even argued that the Indian Act was a codified version of authentic band traditions. Yet, Wayne Roan, one of the plaintiffs in the case, gave some evidence that there were no hard and fast rules for determining membership. His own father had joined the tribe of his wife. He said that his father "did not get along on another reserve, so he tried another reserve where his relatives [were]."[19] Similarly, Professor Alexander Von Gernet, the expert witness for Canada stated that the

> focus on lineality as a criteria (sic) for group membership is merely an artificial construct that confines the notion of 'membership' to a particular theoretical abstraction. The ethnographic sources indicate that an ideal patrilineal system was not an important consideration in decisions made about group affiliation . . . 'membership' was conceived by the

Indians in terms of who was actually part of a functioning group . . . and not in terms of the consanguinal and affinal status of each individual.[20]

Therefore, in the process of trying to establish which were traditional Native standards, Von Gernet offered another, more functional or economic approach to membership, which discarded both biology and affinity. In this analysis, historically, group membership was based upon a contribution to survival, not cultural connectedness, and not biological lineage. Von Gernet, continues, quoting historian J.R. Miller:

The Indian Act's tracing of Indian descent and identity through the father was the unthinking application of European patrilineal assumptions by a patriarchal society; but it accorded ill with those Indian societies, such as the Iroquoian, in which identity and authority flowed through the female side of the family. All these attempts at cultural remodeling also illustrated how the first step in the path of protection seemed always to lead to the depths of coercion.[21]

Thus, all Canadian standards were merely vehicles for coercion because they unified the practices of culturally heterogeneous indigenous groups. This point sheds light on how coercive federal protection transforms itself over time into a debate over authentic traditional practices, which are virtually impossible to authenticate (more on this under the tradition frame).

Judge Muldoon's staunch individualism came out in his discussion of biological standards for membership. He claimed that "'Blood quantum' is a highly fascist and racist notion, and puts its practitioners on the path to the Nazi Party led by the late, most unlamented Adolf Hitler."[22] Thus, like with most other issues that focus on native cultural preservation, Muldoon dismissed any non-consent-based membership standards. This is one extreme in the biology-affinity debate, which is a rather uncommon position to take in the context of indigenous identity. *Sawridge* offers the most power-laden account of the biology-affinity balancing act. Federal protection was acknowledged as coercion, but the bands themselves were the ones who wanted to underplay this domination narrative. This twist was their way of resisting the "modern" domination in the form of sex-equality norms.

The Evolution of Membership Standards: Tipping the Balance Between Biology and Affinity

Since the Indian Act explicitly set out the parameters of Indian status, there were few opportunities to contest those standards. But as the Indian Act was reformed, the affinity-biology debate became central to making federal status and band membership decisions. Under the two-tiered rubric of status and membership, bands were able to assert a small degree of control over their membership standards. In some cases, this came with an increased emphasis on biology (as was the case for Kahnawake). In others, the focus was on maintaining the standards set out in the pre-reform Indian Act (as in the *Sawridge* case). Throughout the cases, the groups that wanted to retain the federal "protection" found in the Indian Act argued for 12(1)(b)'s unique combination of biology and patriarchy as the desired membership standard. Interestingly, as some bands attempted to justify their authority to set membership criteria, they claimed that criteria set out in the old Indian Act echoed their pre-contact traditions. The indigenous women, on the other hand, wanted to stress affinity and human rights norms of sex equality (or non-discrimination) in suggesting standards for membership. The discussion under the next frame will show how the biology/affinity balance is often tipped by conceptions of tradition that are impossible to disaggregate from the colonial experience.

Frame Four: Tradition

Phase One: Lavell/Bedard: Contested Traditions

Lavell/Bedard is an early indication that the struggle to define membership standards is closely tied to a contest over authentic tradition. Interestingly, this debate finds both sides arguing for different federal legislation as the guarantor of their version of tradition. Bands began to embrace the Indian Act as an embodiment of pre-contact tradition, while indigenous women looked to individual civil rights discourse to justify their own construction of authentic band practices. The Alberta chapter of Indian Rights for Indian Women argued:

> It is submitted that S.12(1)b of the Indian Act is a 'law of Canada' as defined in the Bill of Rights which first came into force in 1869. It did not reflect a general custom or tradition

of Indian peoples but imposed common law concepts, as they existed in 1869, upon Indian women. In fact, the Iroquois and Huron societies were matriarchal, and women figured prominently in the constitution of the Iroquois or Six Nations.[23]

The Native Council of Canada agreed with the above assessment and stressed the importance of re-coupling band tradition and membership practices. They wrote:

> The discriminatory sections and definitions [in the Indian Act] are, of course, produced by white men and it has not been left to the Indian community to establish their own definition based on heritage and tribal custom. Native rights should be derived from one's racial and cultural origins rather than from discriminatory provisions of the Indian Act.[24]

Here, race and culture are combined to hint at where tradition might be found. This is fascinating given contemporary accounts of "race" as a colonial construct.

Given that the practices embodied in 12(1)(b) were based on British and Canadian customs, Lavell and Bedard pointed out that with the Bill of Rights, even Parliament wanted to abandon this patriarchal tradition. Their factum states, "It is perhaps worth noting that this 'fiction,' that upon marriage a woman ceases to be a member of her former community and automatically takes on the status of her husband, has finally been repudiated by the Parliament of Canada."[25] Lavell and Bedard also pointed to the changes in the Citizenship Act that allowed Canadian women to retain citizenship even upon marrying a foreign husband as further proof that Canada had abandoned their tradition of coupling citizenship with marriage for women. This change in tradition was used by Lavell to argue that the sex-based membership rule is contrary to more contemporary Canadian conceptions of sex equality. In addition to invoking Canadian cultural norms, Lavell and Bedard also asserted that equality reflected authentic indigenous tradition. Lavell, reflecting on the outcome of her case, said, "Not only was this a legal loss but I felt it was also contrary to our traditional values of recognition and respect for each other."[26] Lavell felt that she was not only invoking the Bill of Rights on behalf of winning herself rights, but that her case was also an attempt to assert what she considered to be authentic indigenous values.

The bands that rallied against Lavell and Bedard made a more direct legal argument based upon tradition. They

> endorse[d] the present system of status determination as an embodiment of native custom . . . And this viewpoint . . . was advanced in the historical arguments made in the court that the purpose of the Act was to 'preserve and protect' and that the classification followed custom.[27]

Tradition was being invoked in order to legitimate the Indian Act and to continue federal protection of indigenous peoples. Thus, the federal government became the guarantor of traditional indigenous practices.

In their factum, The Indian Association of Alberta et. al. stated that they would have liked to preserve the "customary" practices found in the Indian Act. It soon became clear that they were not referring to Native customs, but rather the traditional value placed upon the male head of the family which was a "long standing legislative policy in Canada."[28] Additionally, the IAA wrote, "The special legal regime for Indians and their communities is rooted in the British North America Act and the constitutional history of Canada.[29] It is clear that the customs that the IAA wanted to preserve were British and Canadian ones, because they referenced Canadian legislative policy as an important reflection of historical practices.

Lavell/Bedard presented an inkling of the kinds of tradition-based arguments that would sprout up again in the future. Some argued that the Indian Act represented indigenous tradition. Others argued that norms of equality were truer representations of indigenous tradition. And still others embraced European traditions as the superior guiding principles, without trying to pass them off as authentic indigenous culture.

Phase Two: Lovelace v. Canada: Whose Tradition is Embodied in the Indian Act?

In the *Lovelace* case, the Canadian government offered its own take on tradition in its submission to the UN:

> In what was then a basically farming economy, it was considered that Indian reserve lands were more threatened by non-Indian men than by non-Indian women. This, together with the fact that patrilineal family relationships, rather than

blood quantum (measure of Indian ancestry), were traditionally used as a basis for determining legal claims, led to the introduction, in 1869, of the first legislative provisions dealing with the status of Indian women who married non-Indian men . . . Also reflected in these predecessors of section 12(1)(b) was the prevalent view held at the time by non-Indian society on the position of women and the family: that a man was responsible for providing for the family and protecting the family's interests.[30]

Canada felt that imposing patrilineality (as found in traditional European farming societies) on indigenous peoples would prevent white men from destroying Indian culture. Lovelace responded,

The Government of Canada implies that Indian families were traditionally patrilineal in nature when such is or, at least, was not necessarily the case (many Indian communities were matrilineal in nature, and the Indian Act has successfully destroyed that aspect of their culture).[31]

She assumed that when the Canadian government talked about tradition, it was referring to Native tradition. But instead, by invoking traditional European practices, Canada acknowledged this instance of colonial domination. Canada wanted to continue this cultural domination because it was seen as the best guarantor of future indigenous cultural survival. Thus, the preservation of a colonial tradition was touted as the best route for assuring the preservation of indigenous practices.

Lovelace offered an interesting gender analysis of cultural destruction. She wrote,

The reasoning behind the statement that says that white men were more of a threat is irrational because all non-Indians were a threat male and female. The white man would take the land and the white women would gradually melt down the Native Culture.[32]

Since Lovelace felt that women were the keepers of tradition, she thought that allowing non-Indian women to gain status was a very potent weapon of cultural destruction. She ultimately argued that only those who embrace band practices should be members, thereby offering a less tradition-based account of cultural survival, which would allow for inter-marriage. Thus, in the arguments presented by Canada and Lovelace, tradition was invoked either to legitimate or invalidate patriarchal practices found in the Indian Act.

Canada tried to justify the continuingexistence of this outdated European tradition by stating that it wanted to reform the Indian Act with the input of indigenous peoples themselves. The government cited Native discord as a reason reform was taking a long time. Their submission states, "These sometimes opposing viewpoints have been widely and consistently expressed, underlining the magniture [sic] of the differences of opinion within the Indian community itself."[33] Thus, while acknowledging that European tradition guided the policy, Canada blamed the continued cultural domination on the indigenous people themselves.

The UN HRC's decision did not say much about whether tradition should determine band membership or how best to assure cultural survival. Since it ruled on minority rights, tradition was a secondary concern to an individual's cultural affinity. According to the UN HRC's decision, Canada should not prevent minorities from practicing their culture. But, in asserting this, the committee did not comment on the content of authentic traditions. If anything, the UN HRC's focus on individual affinity was an implicit acknowledgement that tradition is a contested terrain.

In sum, tradition was invoked in *Lavell/Bedard* and *Lovelace* only insofar as it was used to justify or argue against the Indian Act. There was very little "expert" evidence offered and the invocation of tradition was quite instrumental. This changed after the Indian Act was reformed.

Phase Three: C-31 and the Charter: An Aboriginal Right to Traditional Practices

In the conflict between aboriginal and individual rights that emerged after the passage of the Charter and C-31, proving authentic tradition became crucial to the process of giving meaning to aboriginal rights. Sometimes, bands claimed that the Indian Act codified a particular historical practice in order to vouch for its authenticity. In order to counter this claim, advocates for women's reinstatement argued that the original Indian Act defied traditional practices and offered their own account of tradition to justify sex equality. They either argued that the heterogeneity of traditional practices was contrary to the uniformity of the Indian Act, or they stressed that some tribes were matrilineal; or they claimed that exclusivity contradicted communal practices that existed before colonial contact.

Those who resisted the reinstatement process argued that C-31 was contrary to their traditions. The C-31 implementation report states, "Aboriginal people feel that their culture, customs and traditional laws are threatened and undermined by Bill C-31."[34] Some pointed out that the process of reinstatement itself did not reflect their traditional practices. They argued that the requirement for a majority vote of the band to pass new membership was contrary to tradition. The implementation report says:

> Many aboriginal people living in First Nations communities do not vote on any issue, nor do they participate in the election of band councils, as prescribed in the Indian Act. These people adhere to more traditional forms of decision-making such as decision by consensus. In these communities, the requirement of the federal government for a 50% . . . vote of all electors to approve a band's membership code will never be achieved.[35]

This tradition-based argument focused more on the political process itself than on the content of the membership criteria.

Finally, the bands feared that an influx of new members through reinstatement would water down traditional practices. On this point, the implementation report states:

> No one knows what the impact will be of reinstatement and new residents . . . The uncertainty extends to concern about what will be the role in the community of new residents who are not familiar with traditions, culture, language or codes of conduct of the First Nations. First Nations do not know what the impact might be on their traditions, culture, language or community life as a result of new residents resulting from C-31.[36]

The arguments, which focus on the perpetuation of cultural practices and the process by which membership standards are created, both say little about what tradition dictates about the treatment of indigenous women who married out of their community. In a way, these procedural arguments are more forward-looking, considering how future cultural survival would be affected by the new rules, rather than saying that the rules themselves violate historical practices. These procedural arguments eventually become deeply intertwined with the interpretation of the substance of tradition. All of these kinds of tradition-based arguments became much more explicit in the *Sawridge* case.

Phase Four: Sawridge v. Canada: Proving Traditional Membership Practices

The arguments presented in *Sawridge v. Canada* illustrate the contours of the tradition debate. According to Sawridge et. al., the sexism found in the pre-C-31 Indian Act represented their authentic aboriginal practice. They argued that "the plaintiff aboriginal communities have, since aboriginal times, determined membership in their territories through the practice of traditional customs, *inter alia*, whereby women followed their men upon marriage."[37] The plaintiff bands made two related claims about tradition. First, the power to set membership standards was a pre-contact tradition, and second, the traditional standard was based upon patrilineal lineage. They argued that the Indian Act embodied this age-old tradition. In order to prove both layers of their claim, the plaintiffs presented both oral history testimony from various band elders and an anthropologist's account of authentic band practices. This evidence was rebutted by Canada's cross-examination of these witnesses as well as their own anthropologist "expert witness" who all offered their own versions of tradition. Judge Muldoon summarizes Canada's and the interveners' counter-argument:

> A number of possibilities, or reasons [for 12(1)(b)], were presented, including a) to protect the reserve communities from the 'marriage-in' of aggressive white males, who would take up an inordinate amount of reserve lands and resources, or were engaging in unscrupulous practices such as bootlegging liquor to Indians or robbing them of their timber; b) to promote enfranchisement and assimilation of Indian persons; or finally c) simply because the Indian Act was amended to correspond with the sexism then rampant in European law, wherein women, of all ages and status, except a 'femme sole' were treated as wards or dependants of the men closest to them, be it their fathers or husbands.[38]

Canada and the interveners agreed that the marrying out regulation was a representation of European patriarchal tradition. This echoes Canada's argument in *Lovelace*. Since C-31 remedied this colonial imposition, Canada stood by the changes. But some argued that the adoption of the new sex equality norms was just an instance of one European "tradition" displacing another.

The oral histories offered on behalf of the plaintiffs provide a fascinating array of claims which show the constructed and contested nature of "authentic tradition." Below is an excerpt from the testimony of Agnes Smallboy, an elder of the Ermineskin Band (into which she married):

> Q: Does the woman always go with the man as you did in the Ermineskin Band? A: Yes, that was the way it was—or has been . . . Q: When an Indian woman of an Indian band decides to leave the reserve and go with a non-Indian, how do the other band members deal with that woman's decision? . . . A: The band would probably counsel her . . . not to marry a non-treaty person . . . The reason she would be advised not to marry a non-treaty is because when she married she would be required to leave the reserve forever and not allowed to come back.[39]

The tensions between modern and traditional discourses are quite apparent in the above quote. Smallboy referred to indigenous peoples as "treaty" or "non-treaty," showing how the colonial terms of membership have completely infiltrated the way that individuals describe their indigenous identity. In the course of talking about a pre-contact tradition, Smallboy made reference to the treaties that were made between Europeans and indigenous groups. Additionally, she was not really able to explain why women traditionally followed men upon marriage. The best justification that she could offer was, "That's the way it was."[40]

Some of the other oral history witnesses tried to fill out why this was the ancient practice of the plaintiff bands. Chief (and Canadian Senator) Walter Twinn said,

> The woman always followed the man . . . [b]ecause of . . . territory. If . . . for instance a bush Cree woman married a prairie Indian, it would be difficult for that prairie Indian to

make a living in the bush. It was a strange environment or vice versa. That was one of the reasonings for it.[41]

Wayne Roan, another one of the plaintiffs in the case, offered similar testimony adding a gendered task-oriented spin:

> Q: And the second law you enunciated was that the woman follows the man? A: That's true, that's the Indian way. Q: And the explanation you gave for that was because the man was strong enough to clear the land, that's what you said? A: yes . . . God . . . created a woman to do specific things and a man to do specific things.[42]

These two arguments combine economic or utilitarian motivations with tradition.

The above arguments articulate a gendered division of labor, which was responsible for denying women's practices outside the home. Many contemporary feminist scholars have drawn upon accounts such as these to critique the split between the public and private spheres, which inevitably prevents women from fully participating in society. Add to that the fact that this division of labor was being presented as a traditional indigenous practice, and indigenous women's intersectional constraints become quite apparent. Even if this was not the "authentic" indigenous practice, its prominence in a legal case in the 1990s shows that some are not only willing to deny indigenous women's ability to articulate their version of tradition, but they are willing to re-construct tradition in order to continue to ex-communicate them from their natal bands.

All of the plaintiff's oral historians had to qualify their account of tradition, which reveals the constructed nature of this "a women follows the man upon marriage" tradition. Under cross-examination, these witnesses revealed that bands, tribes, nations, and marriage are all modern constructs. Wayne Roan's testimony during discovery includes the following exchange:

> Q: According to your customs what is the meaning of the word 'Band'? A: . . . there's no meaning. We don't understand the word 'Band' from my customs, no. Q: According to your customs, what is the meaning of the word 'tribe'? A: From my customs, we don't have no word 'tribe'. Q: According to your customs, what do you understand by the

word 'nation'? A: There's no word 'nation' in my customs . . .
But if he was of the same tribe, if he was a Cree, there was no
reason why a woman could not bring her husband and there
would be no problems becoming members of the Band. A:
There would be no problems.[43]

Roan asserted that, traditionally, there were no such groupings as band
or tribe. Yet, in the next breath he talked about the fluidity of group
affiliation using the term "band." George Ermineskin echoed this point
when he stated: "Before the white man came, there was not Iroquois."[44]
Ermineskin's testimony also questioned the legal construct "marriage."
He said, "In the old days, people did not legally marry each other; they
just took one another to live together . . ."[45] Because there was no
traditional conception of marriage, Ermineskin's testimony implies that
the Indian Act's marrying out policy did not reflect traditional
indigenous practices. According to the non-marriage scheme that he
described, women could return to their natal band if they chose not to
continue living with the man.

After establishing that many of the basic concepts upon which this
ancient tradition was premised (bands, membership, marriage) were
modern constructs, Ermineskin went on to say,

When [women] marry, they're supposed to follow the
husband. And then they were kicked out if they didn't. Q: So
they were in fact kicked out? A: Yeah. They were kicked out,
police, Mounties come [sic] and took them out ."[46]

So, modern Mounties were the enforcers of this "ancient"
tradition.

When asked why the band should decide membership standards,
Elder David Jacobs did not say that it was their traditional practice.
Instead he said, "I think the band should decide . . . Because the treaty
says the money, the land is ours. And we have the privilege of saying
yes or no. And we have all the say on it."[47] The treaties, in his mind,
give him and his band the right to practice their traditions as they see
fit. Thus, the treaties allocate traditional power.

These witnesses were obviously frustrated by the process of
describing their tradition in legal terms. Oral historians were faced with
a great deal of suspicion, which often muddled their testimony. Modern
conceptions of law loomed large; tradition had to be articulated in a
way in which legal actors and institutions could digest, but at the same

time, traditionalists tried, with all their might, to differentiate their practices from modern ones. Note the juxtaposition of tradition and law in the Wayne Roan's testimony:

> Q: . . . Why is it that your elders don't talk about man following woman and only talk about woman following man? A: Because that was their law . . . That was their custom; that was their tradition. Q: I suggest to you, Mr. Roan, that there is no such law. A: . . . I can't know everything. It's the same that you can't know everything, the same as you. You can't understand everything that I say here. You're not trying to understand. You're looking for a lie, but I prayed I will not lie. The best of my knowledge of what the elders have taught me, I will tell you. But anything documented that is legal, my lawyers will take care of that.[48]

First, tradition was referred to as "custom" or "law." Then "legal" matters are said to belong in the realm of lawyers. This quote shows quite vividly how certain kinds of custom and tradition are less legitimate in a courtroom than that which is well-documented and "legal." Custom and tradition had to be authenticated in a legitimate manner, which was determined by Canadian norms.

To supplement and to refute the oral history testimony, both sides in *Sawridge v. Canada* called upon anthropologists to provide more "scientific" input. John Hartwell Moore, Professor of Anthropology from the University of Florida, was the plaintiff bands' "expert" witness. He wrote report entitled "The Ethnology of Traditional Law among Native Peoples of Canada." Professor Alexander Von Gernet, Assistant Professor of Anthropology at Erindale College of University of Toronto was the expert witness for Canada.

Dr. Moore argued that the sexist segments of the Indian Act "might easily have been written by a Chief or Headman of one of the plaintiff bands" and were "consistent with the body of traditional law."[49] Von Gernet analyzed pre-contact practices as well as post-contact practices to show that Moore's conclusions were "absurd."[50] He pointed out that "In 1872, Ontario and Quebec Indians lobbied to have this clause amended so that 'Indian women may have the privilege of marrying when and whom they please without subjecting themselves to exclusion or expulsion from the tribe.'"[51] Von Gernet's analysis concluded that "pre-contact membership appears to have been primarily a function of economics and not blood relationships."[52]

This was echoed by one of the interveners in the case, the Native Council of Canada: "Considerations of kinship and marriage neither defined the boundaries *of* bands, precisely regulated recruitment or admission *to* bands, nor systematically articulated relations *between* bands."[53] Von Gernet also concluded that a marriage between a Native woman and a European man

> created a reciprocal social bond which served to consolidate [the Indian's] economic relationship with a stranger . . . And in return for giving the traders sexual and domestic rights to their women, the Indians expected reciprocal privileges such as free access to the posts and provisions. The marriage of a daughter to a fur trader brought prestige and the promise of security to an Indian family . . . In light of these practices and expectations, it would make no sense whatsoever for the wife's natal group to ostracize or formally sever ties with her. In fact, maintaining such relationships are highly desirable, if not essential in a barter economy.[54]

Thus, membership was determined by economics rather than "tradition." A woman who left her natal band was considered an asset because the marriage fostered trade relations and she would always be welcomed back home if she wanted to return.

Von Gernet adds:

> When it comes to the marriage of Indians and non-Indians, there can be no recourse to prehistoric . . . 'traditions'. By definition, such unions were confined to the Protohistoric and Historic periods. Hence, this particular practice, which originated as an adaptive response to the economic potential afforded by the contact of two groups . . . became the shared 'tradition' of both natives and newcomers. While this tradition served to forge links between Indians and Europeans, the Enfranchisement Act of 1869 was intended to turn Indians into Europeans.[55]

Von Gernet explained how traditions changed and were reconstructed with the colonial experience. And finally, he concluded that "the rescinding of these provisions through the 1985 amendments to the Indian Act was the correcting of an historical misconception of Native practices, rather than an interference with 'traditions' or 'customs.'"[56]

Thus, in one fell swoop, Von Gernet, in presenting his expert scientific input, invalidated the plaintiff bands' interpretation of tradition. He assumed that all practices were economically motivated, and therefore, traditional membership practices were not as inflexible as 12(1)(b).

Judge Muldoon displayed a great deal of suspicion toward Professor Moore's and the oral historians' testimony and quoted Von Gernet's report extensively in his decision. He wrote, "Of the two experts Dr. Von Gernet was the more impressive witness, the more careful and organized professional, and the more resilient and reasoned in cross-examination . . . the Court concludes that Dr. Von Gernet has correctly described the pertinent custom . . ."[57] According to Muldoon, Moore's testimony was completely discredited under cross-examination because he became flustered and questioned Von Gernet's credentials. Muldoon went on to state that "Von Gernet's opinion . . . is thoroughly bolstered by end-note references to support all its own internal quotations and virtually all its assertions."[58] These statements reveal Muldoon's bias in favor of "real science."

Interestingly, no one contested whether this was the proper purview of the Canadian courts. The court's determination of what qualified as authentic tradition was not viewed as a new version of colonial intrusion. Muldoon, the plaintiff, and the defendant all felt that the judiciary could be the proper arbiter of true tradition. Using his reading of the evidence, Muldoon found that "there were no such rights and no such customary laws as pleaded by the plaintiffs . . . Those particulars express a fictitious revisionism . . ."[59] Thus, Muldoon's reading of the evidence, and his bias in favor of scientific norms of documentation, led him to claim that the plaintiff bands' account of tradition was fiction.

Sawridge provides a fascinating example of how claims to tradition can be invoked to legitimize or resist change. This case also shows how the promise of aboriginal rights in the Charter created a legal climate that required the authentication of traditional practices. Muldoon's decision also reveals how this authentication process is very much mediated by modern norms of scientific documentation.

The Evolution of Tradition

The content of the tradition frame does not change a great deal from *Lavell/Bedard* to *Sawridge*. But after the passage of the Charter and C-31, tradition is invoked more often and with greater intricacy. The basic argument that the Indian Act embodied traditional aboriginal practices was first put forth in *Lavell/Bedard* by status Indian organizations. This same argument, in a more detailed form, reappeared in *Sawridge* and was substantiated with expert witnesses.

The basic argument was that before colonial contact, bands were patrilineal and women followed their men upon marriage. The arguments refuting this varied by case. Lavell pointed out that indigenous communities in Canada were quite heterogeneous and, therefore, it was impossible to capture all of those traditions in one sweeping Indian Act. Moreover, she argued that the Indian Act represented a European custom, which was repealed by the Bill of Rights and changing citizenship norms. Lavell also claimed that her individual rights claim was a truer representation of traditional indigenous practices because it stressed equality. Lovelace also argued that the Indian Act represented European traditional practices, and reiterated Lavell's point about the heterogeneity of indigenous peoples in Canada. Canada argued that the imposition of European traditions of patriarchy served to protect Native culture and land and should continue (at least in the short term). And finally, in *Sawridge*, the interveners and the defendants argued that the "woman follows the man" was a warped account of aboriginal tradition and offered a great deal of counter-evidence to prove this point. This counter-evidence was much more detailed, and called upon expert anthropological norms that were not used in earlier cases. Therefore, in this latest case, the debate about tradition and the legitimate measures of tradition became central.

So, as claims to band sovereignty emerged, they were increasingly based upon a particular version of pre-contact tradition. The spheres of legitimate band authority had to be justified in terms of surviving traditional practices. The court in *Sawridge* held these justifications up to the rigors of science. This movement toward authenticating tradition is directly related to John Comaroff's concept of primal sovereignty.[60] He argues that contemporary accounts of indigenous tradition rely upon the colonial construction of indigenous identity. Thus, the colonial tides that constructed indigenous identity (as different from modern, civilized, colonial citizens), also created the forces that would eventually form the basis for contemporary self-determination politics. This reading of identity reveals the strategic necessity of the tradition frame. To maintain indigenous difference, it is necessary to base that difference upon some construction of practices before colonial conquest. Thus, the struggle over authenticity is all about what defines indigenous people as different, deserving culturally specific "rights" or treatment from the Canadian government. Unfortunately, often the delineation of cultural difference prevents indigenous women from having access to those governmental rights. This raises new questions: What governing body has the jurisdiction to decide what is authentic tradition? And how does jurisdiction affect the legal claims of indigenous women in Canada?

Frame Five: Jurisdiction

The jurisdiction frame includes the relationship between the branches of the Canadian government and the distribution of power among the federal government, the provincial governments, and indigenous bands. Under the jurisdiction frame, I will also analyze the judicial methods for deciding cases, since that often has direct influence over how jurisdictional questions are resolved. Since the *Lovelace* case happened in the international arena, the jurisdiction frame also includes the pressures that bodies like the UN can assert over a state. The international community has unique jurisdictional limits. Like the other frames, the discourse of jurisdiction evolves over time.

Phase One: Lavell/Bedard: Judicial Deference to Parliament

Lavell/Bedard was mostly about how far judicial authority can extend in interpreting and enforcing the Bill of Rights. In trying to weigh Lavell's individual civil rights claim against the government's interest in protecting Indians, Judge Grossberg stated that Parliament's exclusive jurisdiction over Indians set clear limits on the judiciary in this arena. He wrote, "Section 91(24) of the B.N.A. Act 1867 gives the Parliament of Canada exclusive legislative authority over 'Indians and lands reserved for Indians'. This provision confers legislative authority over Indians *qua* Indians, and not otherwise."[61] Grossberg felt that if Indians were going to be subject to sex equality norms, it must be spelled out in specific legislation. His ruling reflects a desire to avoid judicial intrusion upon Parliament. In particular, Grossberg did not want to override the only existing "protections" for Indians.

In the Supreme Court decision, Lavell argued first that "in a unanimous judgment, the British Court of Appeal, without relying on any statutory authority, held that discrimination on the ground of sex is . . . capricious, unreasonable and contrary to public policy."[62]

Therefore, she felt that the judiciary could act without explicit statutory instructions. But, she also stated that "Parliament can be taken to have spoken"[63] because the Bill of Rights can act as the explicit legislative statement about sex-based discrimination.

In contrast, the Attorney General argued, "Even with the Canadian Bill of Rights, it [the Indian Act] remains subject to the supremacy of Parliament."[64] According to this argument, the Bill of Rights was not enough to allow the courts to interfere. The Attorney General's factum continues, "The legislative policy of the Indian Act . . . may or may not be socially desirable, but it is not the function of this Court to determine that question."[65] The inequalities found in the Indian Act were mere signs of the social times, rather than being a proper subject for judicial scrutiny, or legal condemnation. This distinction between what is social and what is legal guides the Attorney General's conception of jurisprudential methodology, and, more broadly, its vision of democracy in Canada. The Attorney General stated that it was "not possible for a court to decide that it is a disadvantage for an Indian woman to become disentitled to registration . . . Indian women are treated differently from Indian men in this respect, but it is a matter of opinion whether they are treated more harshly."[66] And the court's opinion on this issue was considered less legitimate than Parliament's.

The majority Supreme Court decision echoes this view. Only an explicit act of Parliament could overturn the Indian Act, and the Bill of Rights was not explicit enough. Justice Ritchie wrote:

> To suggest that the provisions of the Bill of Rights have the effect of making the whole Indian Act inoperative as discriminatory is to assert that the Bill has rendered Parliament powerless to exercise the authority entrusted to it under the constitution of enacting legislation which treats Indians living on Reserves differently from other Canadians in relation to their property and civil rights.[67]

Ritchie felt that the Indian Act made Indians into a special group, whose civil and property rights could only be protected by explicit legislation directed at them as a group. The judiciary could not step in and "protect" a subset of this group using other legislation that was not directed at Indians *qua* Indians. Pigeon echoed this point, stating that the enactment of the "Canadian Bill of Rights was not intended to effect a virtual suppression of federal legislation over Indians."[68]

Pigeon articulated the Supreme Court's great fear that if the Indian Act fell, the Parliament would have no vehicle to "protect" indigenous peoples, and the judiciary would be blamed and accused of overstepping its jurisdictional bounds.

Laskin's dissenting opinion offers an alternative account of how to divide jurisdictional power between the judiciary and Parliament. He was unimpressed by the claim that the Indian Act was a valid exercise of Parliament's exclusive legislative power in relation to Indians. He wrote, "Discriminatory treatment on the basis of race or colour or sex does not inhere in that grant of legislative power."[69] He also wrote that, according to *Drybones*, the Canadian Bill of Rights should have a "paramount force when a federal enactment conflicted with its terms, and it was the incompatible federal enactment which had to give way."[70] Abbott's dissent echoes this point and states that Parliamentary supremacy should be curtailed by the Canadian Bill of Rights. Thus, Laskin and Abbott did not want Indians to be subject to special legislative status and they felt that the Indian Act should be treated like any other piece of federal legislation that was subject to the Bill of Rights. They read this case as a conflict between two Parliamentary acts in which the Bill of Rights should be deemed more powerful.

One's position on jurisdiction reflects a very specific ideological stance about both the role of the judiciary in a democratic society and the political power of indigenous peoples. Judge Grossberg even went so far as to urge Indians to appeal to Parliament to change the Indian Act. He wrote:

> Indians are rightfully members of a proud and courageous race . . . They properly wish to preserve their culture, customs and heritage. However arguable are the solutions, Indians themselves have the intelligence and capacity to judge what is good or bad for them. Indians desire sincere and purposeful dialogue to solve their own problems. If s. 12(1)(b) is distasteful or undesirable to Indians, they themselves can arouse public conscience, and thereby stimulate Parliament by legislative amendment to correct any unfairness or injustice.[71]

Grossberg assumed that indigenous peoples have a great deal of influence in the political arena, thereby treating them as a monolithic entity. Instead, indigenous peoples have very diverse interests and variable amounts of political power.

Status Indians were the group that had the most power to influence Parliament. In their factum, The Indian Association of Alberta et. al. quoted the latter part of the above passage from Grossberg's decision and agreed that "any alteration of section 12(1)(b) . . . is appropriately the task of Parliament and not the judiciary."[72] Thus, they did not want the judiciary to step in and they agreed with Grossberg's assessment of the jurisdictional boundaries. George Manual, the first president of the National Indian Brotherhood, was afraid of judicial intrusion into Indian affairs. He said, " . . . we cannot accept a position where the only safeguards we have had can be struck down by a court that has no authority to put something better in its place."[73] Not only did status Indians want to maintain federal protection under the Indian Act, they also wanted to make sure that the source of federal power over Indians remained in Parliament's hands. It was unlikely that they were going to lobby for indigenous women. "The consequences of the decision for Indian Women were serious, since they were left with no route of appeal but Parliament and they were politically powerless."[74] Thus, indigenous women, who had much less power than status Indian groups, felt that they needed judicial (rather than parliamentary) protection. Thus, they wanted the judiciary to use the Bill of Rights to override 12(1)(b).

The *Lavell/Bedard* case centered around a conflict between two pieces of federal legislation: The Indian Act and the Bill of Rights. This conflict raised questions about the distribution of power and how far the judiciary should go in resolving this legislative conflict. The Supreme Court decision rendered the Bill of Rights powerless in protecting indigenous women. Not only did it weaken the judiciary's ability to be the guardian of civil rights, but it also bolstered exclusive Parliamentary jurisdiction over Indians as a special group that was subject to its own set of legislation (minus civil rights protections).

Phase Two: Lovelace: The Boundaries of International Jurisdiction

The jurisdictional debate about the conflict between the protection of Indian affairs and civil rights also emerged in the Lovelace case, with the added concern of international pressure. It was unclear how binding the International Covenant on Civil and Political Rights was on the states that ratified it. The New Brunswick Human Rights Commission studied the feasibility of making a claim against Canada on behalf of indigenous women and was not sure how far UN jurisdiction would reach. While the International Covenant enumerated various rights that the Indian Act clearly violated, the New Brunswick Human Rights Commission was not at all certain that Lovelace would get a favorable ruling from the Human Rights Committee.[75] But, one of the official communications that the New Brunswick HRC submitted on behalf of Lovelace, states that Canada "tacitly admitted . . . that section 12(1)(b) of the Indian Act, does, indeed, violate certain rights by which Canada, by ratifying the United Nations International Covenant on Civil and Political Rights, has accepted an international obligation to protect."[76] Therefore, since Canada had ratified this agreement, the New Brunswick HRC felt that international pressure should be exerted on this issue.

The fact that the UN HRC's decisions are labeled "views," which find violations and recommend remedies, shows the lack of implementation ability that the UN has over its member states. Thus, although this case was deemed to be under UN jurisdiction, the committee employed a great deal of caution in reprimanding Canada. The UN HRC ruled narrowly on minority rights (as discussed under the individual civil rights frame), and found that it could not comment on sex discrimination because Lovelace had already "lost her status as an Indian at a time when Canada was not bound by the Covenant."[77] To legitimate its ruling against Canada, the UN HRC focused on continuing repercussions of that moment of sex discrimination. It did not want to appear to be overstepping its jurisdictional bounds by ruling on an event prior to Canada's ratification of the Covenant. Therefore, the UN HRC ruled narrowly because its strength was in the reprimand, and the accompanying international embarrassment.

The Canadian government was aware of the limitations of this international body, but still wanted to avoid its scrutiny. Therefore, it stressed that it was in the process of reforming the Indian Act. Canada's defense revealed a new domestic jurisdictional battle, which was the distribution of power between the federal government and the bands. Even though the Indian Act was being reformed, Canada still stood by it "as an instrument designed to protect the Indian minority in accordance with Article 27 of the Covenant."[78] Thus, Canada found validation for Parliament's jurisdiction over Indian matters in the Covenant's protection of minority rights. To balance the protection of the special rights of indigenous peoples with the civil rights of women,

Canada tried to delimit the boundaries between federal and band jurisdiction. Canada stated that it was considering legislative proposals

> which would ensure that an Indian person, male or female, would not lose his or her status under any circumstances other than his or her personal desire to renounce it . . . Further recommendations are being considered which would give Band Councils powers to pass by-laws concerning membership in the band; such by-laws, however, would be required to be non-discriminatory in the areas of sex, religion and family affiliation.[79]

Thus, the arguments presented in Canada's response to the UN HRC's inquiry introduced the domestic jurisdictional confusion (band vs. federal government) which became more apparent in the wake of C-31 and the Charter.

Phase Three: C-31 & the Charter: An Expansion of Band Administrative Jurisdiction ?

With the passage of the Charter of Rights and Freedoms and C-31, a degree of administrative power over funding and internal reserve by-law powers was transferred to band councils. The effect of this transfer of power was that the bands had to allocate diminishing federal funds as the band population increased (with the reinstated women and their families returning to the reserves). But the jurisdictional lines were not clearly drawn, which resulted in a great deal of buck-passing. Some programs were band-based, some fell under provincial or territorial jurisdiction, and others were still considered federal. For example, Bill Erasmus, President, Dene Nation, NWT, stated, " . . . we are being told that the reason we are not getting additional funding for housing is that we do not have control over our programs. Housing is administered through the territorial government, through CMHC or through the Territorial Housing Corporation."[80] Thus, funding was being withheld because jurisdiction was unclear.

This jurisdictional confusion was further exacerbated by the differences in services offered to on and off-reserve indigenous people. It was unclear where those who had Indian status, but were denied band membership, should turn for services. "In Alberta, some bands [did] not recognize Bill C-31 and, therefore, [did] not attempt to access funds designated to offset the costs of Bill C-31 registrants. As a result, their off-reserve people [were] referred back to DIAND, which in turn refer[red] them to the band."[81] By not recognizing C-31, the band denied membership (and the attached right to move back to the reserve) to women who regained federal Indian status. Even if they had recognized C-31, which increased band power, the same dynamic might still have resulted.

For those reinstated women who were granted band membership, there was also a great deal of discrimination directed at them from other band members. The C-31 implementation report states:

> In situations where families have moved to their home reserve and the children have not successfully integrated into the community or local schools, they return to the city. Their attempts to transfer back to city schools are effectively blocked as a result of jurisdictional debates. DIAND considers the students to be a band responsibility. The band has no authority to provide continued assistance since the student is living off the reserve, and the provincial government attests that responsibility lies with DIAND.[82]

Hence, people who moved away from the reserve after being shunned by resentful band members lost out on services because there was a lack of clear jurisdiction. They also felt that no forum would deal with this discrimination. The C-31 implementation report states, "[T]here is recognition of discrimination within the First Nations, and that the government has been able to wash its hands of these problems."[83] Thus, the devolution of power to the bands allowed the federal government to bow out of mediating the long-term effects of the influx of reinstated women and their families.

Power was bestowed upon the bands without the necessary funding for implementation. Moreover, overlapping jurisdiction robbed the bands of the power to truly gain control of many programs. The C-31 implementation report states that there

> has been a backlash against some First Nations governments. Because band councils must administer certain programs according to DIAND policies, band members assume that all restrictive criteria are imposed by the band councils . . . At a time when many First Nations are striving for greater self sufficiency and control, the essential support of the aboriginal

population is seriously jeopardized by government interference and rigid policies.[84]

This jurisdictional mess resulted in a great deal of resentment directed at both the band councils and the federal agencies. Andrew Joseph of the Tl'Azt'En First Nation in British Columbia describes one version of the blame game that ensued:

> The Department of Indian Affairs camouflaged themselves, and it seems that native leaders within our communities are scapegoats between the members of our communities and the Department of Indian Affairs. Our people are kicking us on our rear and the Department of Indian Affairs would not let us proceed, would not let us change or even negotiate to change some of the policies and guidelines to meet our needs. In doing so . . . the department keeps our people divided.[85]

Therefore, the "expansion" of band jurisdiction over local matters in many ways exacerbated the indigenous peoples' feelings of coercion. The federal government was perceived to be bowing out of a problem that it was responsible for creating, and the band councils were seen as either accomplices or scapegoats in the process of neglect. This resentment in the wake of the jurisdictional morass created by C-31 foreshadows some of the anti-C-31 arguments put forth in *Sawridge*.

Phase Four: Sawridge: Parliamentary Jurisdiction vs. Band Authority

Sawridge et. al. argued that C-31 itself was an instance of the Parliament overstepping its power. To make this argument, the bands stated that their ability to set membership criteria was based on an ancient tradition—not C-31—and the requirement to reinstate women and not be sexist was a violation of this ancient practice. Yet, the bands' jurisdictional claim was founded upon a federal grant of power, the Constitution Act's promise of Aboriginal rights. A fascinating and somewhat circular account of jurisdiction emerged from this case. The bands said membership issues were under their jurisdiction because the Canadian Constitution said so.

Muldoon, in his colorful way[86], disagreed:

> Parliament demonstrated a clear and plain intention to extinguish any Aboriginal right or custom by which the identity and definition of Indians is established as far back as .

. . 1868 . . . The clear and plain intention was clearly to establish a racist apartheid, which would be completely repulsive today, but which was clearly and plainly within the legislative jurisdiction of Parliament.[87]

The Native Council of Canada also denied the aboriginal right claimed by Sawridge et. al. The Council felt that C-31 is a relatively positive way for Parliament to assert its jurisdiction.

Bill C-31 is a compromise to a complex problem. It's not a happy compromise. Practically no one if anybody was happy with it fully. But what it does represent . . . is a valid exercise of legislative power and legislative judgment. And it's a compromise, it's a compromise between the individual rights of bill C-31 and the collective rights of the Indian bands . . . [88]

This debate about jurisdiction reflects the fact that basically all band power is subject to federal approval. Each side looked to a different statutory source to draw legitimate jurisdictional boundaries. Thus, the debate became more about the appropriate exercise of federal jurisdiction in defining band jurisdiction.

The Evolution of Jurisdiction

The jurisdiction frame evolved from being focused squarely on the distribution of power among federal institutions to including the distribution of power between the federal government and the bands. This evolution did not necessarily lessen federal jurisdiction, but it re-framed it in a way that echoes the shift from the federal protection discourse to an aboriginal rights discourse. Instead of focusing on which governmental branch is the best to protect indigenous peoples, the new jurisdictional battle is about how the federal government can define band power. There was some discussion about which level of government (federal or band) should protect civil rights and it looks as though that power will continue to fall squarely on federal shoulders.

In developing the meaning of aboriginal rights, it was necessary to delineate what falls under treaty rights, where federal authority ends and where band authority begins. Bands gained a greater amount of administrative authority, but did not receive the funding or support from the federal government to assert this authority. Moreover, it was unclear how far provincial governments' jurisdiction would extend to indigenous peoples (especially for those who lived off-reserve). What resulted was a legitimacy crisis at the band level, with band members doubting the council's ability to govern, resenting reinstated women and their families, and also blaming the federal government for continuing domination or neglect. Thus, the official expansion of band jurisdiction did not necessarily expand band autonomy, empowerment, or self-determination. "Aboriginal Rights" is a contested concept, which still needs further development.

Indigenous women get caught in the middle of this meaning-making process. Cut and dry delineations of jurisdiction are likely to re-create the dual domination that indigenous women experience. If the federal government were to assert a heavy-handed approach on all issues, then colonial domination would be perpetuated. At the same time, ongoing gender discrimination seems to be tied to the increasing jurisdictional reach of the bands. Also, indigenous women are least likely to appeal to the Parliament, and if the judiciary actively "protects" their individual civil rights, it is condemned for asserting liberal legal discourses on indigenous communities. Therefore, jurisdictional concerns have great implications for the double bind of intersectionality. Jurisdictional confusion exacerbates discrimination because it prevents the delivery of services, which has very real economic impacts upon reinstated women.

Frame Six: Economic and Material Forces

Each party in these cases expressed unique economic concerns. The women themselves focused primarily on the loss of the benefits associated with Indian status, and the bands and the Canadian government focused on the costs of delivering those services to women who had married out. They claimed that there was not enough money to handle all intermarried couples and their children and that the reserves would become overcrowded. Some argued that, with the reforms, the Canadian government should provide funding and expand the Native land base in order to accommodate the influx of status Indians. As was mentioned under the jurisdiction frame, federal funding in the wake of C-31 was not adequate, and indigenous women were often the most economically disadvantaged by this funding failure. All of these economic forces had a direct effect upon the process of reintegrating reinstated women. Many of the arguments that were presented directly link cultural survival with economics.

Phase One: Lavell/Bedard: Losing Benefits or Protecting Meager Band Resources?

Lavell /Bedard introduced the issues that were at stake. According to Lavell's factum, Lavell and Bedard wished mostly to retain their ethnic affiliation.[89] But they also wanted to maintain Indian status, which gave them access to benefits and the ability "own or inherit property on the reserve."[90] When women married out of their band, they lost the ability to live on the reserve unless someone took them in. They also lost access to band annuities and federal health and education programs. Other lost benefits included: school-supplies and equipment, free daycare, post-secondary education expenses, mortgages, loans and grants to start a business, tax-exempt status, free medicine, fishing and hunting rights, and an exemption from a visa requirement for employment in the US. Finally, women who lost their status were unable to vote in band elections, which prevented them from helping influence policy on the distribution of resources.

While exited women might have been allowed to live unofficially on the reserves after marrying out, they had no legal access to any of these services. Also, many of the women who had moved away wanted to return to the reserve after their husbands died or if they were divorced. Many argued that they were subject to discrimination while living in Canadian society and could not earn a living there. Yet, even if they were allowed to return (at the discretion of the band council), they were still economically disadvantaged on the reserve.

As of 1956, when a woman married out of her band, upon leaving the reserve, she was "given twenty years of treaty money (if the band took treaty). Moreover one per capita share of the capital revenue moneys held by Her Majesty on behalf of the band."[91] This came "to a total of between $80 (20x$4) and $100 (20x$5) . . . The total amount paid to both women and men (who were enfranchised) between 1966 and 1977 . . . [was] an average of $261.80 per person."[92] Per capita payments were based upon "what is actually shown in the band's bank balance on the day the woman is enfranchised."[93] This figure did not include any money from band business ventures or funds like oil royalties. Despite the small amount of money involved, some argued that women were so destitute that this lump sum actually served as motivation to marry out and leave the reserve (this point will be expanded under the discussion of the *Sawridge* case). Some indigenous people also saw this lump sum payment as another Canadian assimilation tactic.

The Attorney General's factum states that, "It is . . . a matter of opinion whether it is a disadvantage for a person to be released from the application of the Indian Act. In some respects it may be a disadvantage, in other respects it may be an advantage."[94] Six hundred ten people applied for enfranchisement between 1960 and 1970, which led the Attorney General to conclude that, "These applicants clearly did not regard it as a disadvantage to come out from under the Indian Act."[95] As further proof of the "advantages" of marrying out, the Attorney General listed some legal consequences of maintaining Indian status: not having control over land which is held in trust by "Her Majesty"; having "limited testamentary capacity" because a Canadian Minister could void an Indian's will; not having the ability to make regulations on the reserves; the requirement that Indian children go to Indian schools; and that lands might be confiscated at any moment.[96] Thus, because one gained the benefits of Canadian citizenship and the Indian Act placed an unfair disadvantage on Indian women, the Attorney General felt it was possible that 12(1)(b) did not hurt these women, and might even have helped them. This line of argument acts as validation for indigenous peoples' fears of assimilation.

Rather than focusing on the economic impacts upon men versus women, the Attorney General discussed the transfer of dependence, with an assumption that women must be dependent on someone. The Attorney General's factum says:

> In the case of an Indian woman marrying a person who is not an Indian, this will generally involve a transition from dependence upon the Indian community and its special position under our law to dependence upon her husband in the ordinary circumstances of the larger community.[97]

Here, women's economic dependence is assumed and being dependent upon a white husband is preferable over being dependent upon an Indian band. This is another articulation of assimilation—such a hierarchy of economic dependence has a very serious impact upon cultural survival. The preference for dependence upon a white husband devalues the cultural coherence of the indigenous community.

Osler's ruling in favor of Bedard was based upon the fact that she did not have equal enjoyment of her property rights. He was persuaded by Bedard's claim that she should be allowed to live on the reserve and enjoy the benefits listed above. On the other hand, Grossberg ruled that Lavell enjoyed "the same rights and privileges in matters of marriage and property as other Canadians."[98] He felt that the material benefits that came with Indian status were basically meaningless, and could be replaced by provincial and federal government programs that other Canadians enjoyed. Since the Supreme Court ruled primarily on jurisdictional grounds, there was no explicit argument about the economic consequences of 12(1)(b), but implicitly, these factors were not compelling enough for the majority to find that the Bill of Rights should invalidate the sexist membership rule.

Another economic argument that emerged in *Lavell/Bedard* came from the bands and the organizations that represented status Indians. Bands were afraid of taxing their limited resources with the increased number of members that would come if 12(1)(b) were repealed. The Indian Association of Alberta stated that " . . . it is manifestly the policy of the Indian Act to maintain a viable reserve system and neither to deplete the Indian population nor to expand it unduly (thus placing intolerable pressure on the fixed reserve land base)."[99] To justify the sex-based discrimination found in 12(1)(b), the factum goes on to state: "the entry into a reserve community of non-Indian men can reasonably be expected to have a greater impact than the entry of non-Indian women."[100] This argument was based upon a twofold fear that men would not integrate culturally and would have a greater economic impact upon the reserve communities.

Yet, Jamieson notes that "the numbers of marriages of Indian men to non-Indian women seem[ed] to be increasing and for the years 1973 to 1976 inclusive ha[d] exceeded the number of women marrying non-Indians by 9.7%."[101] Therefore, the number of non-Indian women that gained Indian status was greater than the number of Indian women who lost status. So, Jamieson argues that arguments about the depletion of reserve resources would be stronger if every band member who had married out had lost status. She does not agree that men have a disproportionate economic impact on the reserves. The economic arguments presented in *Lavell/Bedard* reflect the competing interests of the bands, the federal government, and indigenous women.

Phase Two: Lovelace: Bearing the Economic Burden of Reforming the Indian Act

In *Lovelace v. Canada*, The Canadian government made a similar argument to Grossberg's in *Lavell*. Canada's submission says

> [Lovelace] also lost access to federal government programs for Indian people in areas such as education, housing, social assistance, etc . . . At the same time, however, she and her children became eligible to receive similar benefits from programs the provincial government provides for all residents of the province.[102]

For many, this acted as evidence that 12(1)(b) was an assimilation tactic. The attempt to assimilate Indians had a crucial economic component; between the payment of a lump sum upon marrying out and the promise of other government funds, some felt that the federal government was paying women (and enfranchised men)[103] to become Canadian.

Canada articulates the band's fears in its communication:

> Some [Indians] maintain that because amendments to the status provisions of the Act may well increase the number of Indians and thereby place demands on Indian lands and reserve lands, there should be no such amendment without a corresponding increase in the resource base of Indians. Others oppose any changes because it is felt that the present legal situation protects the Indian cultures and land base from erosion by non-Indians.[104]

This point also establishes the link between land base issues, resource limitations and cultural survival. Those who argue for the status quo do so out of a fear of both cultural and economic intrusion.

Lovelace responded to both the cultural survival and the economic assimilation arguments above. While she stressed that the most important consequence of 12(1)(b) was the loss of cultural contact, Lovelace also listed all of the benefits to which she no longer had access.[105] The desire to retain these benefits was not purely economic, according to Lovelace's communications. She pointed out that there is a link between these economic benefits (especially residing on the reserve) and feeling connected to her reserve community, and by extension, the cultural survival of that community. Being a part of an indigenous band includes living on the land and having equal access to band resources. This contributes to the survival of the community because, according to this perspective, those who remain connected will help the community thrive.

Lovelace felt that since the Canadian government created the problem, it should incur the expense of extending status to women. In particular, she thought that the Indian land base should be expanded. This claim reflects Lovelace's intersectional identity, with her competing loyalties. She wanted sex equality but not at the bands' expense. Instead, she wanted Canada to empower the bands (with money and land) so that they could include everyone.

Canada claimed that it was so committed to changing the Indian Act that it funded indigenous women's political groups. The Canadian communication states:

> Lending additional support to this intention [to amend 12(1)(b)] is the fact that the Government of Canada has funded and continued to fund Indian Rights for Indian Women, an organization having as one of its stated objectives the amendment of section 12(1)(b) of the Indian Act.[106]

To which Lovelace responded:

> Bullshit! The Govt. had no intention of changeing [sic] the Indian Act until political pressures forced them to Consider it. I.R.I.W. [Indian Rights for Indian Women] funded [sic] starting 1979, as a result of political pressures created during and after Native Women's Walk. There has been no Continoues [sic] funding.[107]

Canada's eventual funding of political groups that supported sex-based equality probably had a very interesting effect on political and legal mobilization (more on this in chapter 5). But, by using this as proof of its commitment to change, Canada acknowledges that it takes money and time to lobby Parliament, and to take part in the political process. Such an acknowledgement goes beyond merely funding bands to deal with the inevitable influx of new members. It also reveals that the relationship between the federal government and Native groups needs ongoing dialogue, which, in turn, requires money.

The *Lovelace* case reiterated many economic arguments presented in *Lavell/Bedard*. Both cases articulated the connection between economics and cultural survival, and reflected each side's unique fears about reforming the Indian Act.

Phase Three: The Charter and C-31: The Multiple Economic Consequences of Reform

When the Indian Act was finally revamped, many of the expressed fears came to fruition and many unanticipated problems arose. Bands were unable to assert their newfound autonomy because their resources were being strained by C-31 reinstatees. Also, the jurisdictional conflicts discussed earlier were exacerbated by a lack of funding. Throughout the implementation process, indigenous women had to continue their struggle to be reinstated in a way that would not re-invigorate the unique domination at the intersections of race and gender hierarchies.

One huge problem that emerged was that there was no housing for those women who wanted to return to the reserve after regaining status. Thus, one of the most concrete benefits of regaining status often was not realized. To ease this burden, the Canadian government offered grants to help the bands build new homes. But housing subsidies were roughly half of what it would have cost to build a house that met national building code standards.[108] If these problems were not enough, on many reserves, there was also an inadequate land base to build additional homes. The C-31 implementation report details this problem:

> Lands held in common by the band are often already allocated and are held by individual families under Certificates of Possession and Certificates of Occupation. As a result, reinstated members must either purchase land from another band member, if possible, or share land held by their families . . . In other cases, the only available land has been set aside for its development or revenue-generating potential. In communities where there is a dire need for economic development and employment, bands are understandably reluctant to reassign development lands for residential development. In addition, the cost of providing the necessary development infrastructure to make available lands habitable are prohibitive and often impossible to meet . . . Unless the land base is increased and resources provided for development or, alternatively, residency requirements are reversed, reinstated people will be denied access to rights and benefits associated with status, namely housing, employment and economic development programs, etc. While bands have

attempted to expand the existing land base through a number of means (including pressuring government to recognize treaty land entitlement, securing Crown land and submitting specific land claims), their efforts have been stymied.[109]

Thus, the promise to C-31 reinstatees of a home on the reserve often went unfulfilled. Moreover, even when they were housed, the reinstatees were resented by reserve residents because they were perceived to be the recipients of special benefits. Chief Harry Coo of the Lac La Ronge Band stated:

> The special C-31 housing program has created a degree of animosity between lifelong band members and reinstated band members. Lifelong band members have to put in their application for housing and wait as long as eight years for their name to reach a level in the priority listing . . . C-31 members on the other hand, can jump to the head of the lineup as a result of the special C-31 housing program.[110]

So, even if reinstated indigenous women were able to gain access to the reserves, they were not necessarily welcomed back into the community.

The federal government also cut another housing program aimed at indigenous people living off-reserve. The implementation report states:

> The termination of the off-reserve housing program immediately prior to the passage of Bill C-31 effectively blocked one avenue through which the housing crisis may have been eased. Many aboriginal people believe that the termination of the off-reserve housing program by DIAND was carefully planned to avoid responding to the projected increased demands on the program resulting from Bill C-31. It is important to note the sequence of events: Bill C-31 was proposed in March 1985; DIAND's off-reserve housing program was cancelled in May 1985; and Bill C-31 was passed in June 1985.[111]

The termination of this program was just one example of the withdrawal of federal support as C-31 was being implemented. Post-secondary education assistance was also limited prior to the passage of C-31. The funding cuts that coincided with the passage of C-31 offered evidence of continued colonial domination. Indigenous peoples saw this as the withdrawal of even the paternalistic federal protection that many had tried to maintain.

Indigenous people also faced grim employment prospects. The "lack of employment opportunities on reserves . . . result[ed] in a greater number of social assistance payments."[112] Many indigenous people expressed concern that the little funding that was being sent to the reserves was social assistance rather than economic development funding, which would have built a firmer infrastructure on the reserves for future employment. Moreover, "[m]any newly registered Indians either [could not] or [would] not move back to their reserves in the next few years. Because many [were] gainfully employed off reserves and employment [was] scarce on most reserves . . . "[113] While living on reserve would have helped reinstatees reconnect with their ethnic community, economic concerns sometimes prevented them from moving.

In addition to these funding problems, bands also needed funds to develop their own membership criteria. Hugh Braker from the Nuu Chah Nulth Tribal Council said, "We have not got one penny from the federal government to date to administer our membership rules. They promised every single year since 1985 that there would be funding available. Every single year they've said so and not once have we got a penny."[114] Therefore, C-31 gave bands expanded power without the necessary resources to exercise it.

For the women, the process of getting reinstated and gathering the necessary documentation was a costly process. Also, many felt that it was necessary to use the courts to ensure accountability. There was an expectation that the Canadian government would cover these costs. The C-31 implementation report states, "There is a need for greater access to litigation funding for individuals seeking restitution through the courts on matters such as equality and equity of access to benefits and services."[115] Democracy and the implementation of equality are expensive. Parliament must be lobbied and various parties must be brought to court. The Canadian government acknowledged these costs, and indigenous peoples expected that the federal government would provide the funding to implement C-31 properly.

C-31 came with many monetary promises to reinstated women, band councils and other band members. Many of these promises were not delivered. The influx of new band registrants created a great deal of resentment and economic turmoil on some reserves. Chief Louis Stevenson, of the Peigus Band stated:

> [David Crombie] gave an assurance that Bill C-31 would not make reserves worse off than they were at the time. He said that the needs of C-31 registrants would be accommodated within the resources they would make available. However, what we ended up receiving was the people, but not the resources to accommodate them.[116]

Meanwhile, many of the benefits that used to be conferred on status Indians were cut, and reinstated women were economically no better off (and some were even worse off) than before C-31 was passed. These economic constraints did not bode well for the either elimination of sex discrimination or the expansion of band autonomy.

Phase Four: Sawridge: Coveting Band Affluence?

Several kinds of economic arguments were presented in *Sawridge v. Canada*. Some witnesses reiterated the concerns described above about burdening band funds and land resources with an influx of new members. Yet, these particular bands were oil-rich, so a new argument emerged. While bands' legal arguments focused on the traditional and sovereign right to determine band membership, an underlying economic motive became apparent. Rather than focusing on deprivation and a lack of band resources, some band members hinted that there were great economic benefits that came with a woman's reinstatement. The change in focus from the economic impacts upon poor bands to individual desires to get rich affected the way that history was reconstructed.

The oral history testimony of Elder David Jacobs mentioned some of the material forces at play in a woman's choice to marry out and leave the reserve: "Q: Why did these women leave the reserve? A: Because the reserve is so poor at the time and they got paper to sign, collect the share. Demand their share that the band had at the time. She was paid off . . . "[117] Judge Muldoon elaborated on Jacobs's testimony and concludes that the opposite economic motivator was what drove women to want to return to the reserve:

> Elder Jacobs said that some women married out because the band was poor . . . although now with oil and natural gas, and housing partly subsidized by the federal government, and new

capital assets, a sportsplex, an agriplex for rodeos and a school the band 'became richer a few years back now.' Q: And things are better now? A: And that's why everybody wants to come in. And there's a lot of . . . people are looking for their . . . birth right . . . There are thousands—about six weeks ago I heard there were about 500,000 people that are ready to come in and get that paper that says, you know, treaty Indian and tax exempt, the tax exemption for gas and oil, cigarettes . . . And it seems like they're all coming for that.[118]

Therefore, the meager benefits that were being stretched according to some accounts became the major attraction for reinstatees to return to the plaintiff bands' reserves.

As stated earlier, the expert witness for the defense, Von Gernet stated that band affiliation was historically determined by economic forces, and women who had married out had opened up trade relations for their families. This account was twisted a bit by Muldoon and some of the witnesses to conclude that band membership issues were not about cultural access but about individual profit. Tradition and economics were juxtaposed only to disaggregate them. The women and the bands were portrayed as nakedly materially motivated. This reading (in Muldoon's mind) de-legitimized the cultural claims that were central to the plaintiff bands' arguments. Muldoon, who had a great distaste for "special benefits" enjoyed by indigenous peoples, thought that the plaintiff bands wanted to be sexist, not because of tradition, but to limit access to their affluence.

The Evolution of the Economic and Material Forces Frame

What emerges from these cases are several different kinds of economic arguments. In all of these cases, there were three distinct concerns. Women wanted to gain access to benefits. Bands did not want to be burdened by more members. And the Canadian government did not know how to simultaneously establish sex equality and the "protect" Indians without incurring great costs. These different perspectives took on different tones over time.

The Charter and C-31 increased band power and membership, while diminishing federal funding, which made it very difficult for bands to exert their newfound power. Thus, C-31 was seen as a new form of economic colonial domination. Another theme that emerged was the relationship between cultural survival and economics. Women wished to retain their connection to their band and felt that they should benefit equally from services and housing programs. Access to these services would foster a greater sense of community and would help indigenous people carry on their traditional practices. The counterargument presented by C-31 detractors was that reinstatees were unfamiliar with band customs, so intermarriage not only would burden band resources, but it also would have a detrimental effect on culture. Finally, the spin placed on the economic arguments in *Sawridge* shifted away from desires for cultural connectedness to pure economic motivators for reinstatement. In this case, economics served to undermine arguments based upon tradition. This shift reflects a fascinating ideological stance: when money is involved, cultural claims are deemed less legitimate.

Conclusion: Making Sense of the Legal Arguments

In the Canadian cases, the relationship between the six discursive frames is quite complicated. The most consistent tension is between individual civil rights claims to sex equality and bands' attempts to build some level of sovereignty and to give meaning to their promised aboriginal rights. The passage of the Charter and C-31 simultaneously bolstered both streams of legal argumentation. After these reforms, women could make much stronger sex discrimination claims. But the Charter also introduced the language of aboriginal rights, which strengthened bands' autonomy claims (often having detrimental effects upon indigenous women). These two master frames, individual civil rights and sovereignty rights, colored how the other four frames got invoked, and sometimes, creative combinations of the two resulted.

In making legal claims, indigenous women favored the individual civil rights rubric because this formed the basis for sex equality. This influenced the kinds of membership standards that they recommended because they focused more on individual affinity and voluntary membership than on biology or lineage. When tradition was invoked, it was usually used to bolster conceptions of equality and choice. These women's jurisdictional arguments usually stressed judicial protection of civil rights because they had less access to parliament. Moreover, they desired federal enforcement of sex equality on the reserves. There were many explicit arguments that the bands were answerable to the Charter's promises of individual civil rights. Finally, most of the economic arguments that these women made were about how they might regain their individual benefits under the Indian Act, which would allow them to fully access their ethnic identity.

But, these cases show that indigenous women have very complicated views about their identities. While they might not have wanted to have the bands decide whether they are members, they also did not necessarily want to be Canadian citizens. While they fought for their individual benefits, they did so because they felt that their access would foster indigenous cultural survival. Even though they utilized Canadian legal norms, these women embraced their indigenous identity, and they had well-developed critiques of colonialism. They tended to focus on the rhetoric of individual rights because they felt that they were the best tools for gaining access to their Native identity. These points illustrate the complex perspective that indigenous women must have in order to navigate the intersections of power that define their identities.

The bands, on the other hand, sometimes emphasized federal protection over sovereignty, and most did not embrace norms of sex equality. Accordingly, they preferred parliamentary jurisdiction as long as it limited band membership with manageable standards. Claims to sovereignty became more prevalent after the Charter was passed and this led to more appeals to tradition. The Indian Act became a symbol for pre-contact tradition, and it was seen as a shield behind which the bands could be immune to an onslaught of individual civil rights claims. Thus, sovereignty and tradition became vehicles for excluding indigenous women and for defending bands from perceived economic destruction. From the bands' perspective, the narrative of colonial domination became increasingly focused on the "ideological" intrusion of sex equality norms.

The fact that C-31 reinstated many women shows that Canada took the marrying out issue seriously. This can be viewed as the greatest victory of indigenous women's mobilization: political activism, going to the UN, and the legal battles paid off. But, contemporary local power struggles, the increased attention to aboriginal rights, and the diminishing social services going to indigenous peoples created many new hurdles for reinstated women and their families. Unless a particular bands' membership practices were based upon norms of sex equality, it was virtually impossible for women to advocate both aboriginal rights and sex equality because they were usually seen as opposing forces in court (as seen in *Sawridge*).

The influence of international norms of human rights is significant in this case. Lovelace's successful foray into the international arena has sparked some very creative arguments. For instance, Sharon D. McIvor, suggests that international covenants and human rights norms can "prevent both Parliament and Aboriginal communities from discriminating against Aboriginal women on the basis of sex or race in the future."[119] McIvor believes that the federal government should protect women's equal access to aboriginal rights, because "the fundamental human rights of Aboriginal women . . . form part of the inherent right to Aboriginal self-government which is now recognized and protected under section 35(1) of the Constitution Act, 1982."[120] McIvor's position is an example of creatively melding these two kinds of rights that sometimes seem quite dichotomous. It is rooted in a nuanced account of colonial power, and it privileges democratic participation for women. Thus, according to McIvor, band autonomy and sovereignty are unattainable without the participation of indigenous women. This is a terrific example of how one might combine both individual civil rights claims with aboriginal rights claims to help alleviate the double bind of intersectionality.

In 1995, the Native Women's Association of Canada (NWAC) went to court to receive funding and be recognized in the Canadian Constitutional reform process. Native organizations took part in the Charlottetown Accord, but the NWAC did not feel that they represented the unique concerns of indigenous women and therefore, they wanted a direct voice in the constitutional talks. This request was ultimately denied by the Canadian Supreme Court, but the fact that indigenous women in Canada continue to go to court shows that they still feel that legal mobilization and the provisional use of rights logics can help relieve the double bind of intersectionality. At the same time, the content of the decision and the ongoing mobilization reveals that indigenous women still suffer a great deal from their position at the intersections of power. The next chapter compares the Canadian and US cases, emphasizing the similarities and differences in the perpetuation of this double bind. Despite enduring colonial domination, these women must construct a unique account of rights that allows them to turn to the federal government (like taking part in Constitutional reform talks) to assure their access to their indigenous identity.

CHAPTER 5

Comparing the US and Canadian Cases

Assessing Impact

Comparing the US and Canadian cases sheds light on where indigenous women have had the opportunity to re-evaluate the meaning of rights, and to spur future legal mobilization or political participation. Such continuing participation might lead to a more explicit critique of the dual domination that exists at the intersections of power. If one deploys the tools that were constructed to eliminate race and gender against one another, the unique position of women of color might be better articulated. Yet, the consistent use of existing discourses might have a dominating effect, further solidifying the double bind of intersectionality. Looking at the impact of legal mobilization[1] as simultaneous domination and resistance requires one to find the perpetuation of domination in tactics of resistance, and the possibility of resistance in continued domination. Thus, it is necessary to look at several different kinds of impact.

First, one must consider *material* impact. Were the indigenous women that were involved in these cases financially better off in their everyday lives after they mobilized the law? Could they live where they wanted? Did they lose services based upon either their sex or their indigenous identity? Second, *cultural* impact must be considered. Could these women take part fully in their cultural rituals, language, traditions, and governing bodies? Did they have a voice in defining tradition? Finally, there is *ideological* impact. Did indigenous women have to continue to strategically employ the dominant ideals in order to improve their material situation and gain cultural access? Does this lead to greater ideological intrusion, and a perpetuation of the hegemony of liberal legal ideals (problematic and contradictory as they may be)? Ideological impact includes the discursive tools and conventions that are available to indigenous women in their legal claim-making.

The three facets of impact that I describe here are very much intertwined. For instance, not having access to cultural practices has direct material consequences. Moreover, ideological domination has direct material and cultural repercussions. I disaggregate these three facets in order to systematically assess the impact of indigenous women's legal mobilization in the US and Canada. Capturing the double bind of intersectionality requires that rights be re-evaluated in a way that increases the likelihood of impact on all of these fronts. Also, because of their overlapping nature, the three facets of impact allow one to see the complicated forces of power at work when intersectionality is most pervasive. Rights re-evaluation involves the creative deployment of existing narratives in order to gain strategic victories. While these tools might improve one's material and cultural situation, there is still the likelihood of continued ideological domination.

The comparison of the US and Canadian cases sheds light on this dynamic. In Canada, we can fairly say that ongoing legal mobilization did have a positive impact upon at least some indigenous women's material context and improved their cultural access. In contrast, Julia Martinez's children never did gain membership in Santa Clara Pueblo, and they lost access to both their culture and the attached material benefits. But, it is *possible* that the US Supreme Court's deference might prevent future ideological intrusion into tribal practices. On the other hand, in Canada, it is even less clear what the long-term ideological impact of increased legal mobilization will be for indigenous women.

It is important to note that more legal mobilization does not necessarily assure a greater degree of rights re-evaluation. Rather, continuing legal claim-making allows for *potential* rights re-evaluation. Legal mobilization also does not necessarily alleviate the double bind of intersectionality; at best, it may provide greater opportunity to strategically mobilize legal norms, exercising the potential for rights re-evaluation, and opening spaces for future resistance. But, it is also quite possible that it will not.

The Canadian case illustrates how ongoing mobilization perpetuates the debate about the content of indigenous women's rights. But the evolving discourse seems to be moving in a direction that often exacerbates the double bind of intersectionality. While the federal courts step in on behalf of women, they sometimes limit the definition of aboriginal rights or even disparage them (as Muldoon did). Yet, the situation in Canada, in any case, is more positive than in the US case, where the Martinez family was left to deal with the double bind of intersectionality in isolation.

An exploration of the institutional differences between Canada and the US helps explain why there was a greater degree of legal mobilization in Canada. And a look at the different kinds of impact—material, cultural, and ideological—helps show whether indigenous women were really able to re-evaluate rights more in Canada than in the US. While the possibility for future resistance is greater in Canada, that mobilization probably will happen under the rubric of liberal legal norms, which might reinforce ideological domination.

Institutional Differences between Canada and the US

The most important difference between the US and Canadian cases is where the sexist membership rule originated. The Indian Act was federal policy, while the Santa Clara Pueblo's membership rule was at the tribal level. Thus, indigenous women in Canada were, for the most part, mobilizing against colonial power while Julia Martinez used a federal statute (the ICRA) to mobilize against her own tribe. This basic difference makes the use of Canadian legal norms less loaded than employing US legal norms and institutions against one's tribe.

The loaded nature of this kind of mobilization is seen in arguments against the federal courts' role in deciding issues of tribal tradition and, by extension, issues of sex equality. The Indian Act epitomized colonial domination, and the sexism of 12(1)(b) was just another form of colonial intrusion upon indigenous women's lives. Thus, there were fewer contradictions in Lavell, Bedard, and Lovelace's initial mobilization than in Martinez's case. Instead of the women having to justify why they turned to federal courts (as Martinez had to), the bands in Canada were the ones who had to justify their use of federal norms and institutions. Status Indians in Canada defended the status quo by embracing another federal institution: the sexism found in the Indian Act, and they even went so far as to call that an indigenous tradition. In Canada, since the battle was fought largely on federal terrain, the conflict between indigenous women and their bands represented a conflict between two federal statutes (the Bill of Rights and the Indian Act, and later, two aspects of the Charter: individual and aboriginal rights). In the US, the tribe could point to Martinez's claim itself as evidence that she was disloyal to tribal autonomy. Early on in Canada, the bands tried to use convoluted logic to assert that the women were disloyal to the bands. But really, those women were disloyal to an aspect of the federal Indian Act. After the dual membership standards were set up, and some jurisdiction shifted to the bands, this dynamic changed in Canada. Later, the use of Canadian courts became complicated in a way that is quite similar to Santa Clara Pueblo (as seen in the *Sawridge* case). As band power expanded in Canada, those who favored federal remedies found in C-31 establishing greater sex equality were seen as subverting newfound band autonomy.

The fact that 12(1)(b) was a Canadian policy (rather than a band policy) was also what made Canada vulnerable to international scrutiny, under the International Covenant. Since the sex-based exclusion happened at the tribal level in the US, it was less likely that the UN would step in. In fact, the UN might very well have validated the US Supreme Court's deference under the self-determination clause of the International Covenant. Therefore, the origin of the membership rule (at the federal or tribal level) explains the different levels of vulnerability to international pressures.

Another important institutional difference between the two cases is that a greater number of indigenous women were affected by 12(1)(b) than by Santa Clara Pueblo's membership ordinance.[2] Thus, there were more people to mobilize in Canada than in the US. The only amicus brief submitted in favor of Julia Martinez's claim was from the ACLU. The twenty others represented tribes and national organizations that disputed Martinez's suit. In contrast, there was total of nineteen facta submitted in the *Lavell/Bedard* case. Four facta were submitted by women's groups, one was submitted by the indigenous women's group Indian Rights for Indian Women, and fourteen were submitted by status Indian organizations and bands. There was also a great deal of press coverage of the mobilization against 12(1)(b) in Canada. These institutional and demographic differences explain the greater degree of sustained legal mobilization in Canada as compared to in the US.

Also, with each stage of legal mobilization in Canada, there was a corresponding legislative or constitutional change which affected indigenous women's lives. First, the loss in *Lavell/Bedard* acted as a symbolic catalyst for Lovelace's complaint to the UN. While the UN considered Lovelace's claim, it became a potent symbol that spurred further political mobilization in Canada. The Lovelace case eventually led to C-31 and was also followed by the passage of the Charter. These legislative changes provided more to mobilize against. Indigenous women and indigenous bands continued to make legal claims in order to critique these imperfect legislative solutions. The governmental reports document these critiques quite well.[3] Moreover, there was ongoing legal mobilization to gain access to the Constitutional reform process,[4] which shows that indigenous women continued to see the Canadian political process as a viable venue for making their claims.

There were also important textual differences between the statutes and federal Constitutions in the two cases. The word "sex" is not mentioned in either the ICRA or the Fourteenth Amendment of the US Constitution, but sex discrimination is explicitly forbidden in Canadian Bill of Rights, the Charter, and the International Covenant on Civil and Political Freedoms. Thus, Canada had to justify the continued existence of 12(1)(b) despite its defiance of other important legal texts. Both C-31 and the Canadian Charter explicitly set up the tension between sex discrimination and aboriginal rights by codifying both simultaneously. In contrast, the US Supreme Court was able to defer to the tribes without having to make any textual justification. In fact, the US Supreme Court would have had to justify any active protection against sex discrimination because there was no explicit textual basis for such action in the ICRA. This textual difference helps explain the differing legal legacies which contribute to the differing levels of mobilization in the two cases. While textual differences are important, it is crucial to note that if the political climate, legal support structure, and ideological leanings of the justices were different, then the US Supreme Court ruling might have been different (despite the textual absence of sex-discrimination).

Charles R. Epp points to a few pertinent institutional differences between the US and Canada in his book, *The Rights Revolution: Lawyers, Activists, and Supreme Courts in Comparative Perspective.*[5] He notes that Canada had a longstanding history of government funding for legal advocacy.[6] As discussed in chapter 3, the Department of Indian and Northern Development sponsored the status Indians' appeals of the Lavell and Bedard cases. Also, there was a great deal of government sponsored litigation which brought test cases to court under the Charter. Epp labels this the "support structure for legal mobilization," which was partially responsible for the "rights revolution,"[7] in Canada. According to Epp, the Charter alone would not have created the rights revolution. Rather, there needed to be other elements in place for individual rights norms to take hold. In addition to litigation financing, Epp states that the support structure also includes the legal profession, government rights enforcement agencies, and rights-advocacy groups.

This support structure is very relevant to indigenous women's legal mobilization in Canada. Epp notes that there was a proliferation of women's rights groups during the years when Lavell, Bedard, and Lovelace brought their cases to court and to the UN. "[R]oughly a third were formed between 1970 and 1974, another 24 percent between 1975 and 1979, and another 12 percent between 1980 and 1984."[8] Additionally,

> [b]eginning in the mid-sixties, the Canadian provinces and the national government began adopting comprehensive human rights codes . . . ; along with these codes, they created human rights commissions having jurisdiction as quasi-judicial administrative agencies to hear discrimination claims.[9]

The New Brunswick Human Rights Commission was the organization that sponsored Lovelace's case before the UN's Human Rights Committee. The formation and government sponsorship of both women's and human rights groups shows the kinds of support structures that could be mobilized on behalf of indigenous women in Canada. As was noted earlier, Canada partially funded the protest group, Indian Rights for Indian Women, which was formed specifically to fight 12(1)(b). On the other hand, the Canadian government also, through DIAND, funded the opposition status Indian groups. Thus, in its funding patterns, the Canadian government was reinforcing the double bind of intersectionality for indigenous women. This funding was not necessarily all good, because it might have assured that dominant Canadian legal norms would be favored and perpetuated.

In contrast, the US had government funded legal services starting in 1965,[10] but this was aimed primarily at defending the rights of the accused, with some constitutional testing surrounding issues of poverty. Julia Martinez's lawyer was one such legal services lawyer.[11] But a lack of specialized advocacy not only gave Martinez less specific legal representation, but also embodied a symbolic difference between the US and Canada. The federal governments differed in their levels of interest in testing policies that affected indigenous women's lives. The US also experienced a stark growth in women's rights advocacy groups after 1966, but none were federally funded.[12] Moreover, few, if any, of these groups took an active interest in the Martinez case[13] and there were no advocacy groups that specifically mobilized indigenous women. Thus, the US might have had state sponsored lawyers and privately funded rights groups, but Canada had more specialized, publicly financed litigation advocacy groups.

The institutional differences between the US and Canada help explain why ongoing mobilization happened in Canada while there was no mobilization on behalf of indigenous women in the US who had married out of their tribe after the *Santa Clara Pueblo v. Martinez* case. The origin of the sexist membership rule, the number of women affected by the rule, and the legal texts and support structure at their disposal all help account for the different levels of legal mobilization in these two cases. These institutional differences also help explicate the varied impact of legal mobilization upon the double bind of intersectionality.

Material Impact

The analysis of the *economic and material forces* frame in chapters 2 and 4 shows that in both the US and Canada, legal mobilization had very concrete material implications. The Martinez children were going to lose access to their home on the reservation after their mother died. The Pueblo argued that the sex-based rule was the best way to deal with the distribution of scarce resources, and that they would be less vulnerable to litigation costs if the ICRA were weakened. Ultimately, the Supreme Court ruling sent the message that the Pueblo's stated economic concerns were more important than Martinez's. The Pueblo did not have to reassess its sex-based scheme for distributing tribal resources and Martinez's children continued to be excluded.

In Canada, while there were many indigenous women who regained the benefits that accompanied federal status, and some who were readmitted as band members, the reinstatement process imposed new material burdens upon them. Over time, the bands in Canada also gained administrative power, but this was accompanied by shrinking resources. So, while the material impact for indigenous women was more positive in Canada than it was in the US, both the women and bands in Canada still continued to experience a great deal of material domination.

It is important to note that in both cases, the motivations for mobilizing and consequences of the court decisions were rarely purely material. Sometimes material motivations or projected impacts were used to delegitimize cultural claims. For example, if it had been proven that the *Santa Clara Pueblo v. Martinez* membership rule was adopted to respond to changing economic times, then it would not have been viewed as representing authentic tradition. Given this concern, most of the legal arguments that were presented blended material and cultural survival arguments. This underscores how a tribe or band's material survival is directly related to the survival of its cultural traditions.

Cultural Impact

The cultural access facet of impact was similarly complicated in both cases. The Martinez children were physically and culturally excluded from Santa Clara Pueblo. But, equally important, the Supreme Court ruling in the US foreclosed any voice that Martinez and similarly situated women would have in defining tradition and determining the Pueblo's membership practices. Unless the tribal government's policies changed, indigenous women would not be able to assert their conception of tradition because, on this issue, the federal courts were no longer available to them.

In Canada, many reinstated women regained cultural access, and continued to have a voice in describing some cultural practices. But, the two-tiered membership system that was developed in C-31 created discord on many reserves, which limited many indigenous women's cultural access. The antagonisms that have been created by C-31 and the Charter have kept the dialogue about intermarriage going, but sometimes that dialogue has exacerbated indigenous women's cultural exclusion. It is also unclear how cultural practices will survive if women's access is dependent upon the federal government's intrusion. This points to the direct relationship between cultural and ideological impact.

Ideological Impact

The ideological dimension of impact is probably what is best described by the discursive analysis found in chapters 2, 3, and 4. The interplay between the individual civil rights and sovereignty rights discourses shows the complicated relationship between colonial and patriarchal power. The kind of ideological domination that exists is also well-illustrated by the jurisdictional arguments and the narratives about tradition that were put forth in both cases. When one reads these cases through an intersectional lens, it becomes clear that ideological domination continues in both the US and Canada.

The jurisdiction frame is crucial to this comparison because it helps explain the balance between individual and sovereignty rights that the US and Canada develop, and it also helps predict how indigenous people will be able to define contested tradition. The jurisdictional disputes between the federal and indigenous governments are an institutional manifestation of ideological domination. While the US judiciary defers to the tribes and/or Congress (possibly to a fault), in Canada, the Charter empowers the judiciary to take an active role in both sex-based claims and aboriginal rights. Deference might seem like the best way to prevent ideological domination, but this conclusion is not necessarily true.

In the US, the Supreme Court's deference re-entrenches patriarchal values which might have been the result of colonial intrusion upon Santa Clara Pueblo. The outcome in the US case reflects the role of the state in sanctioning gender discrimination or relegating gender issues to the private sphere. Thus, by consigning the membership rule to the private sphere of tribal tradition, the US Supreme Court re-inscribes a hierarchy of political importance that is gendered and thus continues indigenous women's dual domination. Therefore, the jurisdictional deference in the US is not necessarily going to lead to greater tribal autonomy, nor does it represent an area completely absent of federal intrusion. Moreover, the judiciary refuses or is unable to step in on behalf of indigenous women, but instead it cloaks these institutional constraints in the narratives of sovereignty and jurisdictional reach.

The ideological domination in the US case is found in the lack of acknowledgement of the historical role that the US government played in the creation of the *Santa Clara Pueblo v. Martinez* membership rule. This kind of ideological domination is somewhat abstract because it is less about forcing dominant ideals upon a particular group, and more about not acknowledging historical power relations. One might argue that institutionally, the only way to prevent future ideological intrusion would be by bowing out of as many internal tribal issues as possible. By not scrutinizing the Pueblo's membership "tradition," the US Supreme Court frees the Pueblo and women who marry out to fight about the tradition without having to make strategic arguments to prevent US input. In the short run, however, judicial deference leaves women like Julia Martinez with no tools for sparking this debate about tradition. Moreover, given the lack of continuing mobilization, and the continued existence of the sexist rule, it seems that the Supreme Court's deference just entrenched existing local political hierarchies.

In contrast, tradition falls under more explicit federal scrutiny in Canada. DIAND must approve band membership standards, and dictates the process by which they may be adopted. Some argue that the process for band membership standard adoption is contrary to traditional practices. At the same time, the legal tools and tactics that are available to indigenous women are rooted in liberal ideals and might be at the expense of traditional modes of conflict resolution. Thus, the ideological impact of this jurisdictional dynamic is twofold. First, the grant of autonomy is limited by federal conceptions of democratic process, and the approval of federal institutions. Second, while women have a greater ability in Canada to dispute membership practices, that voice only exists at the federal level. It is unclear whether women will ever be able to advocate for a version of indigenous tradition that differs from Canadian individual civil rights logics. So, the ideological domination happens when the federal judiciary sits in judgement of aboriginal tradition and bases that judgement on particular conceptions of scientific knowledge and liberal individualism. This kind of federal intrusion has the potential for future ideological domination of both indigenous women and bands.

While the US Supreme Court did not scrutinize tradition (the lower courts did), it also did not provide indigenous women with any judicial remedy. Instead, it deferred to a static notion of tradition. Both Canada and the US adopted a conception of tradition which relies on the scientific authentication of pre-contact practices. The Canadian actors acknowledged the colonial influence upon tradition to a greater degree, but there was a great deal of distrust of both the bands' and women's accounts of tradition. The predilection to authenticate tradition, or to defer in spheres that are deemed to encompass tradition, foreshadows the differing biases in the US and Canada on the individual versus sovereignty rights debate.

Due to the dominance of the federal venue in Canada, the discursive frame that was mobilized most consistently was individual civil rights. This took on many forms. The ruling in *Lovelace* led to a continued assertion by women of their individual human right to access their minority culture. Another recurring version of the individual civil rights frame was the debate over what counted as sex or race-based discrimination. This focus on discrimination exacerbated the double bind of intersectionality because there was great difficulty in considering both strands of discrimination simultaneously. Moreover, there was little or no discussion of equality. After the Charter was passed, aboriginal rights became another frame that competed with individual civil rights. But, even aboriginal rights were whittled down to an individual's right to associate in *Sawridge*. Granted, this use of the individual civil rights frame was very strategic (explicitly so), but it illustrates the prevalence of individual civil rights norms in the Canadian legal system.

Sovereignty became stronger in Canada as the discourse shifted from federal protection to aboriginal rights. But, the legacy of mobilization set up an infrastructure for future questioning of band practices in federal court. With the withdrawal of explicit federal sexism, bands began to assert that sexism was an aboriginal tradition. This led the Canadian government to apply the Charter's anti-sex-discrimination norms to the bands. The end result was a nominal increase of band administrative power with a great deal of federal oversight. Meanwhile, federal jurisprudence was torn between two narratives: aboriginal and individual civil rights. Ultimately, that tension led to more mobilization by both women and the bands. The predominance of federal jurisdiction assures that individual civil rights norms will guide the still evolving definition of aboriginal rights. The balance between individual and sovereignty rights thus tips toward individual rights in Canada.

In the US, many of the arguments explicitly combine the individual and sovereignty rights frames in order to construct a unique form of equal protection under the ICRA. The ultimate outcome, and the federal deference to tribal practices, shows that there is a more coherent account of sovereignty in the US than in Canada. This deference robs indigenous women of judicial protection of their individual civil rights, relegating issues of sex equality to the tribal level. This bias in favor of deference to tribal sovereignty in the area of membership standards contrasts nicely with the general Canadian bias toward individual civil rights. But, it is important to note that the construction of sovereignty in the US is very much informed by colonial legal norms.

Deference does not necessarily grant tribal autonomy for two reasons. First, the Supreme Court was deferring as much, if not more, to Congressional plenary power over Indian affairs as it was deferring to tribal self-determination. Second, the conception of sovereignty that the Court was deferring to is very much modeled upon the US system of governance (as seen in *Santa Clara Pueblo v. Martinez*'s constitution). This kind of deference also shows that, ultimately, it is up to the federal government to decide what properly falls under tribal sovereignty. While the process of deciding the limits of tribal sovereignty is not as intrusive in the US as it is in Canada (especially in the sphere of membership and intermarriage), there is always the possibility of future Congressional action in the US, which could be incredibly oppressive.

Thus, while the individual civil rights logics that mark Canadian jurisprudence might be a more potent form of ideological domination, the kind of sovereignty that is fostered by the ruling in *Santa Clara Pueblo* is also a result of ideological domination. The link between colonial and patriarchal practices shows that the US Supreme Court deferred to a static notion of tradition. This kind of deference leaves the double bind of intersectionality intact and leaves indigenous women with no venue for future claims. The different levels of emphasis on sovereignty or individual civil rights point to the varied forms of ideological impact. Both narratives have a direct effect upon the possibility for rights re-evaluation and, by extension, possible remedies for the double bind of intersectionality.

Impact on Intersectionality

How likely is it that rights will be re-evaluated in a way that will alleviate the double bind of intersectionality? There are several dynamics at work here, which have direct repercussions for intersectionality. In both cases, individual civil rights logics might alleviate indigenous women's sex discrimination claims, but once a woman makes an individual civil rights claim, bands/tribes mobilize in favor of sovereignty (as seen in *Sawridge* and *Santa Clara Pueblo v. Martinez*). In the process of defending an "ancient" tradition, indigenous peoples often rally around sexist practices. Since sex-based claims are perceived as a direct attack on sovereignty, a local backlash against sex equality ensues. The two forces—sex equity and indigenous sovereignty—continue to be considered mutually exclusive, which is exactly the dynamic that the double bind of intersectionality describes. Both strands of power affect indigenous women's lives. They will benefit from both increased sex equality and increased indigenous self-determination.

In Canada, the tension between aboriginal and individual rights ultimately set up a situation where sex equality was protected (somewhat) on the federal level but, as autonomy over band membership standards increased, sex equality was not necessarily protected at the local level. The continued tension between individual and sovereignty rights reflects the continuation of intersectional domination in both the US and Canada. The variation between the US and Canada exists in the degree to which this is a zero-sum binary. In both cases indigenous women still battle with their tribes on the local level, but the US case provides absolutely no federal remedy for indigenous women.

Table 1: Were Tribes/Bands and Indigenous Women Better or Worse Off After Legal Mobilization?

	Indigenous Tribes/Bands		Indigenous Women	
Type of Impact	**US**	**Canada**	**US**	**Canada**
Material	Better	Worse	Worse	Better
Cultural	Better	Better	Worse	Better
Ideological	Better	Mixed	Worse	Mixed

The table above shows where both indigenous bands and women stand after the legal mobilization in the marrying out cases. When one compares the basic outcomes for women versus the bands, the differences between the US and Canadian cases become more clear. While many of the subtleties of the discursive analysis are lost in the presentation of these outcomes in a table, the illustration clarifies where Canada and the US stand on a relative scale.

In the US, the Pueblo was generally much better off than before Martinez went to court because it won the Supreme Court case, which weakened the ICRA and strengthened tribal self-determination. Martinez, on the other hand, not only lost her claim but also the possibility for future legal mobilization at the federal level. While the ideological impact is more nuanced than is indicated in the table, the stark comparison shows how Martinez and similarly situated women were much worse off after mobilizing, while the Pueblo did win precedent that could be construed as bolstering self-determination. While Congress could still assert its plenary authority in a very coercive way, that was a power that existed prior to the *Santa Clara Pueblo* case and it was neither strengthened nor weakened. That is why the Pueblo was better off overall than before mobilization. These conclusions contrast very nicely with the outcome after the Canadian cases.

The table shows that the Canadian outcome is much more complicated. Since Canada had ongoing mobilization on behalf of indigenous women, it is more difficult to make simple assessments of better or worse off. The most telling part of the table is that in many ways, both the bands and the women benefited from the continuing mobilization. Both gained new discourses which could continue to be mobilized for future change. In some cases, the outcomes will have opposing consequences for each party, but overall, in terms of tactics, indigenous women in Canada still have greater opportunities for legal mobilization.

The previous section explains more fully why I put "mixed" under ideological impact for both the bands and the women. First, women might benefit from the individual civil rights logics that guide their claims, but, in the long run, it is unclear what effect these legal tactics will have upon their cultural access. On the other hand, aboriginal rights discourses are still developing and are more than indigenous bands had prior to the Charter, but they certainly have not gained even the level of self-determination that exists in the US. Moreover, the Canadian courts have rather consistently required aboriginal rights to be answerable to norms of sex equality. These mixed results are positive in that there are new legal discourses available to both the bands and to indigenous women. But the extent to which these new discourses will conform to the dominant Canadian legal narratives will determine the possibility for future ideological domination.

The US case acts as a strong precedent for sovereignty and federal deference.[14] Yet, *Santa Clara Pueblo v. Martinez* leaves little space for indigenous women's future mobilization. On the other hand, the Canadian case is a positive account of increased and successful mobilization over time, but the courts are more willing to scrutinize the content of tradition. This possibility for continued ideological domination changes the terms of intersectional power, but does not necessarily alleviate the double bind of intersectionality. Indigenous women are still not able to actualize both aspects of their identity fully. The Canadian case shows more promise for future action, but whether rights will be re-evaluated in a way that better captures indigenous women's intersectional identity is still unclear. The silences and categorical cracks still exist and exclude indigenous women from full political participation.

Potential for Future Rights Re-Evaluation?

Both the US and Canada acknowledge that indigenous women's claims are different from others, but the US outcome re-imposes their silence on the federal level and it is unclear whether the Pueblo will ever reconsider their claim locally. In Canada, the silencing takes on a different tone and indigenous women continue to have to fight new battles. Instead of fighting for reinstatement from the federal government, the battles have become more localized and therefore more similar to those in the US. Canada takes an active interest in this process, but sometimes negates band autonomy with its involvement (by scrutinizing tradition) and often re-inscribes the dominance of individual civil rights norms.

The US case does not seem to present many creative legal arguments that capture the double bind of intersectionality, and the jurisdictional deference leaves no place for indigenous women to turn. Not only does the outcome strengthen existing power dynamics, but it also forecloses future legal mobilization, making rights re-evaluation highly unlikely. An example of a creative legal argument would be to tie gender equity to tribal autonomy. Somehow, excluded women might be able to argue that tribal power would be strengthened by changing the sexist membership rule. Given the Supreme Court ruling, this would have to occur at the tribal level. But, this could be one way that rights might be combined to better capture the dual domination that exists for indigenous women.

Canada is experiencing continuing legal mobilization, leaving open the possibility for future creative and strategic deployments of rights. From the cases that I analyzed, there were strategic invocations of rights for both sides of the marrying out issue. Sawridge et. al. proposed a version of aboriginal rights as individual rights. Some women, drawing upon the UN HRC's ruling in *Lovelace*, embraced minority rights as an individual's right to cultural access. While both of these arguments rely heavily upon individual rights norms, the act of tying together the two identity strands does change the nature of those individual rights. A different kind of creative argument was presented by McIvor, discussed in chapter 4. She ties sex discrimination claims to aboriginal rights, arguing that gender equity should be considered an aboriginal right, and playing up the positive cultural impact of gender equality.[15] All of these arguments show that the discourse is still evolving, making the possibility for future rights re-evaluation greater in Canada than in the US.

However, the overall victory of individual civil rights discourse shows the continuation of a more subtle and pervasive form of ideological domination in Canada. The willingness for the federal government to continue to authenticate tradition and to validate band membership standards also shows that this domination continues. When cultural access is externally dictated, that culture changes, and indigenous women's access becomes qualitatively different. Federal ideological intrusion upon band autonomy oppresses indigenous women just as much as it does the bands, because both are being overshadowed in the process of defining what cultural practices are "authentic."

In the end, Canada seems to be closer to where the US was at the time of *Santa Clara Pueblo v. Martinez.* Canadian cases sometimes quote or refer to US jurisprudence, but the opposite rarely occurs. Many indigenous legal actors point to jurisprudence and the indigenous rights movement in the US as a more positive example of indigenous-federal relations. This might indicate that Canada might eventually move in the direction similar to the US, eventually favoring band sovereignty over individual civil rights for indigenous women. Granting greater autonomy to indigenous peoples in places like Nunavut also show that sovereignty is becoming a stronger discourse in Canada. The next question will be: if bands get their aboriginal rights in the form of federal deference to sovereignty, will they be more likely to reinvigorate sexism as a way to resist future ideological domination? Herein lies the enduring vicious cycle of intersectionality. Remedies for one aspect of domination might reinvigorate others and, when the others are alleviated, then a backlash might rediscover the first oppression, leaving intersectionality back at square one.

In sum, the possibility for rights re-evaluation is much greater in Canada than it is in the US. This is true because indigenous women continue to mobilize, have an infrastructure of advocacy groups geared to their unique claims, and enjoy a legal legacy that favors their continued employment of legal tactics. Yet, my discussion of ideological impact cautions that in each case there is a great possibility that future legal mobilization will perpetuate the dominance of certain legal norms. But the contrasting levels of accessibility of the legal systems in the two cases show that greater access and continued mobilization, in any case, does increase future chances for resistance. So, while there has not been a great deal of radical rights re-evaluation in either case, the potential for future creative combinations and reconstructions of rights discourses is much greater in Canada than in the US.

CHAPTER 6

Legal Mobilization at the Intersections of Power

Multiple Meanings, Multiple Opportunities, Multiple Constraints

> Law is a resource in signification that enables us to submit, rejoice, struggle, pervert, mock, disgrace, humiliate, or dignify.[1]

> [H]egemony is always in flux.[2]

Once power is conceived as a complicated web, the impact of legal mobilization must be expanded to include rights re-evaluation. It is very difficult to re-evaluate rights at the intersections of power, where multiple hierarchies such as race and gender combine to create a new, often more constraining form of power. Given the effects of such power dynamics, maintaining the potential for future struggle is a victory in itself. Presenting legal mobilization theory with the conundrum of intersectionality shows how many meanings and new interpretations can be applied to the same legal constructs. With increased attention to the web of power that mediates political action, one sees the constructed nature of legal norms much more clearly. The intersectionality puzzle both confirms and complicates the assumptions behind a constitutive account of legal power.

Mobilizing Legal Legacies

As stated earlier, "law" is a cultural form, with malleable meanings that represent multiple relations of power. Legal mobilization has been discussed as a very important form of political participation by many legal scholars.[3] The mobilization of law exists within a complicated web of power, which has patterned and recurring logics. These patterns can be strategically invoked to win material benefits, to gain cultural access, or to fight ideological domination. But, the nature of legal mobilization is such that it often strengthens dominant norms, even while winning the potential for future change. E.P. Thompson explains how legal rhetoric both constrains dominant power and structures resistance.

> And the rulers were, in serious senses, whether willingly or unwillingly, the prisoners of their own rhetoric; they played the games of power according to rules which suited them, but they could not break those rules or the whole game would be thrown away. And, finally, so far from the ruled shrugging off this rhetoric as hypocrisy, some part of it at least was taken over as part of the rhetoric of the plebeian crowd.[4]

The analysis of legal texts in this study shows how different parties might employ the same legal rhetoric to reach very different conclusions. The cases that I have studied are moments when indigenous women, with varying degrees of success, used the rhetoric of the law to call their "rulers" at their own game. For indigenous women, and others who occupy the intersections of power, there are multiple sets of "rulers," who have different stakes in the legal rhetoric game.

In many ways, the case of indigenous women's legal mobilization further solidifies many of the constitutive theorists' insights about legal mobilization. For them, "law is understood to consist of a complex repertoire of discursive strategies and symbolic frameworks that structure ongoing social intercourse and meaning making activity among citizens."[5] My analysis of the discursive frames in chapters 2, 3, and 4 helps to show the complexity of this repertoire. Legal frameworks structure political participation, set the terms of future struggle, and help political actors re-describe power.

In his book *Rights at Work*, Michael McCann lays out the stages of political struggle at which legal tactics might be employed. They are 1) the political movement building process; 2) the struggle to compel formal change in official policy; 3) the struggle for control over actual reform policy development and implementation; and 4) the legacy of legal action, which might act as a spark for future empowerment or transformation.[6] In this study, the juxtaposition of the US and Canadian cases shows different levels of success at the different levels of political struggle, but it sheds the most light upon the process of competing to define legal meaning. McCann stresses the importance of this last element—the transformative legal legacy—when he states that "[t]he flexibility and plurality of our rights traditions allow for adaptation to changing circumstances, for new types of claims by new groups over time, and for continued contests over the legitimacy of prevailing arrangements."[7] He shows that women who fought in the pay equity movement drew upon legal constructs to frame their claims, even when litigation failed. McCann focused on how a legal legacy influences the consciousness of political actors. In contrast, I focus on how the legal legacies of prior movements might be molded for contradictory purposes by competing sides in the most formal legal institutions.

A legal legacy represents the historical contest over giving meaning to legal discourses. It also serves as a catalyst and legitimation for subsequent political movements. By using legal rhetoric and institutions, political movements can gain a degree of legitimacy from the support of the state as articulated in prior rulings. Thus, an indigenous woman going to the UN and getting a successful ruling empowers other women like her to continue the battle in Canadian courts. Even when there is a "loss" in court, the presentation of a coherent argument, and the state's consideration of that argument, has a great deal of mobilizing potential, as McCann's study of the pay equity movement illustrates.

There is a unique form of legitimacy that comes with using legal tactics, because they are grounded in the norms that supposedly form the foundation for the existing political system. But, it is important to note that the legitimacy which legal action may confer upon political movements can also be a source of further domination. As discussed in chapter 1, the stamp of approval of the state carries with it the possibility of co-optation and the further entrenchment of existing relations of power. Stuart Scheingold states, "Beyond acquiescence, the myth of rights can generate support for the political system by legitimating the existing order."[8] Marx's distinction between political and human emancipation, as well as Gramsci's conception of hegemony, also underscore this idea. My discussion of both the US and Canadian cases adds empirical fodder for this point. The multi-faceted nature of a legal legacy—as the stamp of state legitimacy, as the spark for future mobilization and legal meaning-making, and as the representation of continued ideological domination—is captured by my conception of legal mobilization as simultaneous domination and resistance.

Some might argue that since the conception of power and law presented in this study focuses on multiplicity and malleability, the terms "domination" and "resistance" might be too binary and static. This assumes that an act is either domination or resistance, but both cannot be represented by the same act. To the contrary, I argue that domination and resistance can be temporally simultaneous, and certain acts can serve to continue historical domination and spark resistance or micro-change. Therefore, the same political act can be viewed as both domination and resistance by the same parties, as shown in much of the discursive analysis found in prior chapters. The conception of domination and resistance that informs this study privileges the position of those who occupy the intersections of power because their experience exemplifies the internal contradictions and multiple motivations with which most political actors must contend. Therefore, using terms that seem simple and binary, such as domination and resistance, but turning them on their head so that they both can happen simultaneously, actually uncovers the problematic of intersectional power quite well. The kinds of legal legacies available to indigenous women epitomize the simultaneity of domination and resistance.

For indigenous women in the US, the legal legacy of the *Santa Clara Pueblo* ruling failed to open new spaces for future movement building. The *Santa Clara Pueblo* case foreclosed any control over the federal policy process for indigenous women. But, it did establish a line of jurisprudence that was invoked again and again on behalf of indigenous tribes to bolster sovereignty claims and to assure their tribal immunity to suit. So, to assess the transformative legal legacy for these cases, it is necessary to examine its effect on two fronts: indigenous women's advancement against sexism and their tribe's advances in favor of sovereignty. Considering both of these forces at once illustrates how legal legacies might actually reinforce domination at the intersections of power. One aspect of power that dominates indigenous women actually was reproduced and strengthened by an apparent "victory" along the other strand of power. The increased power of tribal self-determination was used to reinvigorate gender domination, and left little space for indigenous women to resist in the future.

In Canada, the legal legacy for indigenous women is even more complicated because there was ongoing mobilization. Indigenous women gained some influence in the policy process. There was great potential for their continued legal mobilization to fight indigenous women's dual domination (i.e., there are continuing disputes over band membership policies and the implementation of C-31). Additionally, the marrying out cases and the resulting legislative changes provided the bands with a competing legal legacy (aboriginal rights). This shows that legal legacies, even when there is relative success, can invigorate the dominating forces that led to movement mobilization in the first place. In sum, when studying dynamic intersections of power, the operation of legal legacies is quite complicated.

Therefore, the marrying out cases show that a legal legacy continues to evolve depending on how different parties invoke certain legal discourses. Intersectionality allows us to see, in very concrete terms, how a legal legacy—and the meanings attached to it—can multiply when two simultaneous strands of power are exposed. For example, individual rights discourses can be deployed by indigenous sovereignty advocates as well as women fighting for gender equity. The bands in the *Sawridge* case in Canada were able to articulate their desired sovereignty in terms of an individual's right to associate freely. At the same time, concepts of individual access and freedom from sex-discrimination were the foundations for indigenous women's claims to be reinstated. Additionally, indigenous women often drew upon their version of indigenous tradition when articulating their conception of gender equality. The use of the same discursive frame by parties with opposing interests shows the malleability of the legal legacy that results from litigation. Moreover, it reveals that the discourse itself must be deployed provisionally if the same person/identity group has a stake in both interpretations. Indigenous women value the freedom of their natal tribes/bands from colonial intrusion, but they also desire access to the local processes that would allow them to partake in creating and upholding tradition. In sum, the phenomenon of intersectionality creates multiple legal legacies and, by extension, more sites for simultaneous domination and resistance.

As I have noted earlier, legal legacies not only spur future action for the original parties that mobilized, but they might also provide the discursive foundations for counter-mobilization. Thus, the cycle of protest that McCann describes becomes even more complicated when intersectional concerns are factored in. A process-oriented model takes time into account and acknowledges the ongoing nature of legal mobilization, allowing one to see the evolving impact of legal action. This study is informed by this process-oriented approach to legal mobilization, but focuses primarily on legal argumentation and discourse. Robert Cover's work has a great deal to say about the relationship between legal discourse and power.

Meaning Making at the Intersections of Power

Robert Cover's essay, "Nomos and Narrative" helps flesh out the meaning-making struggle that is central to this study. He states that, "Law may be viewed as a system of tension or a bridge linking a concept of a reality to an imagined alternative."[9] In Cover's terms, I study legal argumentation in order to illustrate the process of *jurisgenesis*, or the creative construction of legal meaning, which he feels "takes place always through an essentially cultural medium."[10] He contrasts this with the *jurispathic* influence of the courts. "By exercising its superior brute force . . . the agency of state law shuts down the creative hermeneutic of principle that is spread throughout our communities."[11] So, according to Cover, while cultural communities are the source of discursive creativity and dynamic legal meaning-making, the state is the seeker of stability, and violently imposes limited legal meanings to preserve the status quo. My analysis of indigenous women's legal mobilization shows that the culture/state dichotomy is not so cut and dry, and that both jurisgenesis and jurispathy exist in cultural and state contexts. Also, a process-oriented approach to legal mobilization and meaning-making shows that there is a kind of dialectic between these jurisgenerative and jurispathic forces.

Reading Cover and McCann together, one can describe the relationship between the creation of legal meaning and political actors' responses to court decisions in a less binary way. The conception of power that allows us to see intersectional domination and resistance and continuing legal struggle underscores the dialectical nature of legal meaning-making. As the cases under scrutiny in this study show, jurisgenesis happens both before and after court decisions have been handed down. Jurisgenesis also results from conflicting rights logics that emerge from court decisions, and the jurisdictional confusions that often result when attempting to implement those decisions.

Jurisgenesis

Cover agrees with many legal scholars when he describes the relationship between social movements and legal meaning-making.

Legal language simultaneously serves as a legitimating force in the process of jurisgenesis, but it also has a constraining or dominating effect because it is what legitimizes state power.

> And just as constitutionalism is part of what may legitimize the state, so constitutionalism may legitimize, within a different framework, communities and movements. Legal meaning is a challenging enrichment of social life, a potential restraint on arbitrary power and violence.[12]

Thus, Cover's account of jurisgenesis describes the continuing struggle to define legal legacies, which is about giving meaning to what is officially acknowledged. He articulates the point made by E.P. Thompson about "rulers" being constrained by their own rhetoric, while the "ruled" make use of that rhetoric to make sure that the rulers continue to be constrained.

Cover writes, "By provoking the response of the state's courts, the act of civil disobedience changes the meaning of the law articulated by officialdom."[13] Not only does the use of legal rhetoric lend legitimacy to official power, but its meaning changes when it is used as a tool for resistance. Thus, jurisgenesis captures quite well the simultaneity of domination and resistance on legal terrain. Cover continues, "The significance lies in the group's creation of jurisprudence that orders the forms and occasions of confrontation, a jurisprudence of resistance that is necessarily also one of accommodation."[14] Here, Cover emphasizes the accommodation to state power that is inherent in invoking legal norms. Such accommodation is even more necessary but also more subversive at the intersections of power.

Through the process of jurisgenesis, cultural movements draw upon and redefine the legal legacy of prior social movements. The discursive analysis of indigenous women's legal mobilization shows how different outcomes create contested legal meanings. The indeterminate nature of legal discourse has been exhibited on many levels throughout this study. There are contradictions and cracks in the norms that inform legal decision-making, which open up spaces for future legal action. The struggle to define rights and to describe wrongs is an ongoing one. Once we add the complexity of intersectional power to Cover's analysis, we see where competing forces of jurisgenesis multiply the sites for confrontation and contradiction.

The cases under scrutiny in this study show that women who occupy the intersections of power must create legal meanings from conflicting and contradictory rights logics and colonial legacies. In a way, this is a kind of jurisgenesis gone wild. Individual and sovereignty rights exist side by side, and there are multiple meanings that could be attached to each set of rights. Since indigenous women have a stake in defining both strands of rights, it is difficult for them to choose between the two. Indigenous women's creative combinations of two kinds of rights show how they must invoke rights strategically in an effort to describe their unique oppression (even before the most formal of legal institutions). Plus, there are multiple institutional levels at which this plethora of rights-definitions might be invoked, which further complicates the process of jurisgenesis. Since basic conceptions of fairness and equity are much more complicated for indigenous women, their definitions become more nuanced and sometimes more problematic than other, more straightforward singular strands of rights. Thus, the existence of two very distinct rights discourses which equally affect indigenous women's lives adds a new wrinkle to the process of jurisgenesis that Cover describes.

In a way, the account of power that informs this project multiplies the insights gleaned from Cover. Jurisgenesis happens between communities and within them. Intersectionality allows one to see sub-communities and the intra-community struggle over defining cultural legal meanings. The cultural nomos becomes much messier, more contested, and unsavory than Cover implies. Multiple and simultaneous instances of jurisgenesis may be liberating for some and dominating for others. Therefore, multiple sites for jurisgenesis inevitably create more sites for both domination and resistance. The same insight can be applied to Cover's notion of jurispathy.

Jurispathy

Cover focuses upon the conflict between jurisgenesis, or the proliferation of legal meaning, and the state's social control function. The imperial form of constitutionalism is all about world maintenance and validating the status quo, which Cover feels is the overriding function of the courts.

It is the problem of the multiplicity of meaning—the fact that never only one but always many worlds are created by the too fertile forces of jurisgenesis—that leads at once to the imperial virtues and the imperial mode of world maintenance.[15]

In Cover's view, the legitimacy of the state rides upon imposing order and exerting power (by committing or implying violence). Cover continues, "The uncontrolled character of meaning exercises a destabilizing influence upon power."[16] In my analysis, power is inherently unstable and sometimes the jurispathic influence of the courts exacerbates this instability. Thus, while the force and violence of the state might give extra weight to court interpretation, that does not assure order. Cover agrees, but seems to grant a great deal more weight to the state's ability to impose order through definitive legal interpretation than my conception of power would allow. State power is not necessarily the imposition of order, but more like a unique form of constraint. Thus, there are several ways that my conception of legal power differs from Cover's. Not only does the state constrain or exert jurispathic power over legal meaning, but it also can be part of the process of jurisgenesis. Second, intersectionality reveals that jurispathy can be found both in official rulings as well as in cultural communities, in the form of counter-mobilization or local re-assertions of traditional control.

The courts are not the only jurispathic influence upon indigenous women's lives. The tribes, the communities, the combinations of power all wield potentially jurispathic power over indigenous women's jurisgenerative impulses. Attention to intersectional power reveals that multiple movements were empowered by the invocation of legal norms by indigenous women. In both the US and Canadian cases, tribes/bands created their own set of legal meanings to contradict indigenous women's legal interpretations. This happened both before and after formal court rulings were handed down. Since tribes and bands hold an official, sometimes "state-like" position vis-à-vis indigenous women, their interpretation of legal norms carries the same kind of legitimating constraint through violence as the colonial state (i.e., jurispathy).

Cover's problematic dichotomy between the state as the primary source of control and jurispathy and culture as an autonomous sphere of vital jurisgenesis comes through when he invokes the *Santa Clara Pueblo* Case. He states that it is an example of how "[r]espect for a degree of norm-generating autonomy has also traditionally been incident to the federal government's relations with Indian tribes."[17]

Here Cover assumes that the Supreme Court's deference to the Pueblo maintained its autonomy and jurisgenerative potential. But, from the perspective of Julia Martinez, the court exerted jurispathic control over her ability to define legal meaning for herself and to counter the tribal council's definitions. At the same time, rather than being a jurisgenerative force, the tribe also served a jurispathic function because it had the very real power to exclude Martinez's children from the reservation.

It is important to acknowledge that jurispathic force is exerted in extra-state settings. When intersectional power is considered, multiple sources of social control soon become evident. The Pueblo proposed its definitions of tradition and sovereignty, which were quite different from both the federal government's and Julia Martinez's. In the process of trying to keep the tribal community insular and autonomous, the Pueblo tried to squelch Julia Martinez's meaning-making ability. The version of sovereignty put forth by the Pueblo was not explicitly accepted by the Court, and so it would not be fair to say that the Court exerted all of the jurispathic force found in this case. Rather, it was the Pueblo's jurisgenerative input that served a jurispathic function in regards to indigenous women. Moreover, the Pueblo's account of sovereignty was neither negated nor supported by the Supreme Court's decision.

The Court deferred to Congress more than it did to tribal sovereignty. Yet, since that ruling, other tribes have been able to use the precedent value of *Santa Clara Pueblo* in order to bolster the Pueblo's conception of sovereignty. Thus, the legal legacy of the Court's deference to Congress has been strategically used to strengthen a degree of tribal self-determination and control over its members. Since this precedent and legal meaning was constructed by ignoring Martinez's claim, I would argue that both the Court and the Pueblo had a jurispathic influence on indigenous women's creative legal meaning-making ability. Cover implies that the only coercive force lies with the state. Looking at intersectional power makes it clear that there are quite a few more sources of social control than he implies. What Cover labels "culture" can control just as much as the state can, especially when cultural forces take on a state-like power, as indigenous tribes/bands do.

Cover focuses on the state's ability to commit violence as the source of social control. In my cases violence is not in the form of "pain and death,"[18] but it involves the expulsion from one's community, which is quite traumatic. In the US case, the Pueblo, along with the US Congress and the Supreme Court, commit acts of violence against indigenous women. Each kind of violence is different, but one is no less violent than another. Therefore, Cover's conception of power, and the linkage between judicial meaning-making and violence, contributes an important element to the theoretical underpinnings of this study. But, at the same time, when this linkage is considered in light of intersectional power, the multiple sites of legal meaning-making also become sites of coercive power.

Cover says a great deal about the rhetoric of jurisdiction, and the kind of power that the courts wield when they defer to other institutions. "Just as those who would live by the law of their community are led to the texts of resistance, the judge who would kill that law resorts to the texts of jurisdiction."[19] This kind of jurispathy applies to the US case quite well, because there were two kinds of jurisdictional arguments offered; the court deferred both to Congressional plenary power over tribes and to tribal self-determination of traditional practices. With added attention to the intersections of power, the force of jurispathy and the violent effects of jurisdictional arguments become more potent and multi-dimensional. *Santa Clara Pueblo* shows the failures of jurisdictional deference to a problematic notion of sovereignty. Cover offers a relevant observation when he states that, " . . . some principles of deference—whether to states, administrators, or legislative majorities—requires that equity, the only effective remedy, stay its hand."[20] This was the outcome from Julia Martinez's perspective. Yet Cover focuses upon the court's deference to the violence of state administrative power. While the Supreme Court primarily deferred to Congressional administrative power and the attached violent control of Native Americans, it also deferred to a very problematic notion of tribal tradition, which wielded control over women like Julia Martinez. Thus, Martinez and her children were subject to the violence of both Congressional neglect and tribal exclusion, and both forms of violence were strengthened by the rhetoric of jurisdiction.

Additionally, in the cases that Cover critiques, the Court makes jurisdictional rulings and defers to state authority without offering any kind of normative reasoning. Cover claims that by making "no interpretive gesture at all," the Court is directly implicated in the violence of the state. In the *Santa Clara Pueblo* case, the Court does offer a normative explanation for its deference. It claims to be unwilling to interfere with tribal tradition, putting forth a notion of tradition that is uncontested and extricated from colonial influence. By interpreting tradition in this way (which is laden with normative judgement), the Court inadvertently creates a foundation for tribal self-determination (or at least immunity from suit) right upon the backs of indigenous women and their children. Cover's analysis applies quite well to the *Santa Clara Pueblo* case, but when one views it through an intersectional lens, the problem of jurisdictional deference becomes even more destructive. In sum, the unique double bind that results from the intersectional identity helps describe power in a way that complicates Cover's (and others legal scholars') constitutive and pluralistic account of law.

The evolution of the sovereignty frame in Canada (as discussed in chapter 4) is a very good example of the multiplicity of jurisgenesis and jurispathy. First, sovereignty evolved from federal protection to aboriginal rights, which was at least a discursive turn away from a colonial conquest toward a more rights-based rubric. But, in trying to fill out the meaning of aboriginal rights, there were many versions offered. One interpretation was focused on complete judicial deference (similar to the version found in *Santa Clara Pueblo*), while others tried to construct a version of aboriginal rights that was similar to an individual's right to associate freely, which were more rooted in the Canadian legal tradition. Plus, indigenous women wanted to build sex-equality into the meaning of aboriginal rights. Thus, the contest over giving meaning to this package of rights sheds some light upon the indeterminate nature of rights discourses more generally. The many meanings given to aboriginal rights in Canada exemplify the power of jurisgenesis, showing the multiple sites at which it occurs (the state, bands, women). Hence, there were many different ways to conceive of aboriginal bands increasing their legal clout.

But as *Sawridge* shows, old meanings can be revived to reconstruct the prevalent legal legacy. Prior rulings and legislation were unable to exert the definitive jurispathic influence that Cover implies. The Sawridge band claimed that the Indian Act was an embodiment of their pre-colonial tradition, preferring the Indian Act's colonial domination over norms of sex-equality found in C-31. This was a fascinating use of the old "federal protection" rhetoric as the foundation for a uniquely post-colonial version of sovereignty, which is explicitly contrary to sex equality. Thus, in the process of jurisgenesis, the band offered a legal meaning that was inherently jurispathic because it precluded future meaning-making activity by indigenous women. By looking back to an old legal meaning (that of the Indian Act), Sawridge et. al. not only hoped to exclude women who might deserve to be band members, but also wanted to squelch their ability to offer new and contradictory legal meanings.

This example shows several things. First, the state, again, is not the only source of control from the indigenous women's perspective. The state may be complicit in reinvigorating sexist meanings, but the bands themselves are just as constraining on this front. It also reveals that jurispathic force can inhabit jurisgenesis itself, depending upon the perspective of the political actor. This emphasis on perspective and multiple legacies is an insight that comes directly from considering the intersections of power.

Revisiting the process-oriented account of legal mobilization allows one to systematically address the simultaneous forces of jurisgenesis and jurispathy. McCann's model of legal mobilization emphasizes the ongoing nature of political struggle, making legal legacies more available for future movements than jurispathy allows. In addition to acknowledging the continuing and ever-changing nature of the legal meaning-making struggle, an intersectional account of power shows that jurisgenesis and jurispathy co-exist at multiple sites and they have a kind of dialectical relationship to each other. This is why, throughout this study, legal mobilization is portrayed as a process of simultaneous domination and resistance. Domination and resistance capture the simultaneity of control and opportunities for future legal meaning-making that are not necessarily captured by jurispathy and jurisgenesis.

By focusing on intersectional power, one can see both the positive and problematic aspects of the notion of sovereignty that was bolstered by the US case. It also reveals the possible future dominating effect that liberal conceptions of equality might have upon indigenous women in Canada. Looking at the intersections of power forces one to insert an analytical feedback loop between jurisgenesis and jurispathy, offering a more nuanced analysis of legal power. Instead of assessing the failure or success of singular instances of legal mobilization, it is helpful to see what aspects of legal meaning-making create future opportunities for political action.

The juxtaposition of the lack of mobilization in the US and the continuing mobilization in Canada exemplifies the relative success that legal tactics can have. The outcome of the US case has a greater jurispathic effect upon indigenous women, while the Canadian case seems to show more promise for potential rights re-evaluation because there are more opportunities for jurisgenesis and future action. This comparative analysis is quite useful for assessing the efficacy of legal mobilization because it reveals relative levels of ongoing struggle and potential for future rights re-evaluation. Neither case completely precludes future action, but the Canadian case offers more opportunity for indigenous women to re-evaluate rights to better describe the intersections of power.

The Intersections of Global Power

To better convey the broader significance of this study, it is helpful to turn to Boaventura de Sousa Santos's work. His insights about globalization and transnational movements help uncover the global implications of my model of power and law. Santos embraces the contingency and plurality of history, politics, and law. He argues that the legal field is being transnationalized, or increasingly marked by interactions between states and international non-state groups. As a result, law is no longer bound to a particular nation-state. He argues that

> national legal fields (state legal orders and local, infrastate legal orders) . . . are transformed by transnational legal movements. The state monopoly of production of law is . . . questioned . . . because the national legal field is increasingly interpenetrated by transnational legal forms which unfold in complex relations with both the state legal order and the local legal orders.[21]

He looks at the multiplicity of power relations on a global scale, stressing the importance of diverse histories and the multifaceted nature of modernization. As one sees political movements as crossing national boundaries, and becoming rooted in multiple legal systems and global economies, looking to intersecting structures of power and the contingency of rights becomes rather important.

Santos states that "the process of globalization is highly contradictory and uneven" because it happens alongside new localisms (new infrastate political and legal innovations).[22] "The world system, and more specifically, what in it is designated as globalization are a web of localized globalisms and globalized localisms."[23] His account of the dialectic interpenetration of the local and global is very much in keeping with my conception of power as a web, with many different layers weaved together. These insights by Santos expand this conception of power and politics, making innovation both more far-reaching and complicated. Santos is very aware of the simultaneity of domination and resistance, but from these forces, he constructs a model of political innovation on a global scale as cosmopolitanism.

Cosmopolitanism is marked by transnational "counter-hegemonic practices and discourses."[24] He argues that human rights norms can be localized and deployed strategically in order to form the basis for transnational cosmopolitan coalitions.

> [C]osmopolitan coalitions have no essentialist class base. They can be rather mixed in their class composition and formed along nonclass lines, such as ethnicity, gender or nationality. In part for this reason the progressive character of cosmopolitan coalitions can never be taken for granted. It is, rather, intrinsically unstable and problematic, and can only be sustained through permanent self-reflexiveness . . . Cosmopolitanism is nothing more than the networking of local progressive struggles with the objective of maximizing their emancipatory potential *in locu* through translocal/local connections.[25]

My argument about rights re-evaluation at the intersections of power is an example of how cosmopolitan coalitions can be self-reflexive. For example, such reflexivity can result from the contest of legal meaning that takes place between indigenous women and others in formal legal forums. Action spurs on new legal interpretation, and further action, which, in turn, sets the terms for further reflection and re-definition. Santos's attention to the emancipatory potential of global action expands this meaning-making contest beyond state borders, thereby multiplying the possibilities for alliances at the intersections of power.

Two examples of cosmopolitan coalitions are international human rights groups and transnational non-governmental organizations representing indigenous peoples. Many of Santos's points about these two groups echo the domestic struggles that I analyze. Santos rightly argues that formal equality in the form of minority rights will not assure indigenous self-determination, and he argues that self-determination must come prior to individual human rights.[26] I would add that as long as indigenous self-determination and human rights are seen as mutually exclusive, disputes like the marrying out cases will inevitably continue to arise. Yet, his construction of cosmopolitanism allows for the two discourses to be combined in creative ways. This process hinges on the acknowledgement that each discourse has multiple interpretations, both at the global and local levels.

Santos describes an aspect of transnational jurisgenesis, when he states that "alongside the dominant discourse and practice of human rights conceived as a globalized Western localism, a counter-hegemonic discourse and practice of human rights conceived as a cosmopolitan politics has been developing."[27] And he acknowledges the double gesture of rights logics as the simultaneous legitimation of current power relations, and the seeds for future resistance. Santos writes, "The emancipatory energy of human rights struggles has always lain in the ever-incomplete list of granted rights and, consequently, in the legitimacy of the claim to new rights."[28] Thus, the process of re-defining human rights can serve both emancipatory and constraining purposes. This simultaneous domination and resistance becomes even clearer when the intersections of power are examined.

The process of assigning counter-hegemonic meanings to the human rights script might clear some space for the consideration of intersectional concerns.

> The contradictions in the regulatory functions of human rights must therefore be taken as the starting point for an emancipatory politics. Because they are experienced worldwide, albeit very differently, such contradictions bear the seeds of translocal intelligibility and the formation of cosmopolitan transnational coalitions. In their conventional conception, human rights are falsely universal because they

obliterate the inequalities in the world system, the double standards, and the differential cultural embeddedness. It is up to cosmopolitan politics to transform such false universality into the new universality of cosmopolitanism. Human rights are a political Esperanto, which cosmopolitan politics must transform into a network of mutually intelligible native languages.[29]

This process parallels the provisional activity at the intersections of power that I have described throughout this book. It describes transnational jurisgenesis, as Cover would put it, which multiplies the discourses that indigenous women might draw upon in the process of resisting the dual domination of intersectional power. It also shows how transnational logics can be adapted for local purposes, which are likely to better serve indigenous women in their struggles, because, through this process of adaptation, they become more intelligible for naming local hierarchies. At the same time, local struggles can inform the transnational meaning-making process. In other words, transformative legal legacies take on global proportions, creating new spaces for resistance as well as new kinds of domination.

The *Lovelace* case, and the subsequent legal mobilization, hints at the dynamic that results from global-local interpenetration. Minority rights logics continue to inform indigenous women's legal arguments, but they have been localized to accommodate the Canadian Charter, C-31, and the particularities of band practices. Thus, what Santos labels cosmopolitan activity echoes the meaning-making activity that happened in Canada and in the US. A global account of human rights might draw upon the contradictions of multiple localisms to create a discourse that might have some provisional emancipatory potential in both local and transnational struggles.

[I]n order to build new emancipatory constellations in a period of paradigmatic transition, it is imperative to learn from the suppressed, marginalized traditions which, in most instances, are the traditions of suppressed or marginalized people. To use the metaphor of hierarchy in the world system, we have to learn from the South. What can we learn from the indigenous peoples who, in a sense, are the South of the South? To answer my question I suggest we consider three perspectives:

neolaw, neocommunity, and neostate. The prefix *neo* is meant to emphasize that we are not learning from the past 'as it really happened,' but rather from the past as it is being reinvented or reimagined by those entitled to it, the retrospect of the self-determined future they want to live in and pass on to their children.[30]

According to Santos, neolaw and neostate involve radical critiques of their modern equivalences. Law and the state become more plural and heterogeneous, able to accommodate a uniquely postmodern citizenwith multiple loyalties (such as indigenous women). Neocommunity is "a complex constellation of social and political meaning, in which premodern, modern and postmodern elements are tightly intertwined."[31] Santos's unique notion of history, community, and politics leaves a great deal open to the imagination. That is central to cosmopolitanism, which is all about re-conceiving social relations in a way that emancipates historically oppressed groups. If we add my notion of intersectionality to this account, it becomes clear that indigenous women might occupy the metaphorical South of the South of the South,[32] and it is crucial for their voices to be heard in this process of defining what is "neo" about neostate, neolaw, and neocommunity. As I argued earlier, indigenous women must be able to define and invent the meaning of tradition in order to fully express their indigenous identity. On the global scale then, it is crucial to create spaces where those who suffer from the dual domination at the intersections of power might be able to describe their position, and to have the opportunity to re-evaluate rights.

Therefore, the continuing struggle to define rights, and to make meanings that might describe complicated power relations is a transnational struggle. The proliferation of meaning in the US and Canadian cases is echoed and expanded when one looks beyond state boundaries. Future studies that attempt to re-evaluate the ability of rights discourses to describe the intersections of power will benefit from attention to these global dynamics. The process of domination and resistance will become more complicated because power strands will multiply, and identity will become all the more malleable. Replacing the state with the interactions of states and supra-state powers will inevitably make the interpretation of legal discourse even more contingent. Thus, an eye to global politics will multiply the insights to be gleaned from this account of intersectional power, but it will also further mystify the process of making political claims.

Conclusion

The preceding discussion of political struggle and the dynamics of legal meaning-making suggests how one should analyze and assess legal mobilization. The deployment of rights is a part of an continuing historical process, whose endpoint is dynamic and impossible to imagine. Attention to the intersections of power complicates this process even further. Intersectionality uncovers the simultaneity of domination and resistance better than a study that focuses on one strand of power (such as race or gender). Analysts should examine the process of struggle when attempting to assess whether legal tactics are worthwhile. The analysis of the marrying out cases shows that it is difficult for the meaning of rights to ossify. Co-optation is therefore not the entire story, because with new sites of power come new opportunities for debate and resistance. Rights re-evaluation is about re-assessing the meaning of specific rights discourses while remaining aware of their role in continued domination. The study of indigenous women's legal mobilization underscores this conclusion.

Notes

CHAPTER 1: INDIGENOUS WOMEN'S LEGAL MOBILIZATION

[1] *Santa Clara Pueblo* v. *Martinez* 56 L Ed 2d 106 (1978) at 111.

[2] Indian Act I S.C. 1951, C.29 (throughout the rest of this book, this section will be referred to as 12(1)(b)).

[3] Indian Act I S.C. 1951, C.29.

[4] Crenshaw, 1995.

[5] Jaimes Guerrero, 1997, 106.

[6] McCann 1995, 232.

[7] Kimberlé Crenshaw, 1992, 404-405.

[8] This point is echoed by many: Patricia Hill Collins, 1991; Patricia Williams, 1991; Cherrie Moraga, 1983; Mari Matsuda, 1996; and Audre Lorde, 1984 to name a few.

[10] Crenshaw, 1995, 1244n9.

[10] Jaimes Guerrero, 1997.

[11] Patricia Hill Collins, 1991.

[12] For an introduction on the social construction of race, see West et. al., 1995. For a discussion about the complicated relationships between race and ethnicity for indigenous peoples, see Santos, 1995.

[13] Santos, 1995, 319.

[14] Jamieson, 1978, 79.

[15] Jaimes, 1992, 332.

[16] Jaimes, 1992, 332.

[17] There are many other structures that help define indigenous women's political identities. My analysis focuses upon race, ethnicity and gender, as well as issues of material constraint. There are many facets to political identity construction, some of which do not fit neatly in these categories.

[18] Sawicki, 1991, 220.

[19] Foucault, 1990, 92-93.

[20] Hartsock, 1990, 170.

[21] Foucault, 1980, 13.

[22] Cocks, 1989, 79-80.

[23] Santos, 1995 313.

[24] See Smith, 1997 and Comaroff, 1995.

[25] Here, "individual rights" refers to the civil rights constructs of the dominant culture. These constructions usually use individual persons as the unit of analysis for governmental protection. "Sovereignty rights" refers to the "hands off" stance that many Native nations would like to see the US or Canada take toward their self-government. Yet, these constructions of sovereignty are often tied to the dominant culture's notion of statehood and property. The cases under examination here exemplify the classic conflict between the desired freedom for tribes to govern themselves using their sovereignty rights, and "Liberal" rights to individual autonomy (which are protected by federal civil rights statutes at the expense of tribal-level solutions). This conflict is often articulated as communal tribal tradition being impinged upon by individual-based remedies (i.e., gender equality vs. tribal sovereignty). This conflict will be explored throughout this book. Rogers Smith (1997) describes how US culture was not singularly influenced by liberal ideals, and competing impulses such as civic republicanism or ascriptive ideologies injected contradictions in the legal system, which were extra-legal.

[26] Foucault, 1990

[27] Grewal and Kaplan, 1994, 8.

[28] See Nagel, 1997. It is important to note that pan-Indianism creates a unified racial category that plays up the racial, rather than the ethnic aspects of indigenous peoples' domination.

[29] See Comaroff, 1995 for a discussion of this as a result of colonial conquest.

[30] These examples show how indigenous women and African-American women experience of intersectionality differently.

[31] Sometimes referred to as "post-realist" (McCann), this theoretical stance derives from realist accounts of law as political power, but take it a step further to acknowledge the unique influence of legal norms in society. Scholars such as McCann (1995), Merry (1988), Yngvesson (1993), Hunt (1993), and de Sousa Santos (1995) adopt this conception of law.

[32] Some call this multiplicity of normative orders "legal pluralism." See Merry, 1988.

[33] See Merry, 1988.

[34] See Smith, 1997; Kymlicka, 1995.

[35] See Kairys (1990) for an introduction to Critical Legal Scholarship.

[36] See Rosenberg (1991) for an example.

[37] Marx, 1978; McCann, 1995; Thompson, 1975; de Sousa Santos, 1995; Crenshaw, 1995; Brown, 1995.

[38] Scheingold, 1974.

[39] McCann, 1995; Crenshaw, 1995; Williams, 1991.

[40] Marx, 1978. This essay is problematic in its virulent anti-Semitic language, but if one reads this inflammatory language as a metaphor, some very important ideas emerge about the utility of rights tactics. For an interesting and provocative discussion of Marx's anti-Semitism see Brown, 1995, 90-92.

[41] Marx, 1978, 35.

[42] Marx, 1978, 46.

[43] Brown, 1995, 86-87.

[44] Brown, 1995, 87.

[45] Brown, 1995, 87-89.

[46] Brown, 1995, 101.

[47] Brown, 1995, 107.

[48] Brown, 1995, 107.

[49] Brown, 1995, 130.

[50] Brown, 1995, 130.

[51] Gramsci, 1971.

[52] De Certeau, 1984.

[53] Scott, 1985. See also see also Sarat and Kearns (1995) for essays on the unique power of legal institutions and narratives in everyday life.

[54] Cocks, 1989, 222.

[55] Smith, 1997, 86.

[56] Comaroff, 1995, 197.

[57] Comaroff, 1995, 235.

[58] Comaroff, 1995, 197.

[59] Comaroff, 1995, 226.

[60] Comaroff, 1995, 198.

[61] Comaroff, 1995, 226.

[62] Comaroff, 1995, 231-2.

[63] Comaroff, 1995, 236.

[64] Scheingold, 1974.

[65] This point is emphasized by Critical Race theorists when they respond to the Critical Legal Studies indictments of rights. See Hunt, 1994; McCann, 1995; Santos, 1995; and Williams, 1991.

[66] Thompson, 1975, 265.

[67] Audre Lorde, 1984, 110. While Lorde's speech, entitled "The Master's Tools Will Never Dismantle the Master's House," implies just the opposite of what I am suggesting here, I think the kind of subversive deployment of the master's

tools that I advocate can force dominant society to acknowledge the different kinds of oppression that Lorde writes about so eloquently.

[68] Gramsci, 1971; Thompson, 1975.

[69] See Foucault 1977; Scott, 1985; and Hunt, 1993.

[70] Rosenberg (1991) argues that courts offer a "hollow hope" for social reformers because the expense of litigation and the constraints of courts make them poor institutions for implementing social change. Rosenberg seems to have a very black and white conception of what counts as "change" and the measurements he employs miss the more subtle, symbolic mobilizing effects that court decisions can have. For more on this see McCann, 1993; Feeley, 1993; Rosenberg, 1993.

[71] McCann, 1995.

[72] Crenshaw, 1988, 1357.

[73] See McCann, 1995, chapter 7; and Santos, 1995.

[74] Thompson, 1975, 263.

[75] Yngvesson, 1993; White, 1990; Merry, 1990; Sarat 1995.

[76] Snow & Benford, 1988, 1992.

[77] See Sarat & Scheingold (1998) for a general discussion of how professional constraints might affect the way that lawyers construct their arguments on behalf of indigenous women. Given these insights, one cannot assume that legal argumentation represents indigenous women's consciousness in any significant way.

[78] Galanter, 1983.

[79] Gamson, 1988, 222.

[80] Hunt, 1993, 121.

[81] Santos, 1995, 326.

[82] Snow and Benford, 1992.

CHAPTER 2: "MARRYING OUT" IN THE US

[1] *Santa Clara Pueblo v. Martinez* 1978 at 111.

[2] Telephone interview with Richard Collins, one of Julia Martinez's attorneys, 1/20/98.

[3] "In 1968, Julia Martinez's now-deceased daughter Natalie, suffering from strokes associated with her terminal illness, was refused emergency medical treatment by the Indian Health Service. This was solely because her mother had previously been unable to obtain tribal recognition for her. Only after meeting with Interior Department solicitors did Mrs. Martinez obtain Bureau of Indian Affairs census numbers for her children. At the time of the trial the

Martinez children were encountering no difficulties in receiving medical care, as defendants have noted. Since then, however, Martinez grandchildren have had problems in obtaining medical care from Indian Health Service" (*Santa Clara Pueblo et. al. v. Julia Martinez et. al., Respondents' Brief,* August, 1977, 3).

[4]*Santa Clara Pueblo V. Martinez* at 111-112.

[5] I do not claim to know Martinez's motivations for going to court. My knowledge of Martinez's position comes from interviews with her attorneys. Therefore, when I refer to Martinez, I am referring to the perspective offered by her attorneys, which does not necessarily parallel her own analysis of the case.

[6] 402 F Supp 5 (1975)

[7] 540 F2d 1039 (1976)

[8] *Santa Clara Pueblo V. Martinez* at 115.

[9] *Santa Clara Pueblo V. Martinez* at 116.

[10] *Santa Clara Pueblo V. Martinez* at 118.

[11] 24 Stat 388 (1887), also known as the Dawes Act.

[12] See Smith, 1997.

[13] Resnick, 1989, 703.

[14] 48 Stat 984, also known as the Wheeler-Howard Act.

[15] Resnick 1989, 700.

[16]Resnick, 1989, 716.

[17] 26 U.S.C. §§1301-1341.

[18] 25 U.S.C. §§ 450-451n, 455-458e.

[19] Respondent's Brief in Opposition to Certiorari, December 1976, 8.

[20] Petition for Writ of Certiorari to the US Court of Appeals for the Tenth Circuit, October 1976, 40a.

[21] Petition for Writ of Certiorari to the US Court of Appeals for the Tenth Circuit, October 1976, 42a-43a.

[22] Respondent's Brief in Opposition to Certiorari, December 1976, 9.

[23] Petition for Writ of Certiorari to the US Court of Appeals for the Tenth Circuit October 1976, 25a.

[24] Petition for Writ of Certiorari to the US Court of Appeals for the Tenth Circuit October 1976, 20.

[25] Respondent's Brief (August 1977), Reply Brief (1976), Petitioner's Brief (1976), Brief for Amicus Curiae American Civil Liberties Union (August 1977), Brief of The Shoshone and Arapahoe Tribes of the Wind River Indian Reservation and the National Congress of American Indians as Amici Curiae

(1977), Brief of the National Tribal Chairmen's Association as Amicus Curiae in Support of Petitioners (1977), Brief for the United States as Amicus Curiae (October, 1977), Brief of Amicus Curiae Confederated Tribes of the Colville Indian Reservation in Support of Petitioners (1976), Brief of Amicus Curiae of The Pueblo de Cochiti, The Pueblo of Isleta, The Pueblo of Jemez, The Pueblo of Laguna, The Pueblo of Sandia, The Pueblo of San Felipe, The Pueblo of San Ildefonso, The Pueblo of Taos, The Hualapai Tribe, The Salt River Pima-Maricopa Indian Community, The Confederated Tribes of the Umatilla Indian Reservation and The All-Indian Pueblo Council, Inc. (1976), Brief Amici Curiae of The Seneca Nation of Indians of New York and the Association on American Indian Affairs, Inc.

[26] Petition for Writ of Certiorari to the US Court of Appeals for the Tenth Circuit October 1976, 37a-39a.

[27] Respondent's Brief in Opposition to Certiorari, December 1976, 10.

[28] Respondent's Brief in Opposition to Certiorari, December 1976, 12-13.

[29] Interview with Alan Taradash, 1/20/99, Gig Harbor, WA.

[30] Interview with Alan Taradash, 1/20/99, Gig Harbor, WA.

[31] Petition for Writ of Certiorari to the US Court of Appeals for the Tenth Circuit, October 1976, 28.

[32] Petition for Writ of Certiorari to the US Court of Appeals for the Tenth Circuit, October 1976, 28.

[33] Brief of the National Tribal Chairmen's Association as Amicus Curiae in Support of the Petitioners, 1977, 29.

[34] This is the language employed in the amicus brief submitted by the Pueblo de Conchiti et. al., 1976, 6.

[35] Petition for Writ of Certiorari to the US Court of Appeals for the Tenth Circuit, October 1976, 125.

[36] The ACLU presents the closest thing to a pure individual civil rights argument, as illustrated in its amicus brief, which states " . . . individual rights guaranteed by the ICRA cannot be denied by the mere assertion of 'tribal tradition.'" (August, 1977, 25). But the ACLU also acknowledges that it is necessary to remain sensitive to the unique status of Native Americans.

[37] Petition for Writ of Certiorari to the US Court of Appeals for the Tenth Circuit, October 1976, 12.

[38] Petition for Writ of Certiorari to the US Court of Appeals for the Tenth Circuit, October 1976, 28.

[39] Petition for Writ of Certiorari to the US Court of Appeals for the Tenth Circuit, October 1976, 13.

[40] Petition for Writ of Certiorari to the US Court of Appeals for the Tenth Circuit, October 1976, 25.

[41] Petition for Writ of Certiorari to the US Court of Appeals for the Tenth Circuit, October 1976, 39a.

[42] 1977, 9.

[43] 1977, 13.

[44] Petition for Writ of Certiorari to the US Court of Appeals for the Tenth Circuit, October 1976, 17.

[45] Petition for Writ of Certiorari to the US Court of Appeals for the Tenth Circuit, October 1976, 14 (quoting Trial court—Memo, Op., App. p. 20).

[46] Petition for Writ of Certiorari to the US Court of Appeals for the Tenth Circuit, October 1976, 42a.

[47] August 1977, 18.

[48] August 1977, 33.

[49] 1976, 32.

[50] Comaroff, 1995.

[51] Petition for Writ of Certiorari to the US Court of Appeals for the Tenth Circuit, October 1976, 21a.

[52] 1976, 11 and see appendices.

[53] Respondent's Brief, August 1988, 6.

[54] Respondent's Brief in Opposition to Certiorari, December 1976, 7 (citing 402 F. Supp. at 18).

[55] The category of "Indian ancestry" relies upon a homogenization of diverse indigenous cultures into one identifiable race. See Comaroff, 1995 and Nagel, 1997.

[56] Petition for Writ of Certiorari to the US Court of Appeals for the Tenth Circuit, October 1976, 21a.

[57] Respondent's Brief in Opposition to Certiorari, December 1976, 8.

[58] Respondent's Brief in Opposition to Certiorari, December 1976, 3.

[59] The National Tribal Chairmen's Association quotes Elsie Clews Parsons's analysis of gender roles in the Pueblo to conclude that "[t]he 1939 ordinance in no way reflects a society that discriminates against women . . . The distinctions are a matter of division of functions between the sexes rather than of subordination of one sex to the other." (1977, 27). Parsons goes on to describe the public/private distinction, stating that women's roles fell squarely in the private realm. Not only does this replicate a division of power that has been critiqued by many feminists as a form of subordination, but it does not clarify how the men were responsible for inculcating children with traditional values.

[60] Petition for Writ of Certiorari to the US Court of Appeals for the Tenth Circuit, October 1976, 9.

[61] Petition for Writ of Certiorari to the US Court of Appeals for the Tenth Circuit, October 1976, 19a-20a.

[62] Petition for Writ of Certiorari to the US Court of Appeals for the Tenth Circuit, October 1976, 43a-44a.

[63] Petition for Writ of Certiorari to the US Court of Appeals for the Tenth Circuit, October 1976, 45a.

[64] 1977, 16.

[65] Respondent's Brief in Opposition to Certiorari, December 1976, 8 1976, 3.

[66] Petition for Writ of Certiorari to the US Court of Appeals for the Tenth Circuit, October, 1976, 29 (emphasis added in the brief).

[67] Interview with Alan Taradash, 1/20/99, Gig Harbor, WA.

[68] Interview with Alan Taradash, 1/20/99, Gig Harbor, WA.

[69] Interview with Alan Taradash, 1/20/99, Gig Harbor, WA.

[70] 1977, 25.

[71] Senator Ervin quoted in Petition for Writ of Certiorari to the US Court of Appeals for the Tenth Circuit, October 1976, 20.

[72] Petition for Writ of Certiorari to the US Court of Appeals for the Tenth Circuit, October 1976, 14 (quoting *Lone Wolf v. Hitchcock*).

[73] Petition for Writ of Certiorari to the US Court of Appeals for the Tenth Circuit, October 1976, 20-21.

[74] Petition for Writ of Certiorari to the US Court of Appeals for the Tenth Circuit, October 1976, 21.

[75] Petition for Writ of Certiorari to the US Court of Appeals for the Tenth Circuit, October 1976, 17.

[76] 1977, 12.

[77] Petition for Writ of Certiorari to the US Court of Appeals for the Tenth Circuit, October 1976, 32a-33a.

[78] Respondent's Brief in Opposition to Certiorari, December 1976, 8 1976, 5-6.

[79] Respondent's Brief in Opposition to Certiorari, December 1976, 8 1976, 4.

[80] Petition for Writ of Certiorari to the US Court of Appeals for the Tenth Circuit, October 1976, 17a-18a.

[81] Respondent's Brief in Opposition to Certiorari, December 1976, 4.

[82] Petition for Writ of Certiorari to the US Court of Appeals for the Tenth Circuit, October 1976, 8.

[83] Petition for Writ of Certiorari to the US Court of Appeals for the Tenth Circuit, October 1976, 9.

[84] Petition for Writ of Certiorari to the US Court of Appeals for the Tenth Circuit, October 1976, 18a.

[85] Petition for Writ of Certiorari to the US Court of Appeals for the Tenth Circuit, October 1976, 9.

[86] Petition for Writ of Certiorari to the US Court of Appeals for the Tenth Circuit, October 1976, 19a.

[87] Petition for Writ of Certiorari to the US Court of Appeals for the Tenth Circuit, October 1976, 21-22.

[88] 1977, 12.

[89] Petition for Writ of Certiorari to the US Court of Appeals for the Tenth Circuit, October 1976, 20a.

[90] Petition for Writ of Certiorari to the US Court of Appeals for the Tenth Circuit, October 1976, 44a.

[91] October 1977, 14.

[92] Petition for Writ of Certiorari to the US Court of Appeals for the Tenth Circuit, October 1976, 30.

[93] Nagel, 1997.

[94] See Nagel (1997) for a very interesting discussion of "pan-Indianism."

[95] This echoes points made by Robert Cover (1995a, 1995b) about jurisdiction, which will be discussed in chapter 6.

[96] A cursory Lexis-Nexis search yielded 17 cases in the Supreme Court between 1979 and 1999 where *Santa Clara Pueblo* was cited as precedent. This only covers Supreme Court decisions, so one can assume that there were many more briefs filed for cases before lower courts, which never reached the Supreme Court. Another Lexis-Nexis search for the phrase "Santa Clara Pueblo v. Martinez" yielded 303 law review articles. This acts as evidence that this case is the subject of legal scholarship and also serves as important legal precedent for tribal immunity to suit, Congressional plenary power, judicial deference to Congress, as well as tribal self-determination.

CHAPTER 3: "MARRYING OUT" IN CANADA: PART I

[1] At various times throughout history, this may or may not have included Metis (mixed blood), and Inuit people. Of course, the term Indian refers to multiple cultures, many of which have very little in common aside from their colonial experiences.

[2] Indian Act I S.C. 1951, C.29 (throughout the rest of this study, this section will be referred to as 12(1)(b).

[3] Indian Act I S.C. 1951, C.29.

[4] Jamieson, 1978, 25.

[5] Jamieson, 1978, 64.

[6] Wherrett, 1996.

[7] Canadian Bill of Rights 1960 (Can.), C. 44.

[8] S.C.C. 1969.

[9] *Drybones* at 54-5.

[10] Boldt, 1993, xv.

[11] Couture, 1980, 7.

[12] Murphy, 1975.

[13] Murphy, 1975.

[14] Moss, 1990, 285.

[15] Jamieson, 1978, 84-85.

[16] Jamieson, 1978, 85.

[17] This claim was brought under the Optional Protocol to the International Covenant on Civil and Political Rights, International Bill of Rights.

[18] For a detailed account of the Tobique women's movement, see Silman, 1994.

[19] "Tories will amend the Indian Act, Clark Says." *Globe and Mail* 21 July 1979.

[20] Couture, 1980, 7.

[21] Strauss, 1981.

[22] "Indians opposed to non-status women." *Globe and Mail* 20 Oct 1981.

[23] Malarek, 1981.

[24] Moss, 1990, 280.

[25] Wherrett, 1996, 8.

[26] Moss, 1990, 281.

[27] Moss, 1990, 281.

[28] "Section 6(1) . . . a person is entitled to be registered if (f) that person is a person both of whose parents are or, if no longer living, were at the time of death entitled to be registered under this section. (2)Subject to section 7, a person is entitled to be registered if that person is a person of one of whose parents is or, if no longer living, was at the time of death entitled to be registered under subsection (1)" (Indian Act).

[29] Wherrett, 1996, 6.

[30] Wherrett, 1996, 11.

[31] Section 25 states "The guarantee in this Charter of certain rights and freedoms shall not be construed so as to abrogate or derogate from any aboriginal, treaty or other rights or freedoms that pertain to the aboriginal peoples of Canada including (a) Any rights or freedoms that have been

recognized by the Royal Proclamation of October 7, 1763, (b) Any rights or freedoms that may be acquired by the aboriginal peoples of Canada by way of land claim settlement" Section 27 states "This Charter shall be interpreted in a manner consistent with the preservation and enhancement of the multicultural heritage of Canadians."

Section 35(1) states "The existing aboriginal and treaty rights of the aboriginal peoples of Canada are hereby recognized and affirmed. (2)In this Act, 'aboriginal peoples of Canada' includes the Indian, Inuit, and Metis peoples of Canada . . . 35(4) Notwithstanding any other provision of this act, the aboriginal and treaty rights referred to in subsection (1) are guaranteed equally to male and female persons" (The Constitution Act, 1982).

[32] Boldt, 1993, 74.

[33] 1994 3 S.C.R. 627.

[34] Wherrett, 1996, 12.

[35] [1995] 4 C.N.L.R.

[36] 1972 SCR.

[37] Communication No. R.6/24, U.N. GAOR, 36th Sess., Supp. No. 40 at 166, U.N. Doc. A/36/40.

[38] [1995] 4 C.N.L.R.

[39] *Canadian Bill of Rights* 1960 (Can.), C. 44.

[40] *Re Lavell and Attorney-General of Canada* (1971), 22 D.L.R. (3d) 182. Ontario County Court, Grossberg Co.Ct.J., 21 June 1971.

[41] *Re Lavell and Attorney-General of Canada at* 227.

[42] Jamieson, 1978, 82.

[43] *Re Lavell and Attorney-General of Canada* (1971), 22 D.L.R. (3d) 188 Federal Court of Appeal, Jackett C.J., Thurlow and Pratte JJ. 8 October 1971.

[44] *Re Lavell and Attorney-General of Canada* (21 June 1971) at 234.

[45] *Re Lavell and Attorney-General of Canada* (21 June 1971) at 235.

[46] *Bedard v. Isaac* (1971) 25 D.L.R. (3d) 551 Ontario High Court, Osler J. 15 December 1971.

[47] *Bedard v. Isaac* (1971) at 15.

[48] *A. G. of Canada v. Lavell—Isaac v. Bedard* S.C.R. [1974] R.C.S.

[49] Respondent's Factum, 3.

[50] Respondent's Factum, 4.

[51] Factum of the Intervenants: The Alberta Committee on Indian Rights for Indian Women et. al., 11.

[52] Factum of the Intervenants: The Alberta Committee on Indian Rights for Indian Women et. al., 12-13.

[53] The Universal Declaration of Human Rights of the United Nations was also cited throughout the Factum.

[54] Factum of the Attorney General of Canada, 10

[55] See Rawls,1971; Sandel, 1982.

[56] Respondent's Factum, 6.

[57] Respondent's Factum, 7.

[58] Factum of the Intervenants: The Indian Association of Alberta et. al., 19.

[59] Factum of the Attorney General of Canada, 10.

[60] Factum of the Attorney General of Canada, 12.

[61] 404 U.S. 71 (1971). The Supreme Court invalidated a provision of the Idaho probate code that gave preference to men over women when persons of the same entitlement class apply for appointment as administrator of a decedent's estate. This code was found to violate the Equal Protection Clause of the Fourteenth Amendment.

[62] Factum of the Attorney General of Canada, 21.

[63] *Lavell/Bedard* at 1371-2.

[64] *Lavell/Bedard* at 1383.

[65] *Lavell/Bedard* at 1382.

[66] Lovelace, 29 December 1977, 3.

[67] Lovelace, 29 December 1977, 3-4.

[68] *Lovelace* at 163.

[69] Article 3 reads "The States Parties to the present Covenant undertake to ensure the equal right of men and women to the enjoyment of all civil and political rights set forth in the present Covenant."

[70] *Lovelace* at 164.

[71] *Lovelace* at 166.

[72] *Lovelace* at 167.

[73] Response, dated 6 June 1983, of the Government of Canada to the views adopted by the Human Rights Committee on 30 July 1981 concerning Communication No. 24/1977 Sandra Lovelace Annex XXXI, 251.

[74] Response of the Government of Canada, 1983, 253.

[75] Bands gained by-law powers and the power to set membership standards.

[76] "Correcting Historic Wrongs?", 1990, 26.

[77] "Correcting Historic Wrongs?", 1990, 18.

[78] "Correcting Historic Wrongs?", 1990, 27.

[79] "Correcting Historic Wrongs?", 1990, 59.

[80] "Correcting Historic Wrongs?", 1990, 32.

[81] For an in depth discussion of the complexities of multiculturalism versus sovereignty or minority rights, see Kymlicka, 1995.

[82] *Sawridge v. Canada* at 136.

[83] *Sawridge v. Canada* at 226.

[84] *Sawridge v. Canada* at 226-227.

[85] *Sawridge v. Canada* at 227.

[86] *Sawridge v. Canada* at 142.

[87] Respondent's Factum, 6.

[88] *Re Lavell and Attorney-General of Canada* at 228.

[89] Factum of the Intervenants: The Alberta Committee on Indian Rights for Indian Women et. al., 7.

[90] *Lavell/Bedard* at 1380.

[91] Canada's Submission Concerning the Lovelace Communication, 1 May 1980, 2-3.

[92] Lovelace, 20 June 1980, 57 (Lovelace's handwritten comments).

[93] Lovelace, 2 December 1980, reply to Questions Asked by Committee.

[94] Lovelace, 2 December 1980, reply to Questions Asked by Committee.

[95] *Lovelace* at 167.

[96] *Lovelace* Interim Decision.

[97] *Lovelace* at 163.

[98] *Lovelace* at 163.

[99] Canada's Response, 1983, 250.

[100] Canada's Response, 1983, 250.

[101] Canada's Response, 1983, 252.

[102] Pamphlet: *Changes to the Indian Act*, Ottawa: Indian and Northern Affairs Canada.

[103] "Correcting Historic Wrongs?", 1990, 26.

[104] "Correcting Historic Wrongs?", 1990, 24.

[105] "Correcting Historic Wrongs?", 1990, 52.

[106] "Correcting Historic Wrongs?", 1990, 24.

[107] "Correcting Historic Wrongs?", 1990, 5-6, quoting Touchwood File Hills Qu'Appelle Tribal Council, Saskatchewan.

[108] *Sawridge v. Canada* at 121.

[109] *Sawridge v. Canada* at 149.

[110] *Sawridge v. Canada* at 148.

[111] *Sawridge v. Canada* at 136.

[112] *Sawridge v. Canada* at 136.

[113] *Sawridge v. Canada* at 137.

[114] *Sawridge v. Canada* at 187.

[115] *Sawridge v. Canada* at 191.

[116] *Sawridge v. Canada* at 200.

[117] *Sawridge v. Canada* at 174.

CHAPTER 4: "MARRYING OUT" IN CANADA: PART II

[1] August 30, 1851, 14&15 Vict. c. 59.

[2] Sec. 11(1) of the pre-C-31 Indian Act reads: Subject to section 12, a person is entitled to be registered if that person

> (a) on the 26th day of May 1874 was . . . considered to be entitled to hold, use or enjoy the lands and other immovable property belonging to or appropriated to the use of various tribes, bands or bodies of Indians in Canada;
>
> (b) is a member of a band
>
> > (i) for whose use and benefit, in common, lands have been set apart or since the 26th day of May 1874, have been agreed by treaty to be set apart, or
> >
> > (ii) that has been declared by the Governor in Council to be a band for the purposes of this Act;
>
> (c) is a male person who is a direct descendent in the male line of a male person described in paragraph (a) or (b);
>
> (d) is the legitimate child of
>
> > (i) a male person described in paragraph (a) or (b), or
> >
> > (ii) a person described in paragraph (c);
>
> (e) is the illegitimate child of a female person described in paragraph (a), (b), or (d); or
>
> (f) is the wife or widow of a person who is entitled to be registered by virtue of paragraph (a), (b), (c), (d), or (e). (Indian Act I S.C. 1951, C.29).

[3] Sec. 12(1)(b) reads: 12(1) The following persons are not entitled to be registered, namely . . . (b) a woman who married a person who is not an Indian, unless that woman is subsequently the wife or widow of a person described in section 11.

[4] Respondent's Factum, 9.

[5] Factum of the Intervenants: The Indian Association of Alberta et. al., 9.

[6] Her submission continues, These factors could be combined in the following formula:

(1) If one were born an Indian, one would automatic remain so, until

(a) one requested a change of status or

(b) one voluntarily removed oneself completely from Indian society and culture for a prolonged period of time and it was reasonable to presume that a break with the society and culture had been made;

(2) If one marries an Indian (regardless of sex) one could be granted Indian status if one embraced Indian society and culture. Once Indian status was obtained, one would automatically remain so unless (1)(a) or (b) became applicable.

(3) The children of a mixed Indian/non Indian marriage could attain Indian status only if they embraced Indian society and culture. Again, once the children attained Indian status, they would automatically remain so unless 1(a) or (b) applied.

(4) Determing (sic) whether anyone (either the non-Indian spouse of an Indian or the children of a mixed marriage) embraced Indian society and culture could be determined by an objective test taking into account such things as place of residence, work and social activity, and contributions to the community. Similarly, the test in (1) (b) could be established and applied in an objective manner.

The advantages of the above-mentioned formula . . . for determining Indian status are that:

(1) It is not based upon discrimination by sex or any other violation of human rights;

(2) It does not threaten minority rights, but rather reinforces them by;

(a) guaranteeing the status of those born within the minority who wish to remain associated with it;

(b) permitting those who genuinely embraced the society and culture to obtain status within it; and

(c) preventing those who do not or can not embrace the society and culture from obtaining status in it. (Lovelace, 2 Dec. 1980).

[7] Lovelace, 20 June 1980.

[8] *Lovelace* at 166.

[9] "Correcting Historic Wrongs?", 27.

[10] DIAND, "Correcting Historical Wrongs? Report on the National Aboriginal Inquiry on the Impacts of Bill C-31" 1990 Ottawa, p. 8.

[11] Linda MacDonald, Yukon Native Women's Assoc., quoted in "Correcting Historical Wrongs?", 10-11.

[12] Chief John Meechas, Portage Band, Manitoba "Correcting Historic Wrongs?" 27.

[13] Wherrett, 1996, 12.

[14] Alfred, 1995, 163.

[15] requiring a blood quantum of 50% or more Native blood. Alfred, 1995, 165.

[16] Alfred, 1995, 165.

[17] Alfred, 1995, 177.

[18] *Sawridge* at 163.

[19] *Sawridge* at 193.

[20] *Sawridge* at 215.

[21] *Sawridge* at 218.

[22] Sawridge at 225.

[23] Factum of the Alberta Committee on Indian Rights for Indian Women et. al., 8. The factum cites as an authority a book by A.C. Parker, *The Constitution of the Nations or the Iroquois Book of the Great Law* from 1916.

[24] Factum of the Native Council of Canada, 5.

[25] Respondent's Factum, 9.

[26] Jamieson, 1978, 82.

[27] Jamieson, 1978, 87.

[28] Factum of the Indian Association of Alberta et. al., 7-8.

[29] Factum of the Indian Association of Alberta et. al., 17.

[30] Canada's Submission Concerning the Lovelace Communication, 1 May 1980, 2-3.

[31] Lovelace 20 June 1980.

[32] Lovelace 20 June 1980.

[33] Canada's Submission Concerning the Lovelace Communication, 1 May 1980, 4.

[34] "Correcting Historic Wrongs?", 6.

[35] "Correcting Historic Wrongs?", 25.

[36] Chief John Meechas, Portage Band, Manitoba quoted in "Correcting Historic Wrongs?", 47-48.

[37] *Sawridge* at 188.

[38] *Sawridge* at 208.

[39] *Sawridge* at 189.

[40] *Sawridge* at 190.

[41] *Sawridge* at 204-205.

[42] *Sawridge* at 191-192.

[43] *Sawridge* at 206.

[44] *Sawridge* at 200-201.

[45] *Sawridge* at 197-98.

[46] *Sawridge* at 202.

[47] *Sawridge* at 199-200.

[48] *Sawridge* at 193-194.

[49] *Sawridge* at 218.

[50] *Sawridge* at 218.

[51] *Sawridge* at 218.

[52] *Sawridge* at 214.

[53] Native Council of Canada 1995. *Volume 1: Intervener Expert Report on Ethnographic Evidence.*

[54] *Sawridge* at 216-217.

[55] *Sawridge* at 219.

[56] *Sawridge* at 220.

[57] *Sawridge* at 211.

[58] *Sawridge* at 220.

[59] *Sawridge* at 220.

[60] Comaroff, 1995.

[61] *Re Lavell and Attorney-General of Canada* (21 June 1971) at 228.

[62] Respondent's Factum, 9.

[63] Respondent's Factum, 14.

[64] Factum of the Attorney General of Canada, 16.

[65] Factum of the Attorney General of Canada, 22.

[66] Factum of the Attorney General of Canada, 10.

[67] *Lavell/Bedard* at 1359.

[68] *Lavell/Bedard* at 1390.

[69] *Lavell/Bedard* at 1388-89.

[70] *Lavell/Bedard* at 1382.

[71] *Lavell/Bedard* at 1382.

[72] Factum of the Intervenants: The Indian Association of Alberta et. al., 20.

[73] Jamieson, 1978, 84.

[74] Jamieson, 1978, 86.

[75] New Brunswick Human Rights Commission, 21-22 November 1977, 17.

[76] Lovelace, 20 June 1980, 2.

[77] *Lovelace* at 160.

[78] *Lovelace* at 159.

[79] *Lovelace* at 162.

[80] "Correcting Historic Wrongs?", 42.

[81] "Correcting Historic Wrongs?", 33.

[82] "Correcting Historic Wrongs?", 46.

[83] "Correcting Historic Wrongs?", v.

[84] "Correcting Historic Wrongs?", 36.

[85] "Correcting Historic Wrongs?", 37.

[86] Muldoon's language eventually is what rendered this case invalid. The phrase "racist apartheid," I think, originally meant that a European minority was dominating an indigenous majority. But, in other places, Muldoon applied the same phrase to modern-day special privileges of Indians, implying that an indigenous minority dominates the tax-paying majority. Bizarre, indeed.

[87] *Sawridge* at 224.

[88] *Sawridge* at 228.

[89] Respondent's Factum, 2.

[90] Jamieson, 1978, 62.

[91] Jamieson, 1978, 62.

[92] Jamieson, 1978, 67.

[93] Jamieson, 1978, 68.

[94] Factum of the Attorney General of Canada, 8.

[95] Factum of the Attorney General of Canada, 8.

[96] Factum of the Attorney General of Canada, 9-10.

[97] Factum of the Attorney General of Canada, 6.

[98] *Re Lavell and Attorney-General of Canada (21 June 1971)* at 227.

[99] Factum of the Indian Association of Alberta et. al., 6.

[100] Factum of the Indian Association of Alberta et. al., 8.

[101] Jamieson, 1978, 65.

[102] *Lovelace* at 163.

[103] Enfranchisement, in short, is when one loses Indian status but gains the right to vote in Canadian elections. This term is odd, because enfranchisement, for indigenous peoples was usually more about losing something (Indian status) than gaining anything. This is viewed as one of the classic examples of Canadian colonial coercion.

[104] Canada's Submission Concerning the Lovelace Communication, 1 May 1980, 3-4.

[105] She lists: residing on a tax-exempt reserve, inheriting possessory interest in land, being buried on reserve, receiving loans from Consolidated Revenue Fund, instruction in farming, free seed, medical treatment, borrowing money for housing from the Band Council, cutting timber free of dues on reserve, and finally, she has no traditional hunting and fishing rights *Lovelace* at 164.

[106] Canada's Submission Concerning the Lovelace Communication, 1 May 1980, 4.

[107] Lovelace's handwritten comments in Lovelace, 20 June 1980, 5.

[108] "Correcting Historic Wrongs?", 38.

[109] "Correcting Historic Wrongs?", vii-viii.

[110] "Correcting Historic Wrongs?", 39.

[111] "Correcting Historic Wrongs?", 40.

[112] "Correcting Historic Wrongs?", vi.

[113] "Correcting Historic Wrongs?", 35.

[114] "Correcting Historic Wrongs?", 26.

[115] "Correcting Historic Wrongs?", ix.

[116] "Correcting Historic Wrongs?", 57.

[117] *Sawridge* at 199-200. The share that is being referred to was an average of $261.80 per person.
(Jamieson, 1978, 62).

[118] *Sawridge* at 202-203.

[119] McIvor, 34-37.

[120] McIvor, 35.

CHAPTER 5: COMPARING THE US AND CANADIAN CASES

[1] It is important to note that the impacts I discuss here are not just related to legal mobilization. There was simultaneous political mobilization and legislative change. But, my focus on legal mobilization allows for a systematic analysis of the discourses that constituted both legal and political claims.

[2] As of 1995, under C-31, there were 101,428 new registrants to federal status. See Wherrett, 1996, 8.

[3] *Impact of the 1985 Amendments to the Indian Act (Bill C-31)*, 1990.

[4] *Native Women's Association of Canada v. Canada* 1994 3 S.C.R. 627.

[5] Epp,1998.

[6] Epp, 1998, 182-184.

[7] Epp describes the rights revolution as historical transformation in the kinds of cases that Supreme Courts hear. This shift is marked by increased attention to defending "individual rights against official abuses of power." (Epp, 1998, 1).

[8] Epp, 1998, 190.

[9] Epp, 1998, 186.

[10] Epp, 1998, 60.

[11] The Legal Services project that represented Julia Martinez was originally funded by the Office of Economic Opportunity, and, in the absence of

governmental financing became a private non-profit organization (Taradash Interview). For a very helpful discussion of how legal services blended client-centered advocacy with reform interests, see Lawrence, 1990.

[12] Epp, 1998, 53.

[13] Taradash Interview 1/20/99, Gig Harbor WA. Feminist scholars did analyze this case after the Supreme Court ruling. MacKinnon, 1987; Resnick, 1989.

[14] A cursory Lexis-Nexis search yielded 17 cases in the Supreme Court between 1979 and 1999 where *Santa Clara Pueblo* was cited as precedent. This only covers Supreme Court decisions, so one can assume that there were many more briefs filed for cases before lower courts, which never reached the Supreme Court. Another Lexis-Nexis search for the phrase "Santa Clara Pueblo v. Martinez" yielded 303 law review articles. This acts as evidence that this case is the subject of legal scholarship and also serves as important legal precedent for tribal immunity to suit, Congressional plenary power, judicial deference to Congress, as well as tribal self-determination.

[15] McIvor, *Canadian Woman Studies* Vol 15, Nos. 2&3, 34-37.

CHAPTER 6: LEGAL MOBILIZATION AT THE INTERSECTIONS OF POWER

[1] Cover, 1995a, 100.

[2] McCann, 1995, 307.

[3] Zemans, 1983; McCann, 1995;Galanter, 1983; Williams, 1991; Scheingold, 1974; Crenshaw, 1995 to name a few.

[4] E.P. Thompson, 1975, 263.

[5] McCann, 1995, 282.

[6] McCann, 1995, 11.

[7] McCann, 1995, 307.

[8] Scheingold, 1974, 91.

[9] Cover, 1995a, 101.

[10] Cover, 1995a, 103.

[11] Cover, 1995a, 144.

[12] Cover, 1995a, 172.

[13] Cover, 1995a, 148.

[14] Cover, 1995a, 154.

[15] Cover, 1995a, 109.

[16] Cover, 1995a, 112.

[17] Cover, 1995a,130n94.

[18] Cover, 1995b, 203.
[19] Cover, 1995a, 156.
[20] Cover, 1995a, 158.
[21] Santos, 1995, 250.
[22] Santos, 1995, 262.
[23] Santos, 1995, 263.
[24] Santos, 1995, 264.
[25] Santos, 1995, 264.
[26] Santos, 1995, 317.
[27] Santos, 1995, 339.
[28] Santos, 1995, 347.
[29] Santos, 1995, 348.
[30] Santos, 1195, 325.
[31] Santos, 1995, 327

[32] This concept is quite similar to Nancy Hartsock's standpoint theory. Hartsock wants to ""build an account of the world as seen from the margins, an account which can expose the falseness of the view from the top and can transform the margins as well as the center"" (Hartsock, 1990, 171). The conception of power that I adopt here requires that there be multiple margins, and a very indeterminate center. But, Hartsock and Santos share a common goal in looking to those who suffer from domination in order to invent better tools for resistance. As long as domination, resistance, the margins, or the South do not ossify into static relations or images, these insights are crucial for understanding the transformative potential of rights re-evaluation.

References

Books and Articles

Alexander, M. J., and Mohanty, C. T. Eds. 1997. *Feminist Genealogies, Colonial Legacies, Democratic Futures*. NY: Routledge.

Alfred, G. 1995. *Heeding the Voices of Our Ancestors: Kahnawake Mohawk Politics and the Rise of Native Nationalism*. NY: Oxford UP.

Anderson, O. Ed. 1982. *OHOYO One Thousand: A Resource Guide of American Indian and Alaskan Native Women*. Wichita Falls, TX: Ohoyo Resource Center.

Anderson, O. Ed. 1983. *OHOYO One Thousand Supplement*. Wichita Falls, TX: Ohoyo Resource Center.

Atcheson, M. E., Eberts, M., *and* Symes, B. 1984. *Women and Legal Action: Precedents, Resources, and Strategies for the Future*. Ottawa: Canadian Advisory Council on the Status of Women.

Bartlett, R. H. 1980. "Indian Act of Canada: An Unyielding Barrier." *American Indian Journal*, 6:11-26.

Bayefsky, A. F., and Eberts, M. Eds. 1985. *Equality Rights and the Canadian Charter of Rights and Freedoms*. Toronto: Carswell.

Beaudoin, G.A., and Ratushny, E. Eds. 1989. *The Canadian Charter of Rights and Freedoms* 2nd ed. Toronto: Carswell.

Benford, R.D. and Snow, D. 1988. "Ideology, Frame Resonance, and Participant Mobilization" in *International Social Movement Research*. Bert Klandermans, Hanspeter Kriesi, and Sidney Tarrow, eds. Vol. 1 Greenwich CT: JAI Press, Inc. 197-217.

Blumm, M. C., *and* Cadigan, M. 1993. "The Indian Court of Appeals: A Modest Proposal to Eliminate Supreme Court Jurisdiction over Indian Cases." *Ark.L.R.*, 46:203.

Boldt, M. 1993. *Surviving as Indians: The Challenge of Self-Government* Toronto: U Toronto Press.

Brown W. 1995. "Rights and Identity in Late Modernity: Revisiting the 'Jewish Question'" in *Identities, Politics, and Rights*. Austin Sarat and Thomas R. Kearns, eds. Ann Arbor: U Michigan Press. 85-130.

Cheffins, R. I., *and* Johnson, P. A. 1986. *The Revised Canadian Constitution: Politics as Law*. Toronto: McGraw-Hill.

Christofferson, C. 1991. "Tribal Courts' Failure to Protect Native American Women: A reevaluation of the Indian Civil Rights Act." *The Yale Law Journal*, 101:169-185.

Cocks, J. 1989. *The Oppositional Imagination: Feminism, Critique and Political Theory*. London: Routledge.

Comaroff, J. 1995. "The Discourse of Rights in Colonial South Africa: Subjectivity, Sovereignty, Modernity" in *Identities, Politics, and Rights*. Austin Sarat and Thomas R. Kearns, eds. U of Michigan Press. 193-236.

Couture, S. 1980. "A Question of Status." *Today Magazine*, 29 November.

Cover, R. 1995a. "Nomos and Narrative" in *Narrative, Violence, and the Law: The Essays of Robert Cover*. Martha Minow, Michael Ryan, and Austin Sarat, eds. Ann Arbor: Univ. of Michigan Press. 95-172.

Cover, R. 1995b. "Violence and the Word" in *Narrative, Violence, and the Law: The Essays of Robert Cover*. Martha Minow, Michael Ryan, and Austin Sarat, eds. Ann Arbor: Univ. of Michigan Press. 203-238.

Crenshaw, K. W. 1988. "Race, Reform, Retrenchment: Transformation and Legitimation in Antidiscrimination Law." *Harvard L.Rev.*, 101:1331-87.

_____.1992. "Whose Story Is It Anyway? Feminist and Antiracist Appropriations of Anita Hill." In *Raceing Justice, Engendering Power.* ed. T. Morrison, NY: Pantheon Books.

_____.1995. "Mapping the Margins" in *Critical Race Theory: The Key Writings that Formed the Movement.* Kimberle Crenshaw, Neil Gotanda, Gary Peller, and Kendell Thomas, eds. NY: The New Press. 357-383.

De Certeau M. 1984. *The Practice of Everyday Life* Berkeley: Univ. of California Press.

Donnelly, J. 1985. *The Concept of Human Rights.* London: Croom Helm.

Epp, C.R. 1998. *The Rights Revolution: Lawyers, Activists, and Supreme Courts in Comparative Perspective.* Chicago: U Chicago Press.

Ewick, P., and Silbey, S. 1992. "Conformity, Contestation, and Resistance: An Account of Legal Consciousness." *New England L.R.*, 26:731-49.

Feeley, M. 1993. "Hollow Hopes, Flypaper, and Metaphors." *Law and Social Inquiry.* American Bar Foundation.

Fitzgerald, M., Guberman, C., *and* Wolfe, M. Eds.. 1982. *Still Ain't Satisfied: Canadian Feminism Today.* Toronto: The Women's Press.

Foucault, M. 1977. "Two Lectures." In *Power/Knowledge: Selected,Interviews and Other Writings 1972-1977* ed. C. Gordon. NY: Pantheon.

_____. 1980. "The History of Sexuality: An Interview," trans. Geoff Bennington, *Oxford Literary Review,* 4:2.

_____. 1990 *The History of Sexuality: Vol. I, An Introduction.* Robert Hurley, trans. NY: Vintage Books.

Galanter, M. 1983. "The Radiating Effects of Courts." In *Empirical Theories of Courts,* ed. Keith D. Boyum and Lynn Mather, 117-42. New York: Longman.

Gamson, W.A. 1988. "Political Discourse and Collective Action" In *International Social Movement Research.* ed. Bert Klandermans et. al. Vol.1. Greenwich CT: JAI Press. 219-244.

Gramsci, A. 1971. *Selections from the Prison Notebooks* Q. Hoare and G. Nowell-Smith, ed. and trans. London: Lawrence and Whishart.

Grewal, I. and Kaplan C., eds.1994. *Scattered Hegemonies: Postmodernity and Transnational Feminist Practices.* Minneapolis: U of Minnesota Press.

Harring, S. L. 1994. *Crow Dog's Case: American Indian Sovereignty, Tribal Law and United States Law in the Nineteenth Century.* NY: Cambridge UP.

Hartsock, N. C. M. 1983. *Money Sex and Power: Toward a Feminist Historical Materialism.* Boston: Northeastern UP.

_____. 1990. "Foucault on Power." In *Feminism/Postmodernism.* L. J. Nicholson, ed. NY: Routledge.

Herman, A. M. 1979. *Native American Women and Equal Opportunity: How to Get Ahead in the Federal Government.* U.S. Department of Labor.

Hill Collins, P. 1991. *Black Feminist Thought: Knowledge, Consciousness and the Politics of Empowerment.* NY:Routledge.

Hunt, A. 1993. *Explorations in Law and Society: Toward a Constitutive Theory of Law.* NY: Routledge.

"Indians opposed to non-status women." 1981. *The Vancouver Sun.* 20 October.

Jaimes, M. A. Ed. 1992. *The State of Native America: Genocide, Colonization, and Resistance.* Boston: South End Press.

Jaimes Guerrero, M. A. 1997. "Civil Rights Versus Sovereignty: Native American Women in Life and Land Struggles." In *Feminist Genealogies, Colonial Legacies, Democratic Futures.* M. J. Alexander and C. T. Mohanty, eds. NY:Routledge. 101-121.

Jamieson, K. 1978. *Indian Women and the Law in Canada: Citizens Minus?* Canada: Minister of Supply and Services.

Jeffrey, R. C., Jr. 1990. "The Indian Civil Rights Act and the Martinez Decision: A Reconsideration." *South Dakota L.R.*, 35:371.

Kairys, D. Ed. 1990. *The Politics of Law: A Progressive Critique.* NY: Pantheon Books.

Kealey, L. 1993. *Pursuing Equality: Historical Perspectives on Women in Newfoundland and Labrador.* St. Johns: Institute of Social and Economic Research, Memorial University of New Foundland.

Klein, L. F. and Ackerman, L. A. 1995. *Women and Power in Native North America.* Norman: Univ. of Oklahoma Press.

Kulchyski, P. 1994. *Unjust Relations: Aboriginal Rights in Canadian Courts.* Toronto: Oxford UP.

Kymlicka, W. 1995. *Multicultural Citizenship.* Oxford: Oxford UP.

Lawrence, S.E. 1990. *The Poor in Court: The Legal Services Program and Supreme Court Decision Making.* Princeton: Princeton UP.

Lorde, A. 1984. *Sister Outsider.* Freedom, CA: The Crossing Press.

MacKinnon, C. A. 1987. " Whose Culture? A Case Note on Martinez v. Santa Clara Pueblo." In *Feminism Unmodified: Discourses on Life and Law*. C. A. MacKinnon, ed. Cambridge: Harvard UP.

Malarek, V. 1981. "Kick mixed couples off reserves: Indian Leader." *Globe and Mail*. 6 Nov.

Mandel, M. 1989. *The Charter of Rights and the Legalization of Politics in Canada*. Toronto: Wall and Thompson.

Marx, K. 1978. "On the Jewish Question." In *The Marx-Engels Reader*. R. C. Tucker, ed. NY: Norton.

Matsuda, M. 1996. *Where is Your Body?: And Other Essays on Race Gender and the Law*. Boston: Beacon Press.

McIvor, S. *Canadian Woman Studies* Vol. 15, Nos. 2 & 3. 34-37.

McCann, M. 1991. *Taking Reform Seriously*. Ithaca: Cornell UP.

_____. 1995. *Rights At Work*. Chicago: U Chicago Press.

_____. 1993"Reform Litigation on Trial." *Law and Social Inquiry*. American Bar Foundation.

Medcalf, L. 1978. *Law and Identity: Lawyers, Native Americans, and Legal Practice*. Beverly Hills: Sage Publications.

Merry, S. E. 1988. "Legal Pluralism." *Law and Society Review*, 22:868-96.

_____.1990. *Getting Justice and Getting Even: Legal Consciousness Among Working Class Americans*. Chicago: U Chicago Press.

Minow, M. 1997. *Not Only for Myself: Identity, Politics, and the Law*. NY: The New Press.

Minow, M., Ryan, M., and Sarat, A. Eds. 1995. *Narrative, Violence and the Law: The Essays of Robert Cover*. Ann Arbor: U Michigan Press.

Moraga, C. Anzaldúa, G. Eds. 1983. *This Bridge Called My Back : Writings By Radical Women Of Color.* New York : Kitchen Table, Women of Color Press.

Morse, B. W. Ed. 1985. *Aboriginal Peoples and the Law: Indian, Metis, and Inuit Rights in Canada.* Ottawa: Carleton UP.

Moss, W. 1990. "Indigenous Self-Government in Canada and Sexual Equality Under the *Indian Act*: Resolving Conflicts Between Collective and Individual Rights." *Queen's Law Journal,* 15:279-305.

Murphy, L. P. 1975 "A Thorn in the Side of Indian Bureaucracy" *Edmonton Journal.* 4 June.

Nagel, J. 1997. *American Indian Ethnic Renewal: Red Power and the Resurgence of Identity and Culture.* NY: Oxford UP.

Parr, J. Ed. 1995. *A Diversity of Women: Ontario 1945-1980.* Toronto: Univ. of Toronto Press.

Patiel, F. L. 1972. *Status of Women in Canada.* Ottawa: Information Canada.

Prucha, F. P. Ed. 1990. *Documents of United States Indian Policy.* Lincoln: U Nebraska Press.

Rawls, J. 1971. *A Theory of Justice.* Cambridge: Belknap Press.

Resnik, J. 1989. "Dependent Sovereigns: Indian Tribes, States, and the Federal Courts." *U Chicago L.R.*, 56:671-759.

Rosenberg, G. N. 1991. *The Hollow Hope: Can Courts Bring About Social Change?* Chicago: U Chicago Press.

_____. 1993. "Hollow Hopes and Other Aspirations: A Reply to Feeley and McCann" *Law and Social Inquiry.* American Bar Foundation.

Sandel, M. J. 1982. *Liberalism and the Limits of Justice.* Cambridge: Cambridge UP.

Santos, B. de S. 1995. *Toward a New Common Sense: Law, Science and Politics in the Paradigmatic Transition.* NY: Routledge.

Sarat, A. and Kearns, T. Eds. 1995. *Law in Everyday Life.* Ann Arbor: U of Michigan Press.

_____. and Scheingold, S. Eds. 1998.*Cause Lawyering: Political Commitments and Professional Responsibilities.* Oxford:Oxford UP.

Sawicki, J. 1991. "Foucault and Feminism: Toward a Politics of Difference," *Feminist Interpretations and Political Theory.* Mary Lyndon Shanley and Carole Pateman eds. University Park: Pennsylvania State UP.

Scheingold, S. 1974. *The Politics of Rights: Lawyers, Public Policy and Political Change.* New Haven: Yale UP.

Scott, J. C. 1985. *Weapons of the Weak: Everyday forms of Peasant Resistance.* New Haven: Yale UP.

Seidle, L. Ed. *Equity and Community: The Charter, Interest Advocacy, and Representation.* Montreal: Institution for Research on Public Policy.

Silman, J. 1994. *Enough is Enough: Aboriginal Women Speak Out.* Toronto: Women's Press.

Smith, D. G. Ed. 1975. *Canadian Indians and the Law: Selected Documents, 1663-1872.* Toronto: McClelland and Steward.

Smith, L., and Wachtel, E. 1992. *A Feminist Guide to the Canadian Constitution.* Ottawa: Canadian Advisory Council on the Status of Women.

Smith, R. M. 1997. *Civic Ideals: Conflicting Visions of Citizenship in U.S. History.* New Haven: Yale UP.

Smith, S. and Watson, J. Eds. 1992. *De/Colonizing the Subject.* Minneapolis: U Minnesota Press.

Snow D. and Benford R.D. 1992. "Master Frames and Cycles of
. Protest." In *Frontiers of Social Movement Theory.* Aldon D.
Morris and Carol McClurg Mueller, eds. New Haven: Yale
UP. 133-155.

Stephenson, M. Ed. 1977.*Women in Canada.* Ontario: General
Publishing.

Stetson, C. L. 1980. "Tribal Sovereignty: Santa Clara Pueblo v.
Martinez: Tribal Sovereignty 146 Years Later." *American
Indian Law Review*, 8:158-159.

Strauss, M. 1981."Canada's Indian Act works against women, UN
group States." *Globe and Mail* 15 August.

Thompson, E. P. 1975. *Whigs and Hunters: The Origin of the Black
Act.* New York: Pantheon.

"Tories will amend the Indian Act, Clark Says." 1979. *Globe and Mail.*
21 July.

Tsosie, R. 1994. "Separate Sovereigns, Civil Rights, and the Sacred
Text: The Legacy of Justice Thurgood Marshall's Indian Law
Jurisprudence." *Arixona State L.J.*, 26:495.

Vine Deloria, J., and Lytle, C. M. 1994. *American Indians, American
Justice.* Austin: U Texas Press.

White, L. 1990. "Subordination, Rhetorical Survival Skills and Sunday
Shoes: Notes on the Hearing of Mrs. G." *Buffalo Law Review*,
38:1-58.

Wherrett, J. 1996, "Background Paper: Indian Status and Band
Membership Issues." Ottawa:Library of Parliament Research
Branch.

Williams, P. J. 1991. *The Alchemy of Race and Rights: Diary of a Law
Professor.* Cambridge, MA: Harvard UP.

Yngvesson, B. 1993. *Virtuous Citizens and Disruptive Subjects: Order
and Complaint in a New England Court.* NY: Routledge.

Zemans, F. K. 1983. "Legal Mobilization: The Neglected Role of the Law in the Political System." *American Political Science Review*, 77:690-703.

Case Index

A. G. of Canada v. Lavell -- Isaac v. Bedard S.C.R. [1974] R.C.S.

Bedard v. Isaac (1971) 25 D.L.R. (3d) 551*Canadian Native Law Cases* B. Slattery and S. Stelck, eds. Saskaton:Suskatchewan, U. of Suskatchewan. 7:9-16.

Lovelace v. Canada. Decision on Admissibility. Communication No. R.6/24, U.N. Human Rights Committee. 14 August 1979.

Lovelace v. Canada Interim Decision. Communication No. R.6/24, U.N. Human Rights Committee. CCPR/C/DR(X)/R./24. 31 July 1980.

Lovelace v. Canada Communication No. R.6/24, U.N. GAOR, 36th Sess., Supp. No. 40 at 166, U.N. Doc. A/36/40. *Human Rights Law Journal* Vol. 2, No. 1-2, 1981.

Regina v. Drybones S.C.C. 1969.

Native Women's Association of Canada v. Canada 1994 3 S.C.R. 627

Re Lavell and Attorney-General of Canada (1971), 22 D.L.R. (3d) 182 *Canadian Native Law Cases*, 7:222-229.

Re Lavell and Attorney-General of Canada (1971), 22 D.L.R. (3d) 188 *Canadian Native Law Cases*, 7:230-235

Santa Clara Pueblo v. Martinez 436 US 49, 56 L Ed 2d 106, 98 S Ct. 1670.

Sawridge v. Canada [1995] 4 C.N.L.R. 121-230.

Case Briefs and Supporting Documents

For Santa Clara Pueblo v. Martinez:
Respondents' Brief, August, 1977.

Respondent's Brief in Opposition to Certiorari, Dec. 1976.

Petition for Writ of Certiorari to the US Court of Appeals for the Tenth Circuit, Oct. 1976.

Brief for Amicus Curiae American Civil Liberties Union, August 1977.

Brief of Amicus Curiae Confederated Tribes of the Colville Indian Reservation in Support of Petitioners, 1976.

Brief of the National Tribal Chairmen's Association as Amicus Curiae in Support of Petitioners, 1977.

Brief of Amicus Curiae of The Pueblo de Cochiti, The Pueblo of Isleta, The Pueblo of Jemez, The Pueblo of Laguna, The Pueblo of Sandia, The Pueblo of San Felipe, The Pueblo of San Ildefonso, The Pueblo of Taos, The Hualapai Tribe, The Salt River Pima-Maricopa Indian Community, The Confederated Tribes of the Umatilla Indian Reservation and The All-Indian Pueblo Council, Inc., 1976.

Brief of The Shoshone and Arapahoe Tribes of the Wind River Indian Reservation and the National Congress of American Indians as Amici Curiae , 1977.

Brief Amici Curiae of The Seneca Nation of Indians of New York and the Association on American Indian Affairs, Inc.

Brief for the United States as Amicus Curiae , October, 1977.

For A. G. of Canada v. Lavell -- Isaac v. Bedard
Respondent's Factum, Clayton C. Ruby, Solicitor for the Respondent, 4 Prince Arthur Avenue, Toronto 5, Ontario.

Factum of the Attorney General of Canada, 18 September 1972. C.R.O. Munro, N.A. Chalmer, J.E. Smith, Of Counsel for the Attorney General of Canada. Ottawa.

Factum of the Intervenants: The Alberta Committee on Indian Rights for Indian Women Incorporated, Voila Shannacappo, Monica Agnis Turner, The University Women's Club of Toronto, The University Women's Graduates Limited Toronto, Rose Wilhelm and The North Toronto and Professional Women's Club, Inc. Margaret P. Hyndman, Of Counsel for the Intervenants.

Factum of the Intervenants: The Indian Association of Alberta, The Union of British Columbia Indian Chiefs, The Manitoba Indian Brotherhood, The Union of Ne Brunswick Indians, The Indian Brotherhood of the Northwest Territories, The Union of Nova Scotia Indians, The Union of Ontario Indians, The Federation of Saskatchean Indians, The Indians of Quebec Association, The Yukon Native Brotherhood, The National Indian Brotherhood. Douglas Sanders, Solicitor for the Intervenants, Ottawa.

Factum of the Native Council of Canada. MacKinnon, McTaggart, Solicitors for the Intervenant.Toronto, Ontario.

For Lovelace v. Canada Canada's Submission Concerning the Lovelace Communication. 1 May 1980.

Faulkner, Hugh, Minister, Department of Indian and Northern Affairs, letter to Noel A. Kinsella, Chairman of the New Brunswick Human Rights Commission 8 November 1977.

Kinsella Noel A., Chairman of the New Brunswick Human Rights Commission telex to Honorable Hugh Faulkner, Minister, Department of Indian and Northern Affairs 19 October 1977.

Lovelace, Sandra and New Brunswick Human Rights Commission. Transmittal Concerning the Communication and the Arguments Made by Canada in its submission (includes Lovelace's handwritten comments). 20 June 1980.

Lovelace, Sandra. Communication to United Nations Human Rights Committee. 29 December 1977.

Lovelace, Sandra. Letter to Jakob Th. Möller, Chief Communications Unit of the U.N. Division of Human Rights. 30 May 1979.

Lovelace, Sandra. Letter to Jakob Th. Möller, Chief Communications Unit of the U.N. Division of Human Rights. 28 November 1979.

New Brunswick Human Rights Commission. *Extract of Minutes.* 17 October 1977.

New Brunswick Human Rights Commission, "Case Study: An Illustration of Non- Compliance 'Discrimination against Native Women in Canada'." *Agenda Item: International Covenants on Human Rights and Optional Protocol to the International Covenant on Civil and Political Rights* submitted to the Continuing Federal-Provincial Committee of Officials Responsible for Human Rights. 21-22 November 1977, Ottawa.

Permanent Mission of Canada to U.N., letter to U.N. Human Rights Committee submitted in response to the committee's request for observations on questions of admissibility. Geneva. 26 September 1979.

Response of the Government of Canada to the Decision of the Human Rights Committee Contained in Document CCPR/C/DR(VII)R.6/24 dated 19 September 1979 in the Matter of Sandra Lovelace. 4 April 1980.

Response, dated 22 November 1980, of the Government of Canada to the Questions asked by the UN Human Rights Committee.

Response, dated 2 December 1980 of Sandra Lovelace to questions asked by the UN Human Rights Committee.

Response, dated 6 June 1983, of the Government of Canada to the views adopted by the Human Rights Committee on 30 July

1981 concerning Communication No. 24/1977 Sandra
Lovelace Annex XXXI.

For *Sawridge v. Canada:*Native Council of Canada 1995. *Volume 1:
Intervener Expert Report on Ethnographic Evidence.*

Other Government Documents

American Indian Resources Institute. 1998. *Indian Tribes as Sovereign
Governments* 7 ed. Oakland, CA.

Canadian Advisory Council on the Status of Women. 1973-74. *Annual
Report.*

Canadian Advisory Council on the Status of Women. 1974-75. *Annual
Report.*

Canadian Advisory Council on the Status of Women. 1975-76. *Annual
Report.*

Canadian Advisory Council on the Status of Women. 1976-77. *Annual
Report.*

Canadian Advisory Council on the Status of Women. 1978-79. *Annual
Report.*

Canadian Advisory Council on the Status of Women. 1979. *Towards
Equality for Women: Plan of Action Pamphlet.* Status of
Women, Canada.

Canadian Advisory Council on the Status of Women. 1986-87. *Annual
Report.*

Canadian Advisory Council on the Status of Women. 1989-90. *Annual
Report.*

"Correcting Historic Wrongs?: Report of the National Aboriginal
Inquiry on the Impacts of Bill C-31." 1990. *Impacts of the
1985 Amendments to the Indian Act Bill -C31).* Module 1.
Ottawa: Minister of Supply and Services Canada.

Gathering Strength. 1996. Report of the Royal Commission on Aboriginal Peoples. Vol. 3.

Impacts of the 1985 Amendments to the Indian Act Bill -C31). 1990. Modules 1-4. Ottawa: Minister of Supply and Services Canada.

Looking Forward, Looking Back. 1996. Report of the Royal Commission on Aboriginal Peoples. Vol. 1.

Pamphlet: *Changes to the Indian Act.* Ottawa: Indian and Northern Affairs Canada.

Perspectives and Realities. 1996. Report of the Royal Commission on Aboriginal Peoples. Vol. 4.

Renewal: A Twenty Year Commitment. 1996. Report of the Royal Commission on Aboriginal Peoples. Vol. 5.

Restructuring the Relationship. 1996.. Report of the Royal Commission on Aboriginal Peoples. Vol. 2.

Interviews

Interview with Alan Taradash, 1/20/99, Gig Harbor, WA.

Telephone interview with Richard Collins, 1/20/98.

Index